The
Bedside Book
of Murder

The
Bedside Book
of Murder

RICHARD AND MOLLY WHITTINGTON-EGAN

DAVID & CHARLES
Newton Abbot   London

Acknowledgements

To those who helped us:

On this side of the water – our friends, Annabel Carey, Martin Fido, J. H. H. Gaute, Jonathan Goodman, Melvin Harris, Robin Odell, Donald Rumbelow, Camille Wolff, and John Sinkins and Roy Heywood of Messrs Wildy & Sons.

On the other side of the water – our friends, Albert Borowitz, Tom McDade, and Patterson Smith, for many transatlantic favours.

Our gratitude to our friend Lee Berckman, who insisted that the Black Daahlia (sic) should be given her prideful place, and to whom we dedicate that section of the book. We are most grateful, also, to Franklin Armstrong and his son Bruce, who pursued the Dahlia through California on our behalf.

Our thanks to George Johnson, Chief Librarian of the *Daily Mail,* who never failed when his guidance was sought, and to Jerry Mullaney for his very special photographic expertise.

We also wish to thank those who willingly granted permission to use copyright illustrations. If we have been unable to trace the holders of copyright in any instance, we offer our sincere apologies.

Richard and Molly Whittington-Egan

British Library Cataloguing-in-Publication Data

Whittington-Egan, Richard
The bedside book of murder.
1. Murder, to 1987
I. Title II. Whittington-Egan, Molly
364.1′523′09

ISBN 0–7153–9267–0

First published 1988
and printed in Great Britain by
Butler & Tanner   Frome   Somerset
for David & Charles Publishers plc
Brunel House   Newton Abbot   Devon

Contents

Invitation

Clamber aboard.

It could be an Arabian Nights' flying carpet, or Dr Who's telephone box that transmogrifies. But it is neither. It is a bed which we, like John Donne, invite you 'to make thy center', and from it voyage out, taking this book beside you for your guide.

Clamber abed.

We are as barkers before the galanty show's tent sheets, anxious to button-hole you to diversion. For this, become a magic bed, facture of words, floats safe and smooth across the homicide zones, 'to boldly go' into strange territories of murder.

We shall visit other lands. Four sanguineous pilgrimages to America; one each to Australia and New Zealand.

We shall hover about the time warps, plunging back to view sundry grotesqueries out of the Victorian peep-show. Here be black bombazine bogey-women, avenging She-Devils ... Irish Kate, hatchet-faced cook-general, hawking her gallipots of dripping, rich and creamy, marbled with veins of goodness, skimmed from the copper in which simmered prime cuts of her lately butchered late mistress ... buck-toothed Mary Eleanor Pearcey, wheeling her spindly perambulator of corpses through the dark hinterland of North London ... that dreaded droll, Mrs Amelia Dyer, the terrible Reading baby farmer, acid-milked as Lady Macbeth, aeviternally clutching her insatiably cadaverophagous carpet-bag ... and Christiana Edmunds, that simpering Brighton belle who, in her resentful spinsterhood, wreaked her vengeance against Cupid by poisoning litle children, and ended her days as Dowager of Broadmoor, presiding over the teacups, 'At Home' in the criminal lunatic asylum.

Here, too, in this lost horizon world, lopes Jack the Ripper, mythopoeic cacodaemon of a whole nation's hundred-year imaginings.

Forward then, embedded in the cosy blankets of the surrogate time capsule, to an old dark house on North 14th Street, East Orange, New Jersey, where a drowned Ophelia, death-splayed in the bath, raises the curtain on the blackest black drama of the three weird sisters, shrouded themselves in darkest-dyed mystery, and matching appurtenances of black hats, coats, dresses, scarves and winding-sheet-like veils.

And, west of Sunset, to the raunchy heyday Hollywood of the forties, to find, fugitive from the candy floss, the Black Dahlia, the sawn-in-half woman, who, every drop of blood drained from her body, was discovered, de-petalled, in the place of the weeds. The hideous fate of the sacrificial maiden of Celluloid City still troubles the conscience of Los Angeles Police Department, where her unclosed file gathers no dust.

We change course, dip back to the flickering-out days of the last century, to visit Oscar Wilde in prison and hear the full story of the bloody doings of the man in the scarlet coat that brought him to mortality at the hangman's hands – and immortality in *The Ballad of Reading Gaol*.

Two mysteries of the southern spheres titillate and tantalise.

A man and a woman lie dead amid the scrubby boscage fringing the Lane Cove River, Sydney, Australia. He is one of the world's leading laser physicists. She, an ex-nurse and another man's wife. Love – or sex – yoked this disparate pair; parate forever now in death. A familiar scenario? But *this* one is so very, very different. Batteries of doctors and scientists have analysed those corpses, scrutinised them down to the tiniest atom of flesh, and they can find absolutely no reason why they should be dead. This is the world's supreme, unique 'whatdunnit' unsolved puzzle.

A lone child crying in a deserted New Zealand farmhouse behind its screen of macrocarpa trees. Mother and father slain five days before. By all the rules the child, too, should be dead – starved, frozen. But *some* hand has shooed the reaper from the door. Who fed baby Rochelle is this book's second best bed puzzle.

We travel on, as in a kind of claustrophobic nightmare, into the grim laboratories of poisoners' minds, to watch the brewing there of the skull-and-cross-boned elixirs of death.

Finally, all of evil's ambition and excitement quenched, we broach stone walls, accompanying the malevolent and malfeasant to the very last touching wood of the gallows' beam, there to witness how, in falsehood's inescapable moment of truth, they faced that mote and the hangman's ungloved grip.

Richard and Molly Whittington-Egan

Who Slew the Bogle?

How a satyrical scientist and his misleading lady pose the Sydney police an unanswerable scientific riddle by the immaculate deception of their double death.

We were dining, that early July evening in 1984, with full College silver splendour, in an upper chamber of Wadham. We were, I remember, just relishing the College's celebrated 'green butter', when I, pursuing a topic upon which I had recently been working with some concentration, mentioned to my friend and fellow crime-fancier, Jonathan Goodman, the quite extraordinary affair of the death of the physicist, Dr Gilbert Stanley Bogle.

Now it so happened that my neighbour at table was the extremely distinguished Oxford physicist, Professor Thomas Clews Keeley. He was, incidentally, ninety-one at the time, and had occupied the same set on the same staircase at Wadham since 1924 – surely a record-setting sixty years. Professor Keeley leant over and said: 'Bogle was one of my students, you know. I recall him well. Very bright chap. Most curious the way he died. Mysterious.'

Mysterious indeed. But strange, too, the unexpected links which circumstance forges. Who would have guessed at any connection between the smooth green lawns of Wadham and the scrubby boscage of the Lane Cove river-bank, New South Wales?

In a way, there was a certain appropriateness in the fact that one of the world's leading lights of the almost supranormal sphere of advanced solid state physics, the top laser man of his day, should quit our more mundane orb in a mode so far defying ordinary scientific analysis that it was almost as if he had been 'beamed up' somewhere or other on one of his own lasers. For the plain truth is that even now, we do not have a clue as to what killed him. Nor do we know who. Perhaps we know why.

Victim Dr Gilbert Stanley Bogle.

It is the warm December's evening of the last day of the year 1962. The personnel of our drama are assembling themselves in and about the great Australian city of Sydney. At the verandahed and gabled house of Kenneth Nash and his beautifully groomed wife Ruth, No.12 Waratah Street, Chatswood, on Sydney's North Shore, they lay out the bottles and the canapés for their New Year's Eve party. Ken, a tall, urbane man, occupies a senior position in the Commonwealth Scientific and Industrial Research Organisation, and most of the guests are either his colleagues or members of the professional, executive and artistic classes. The Nashes were anxious to preserve their reputation as providers of fine food, drink and sparkling conversation.

About five miles from the Nash homestead, in his cosy,

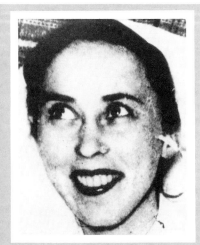

Victim Mrs Margaret Chandler.

unpretentious, brick-built Turramurra home, the brilliant Bogle was busy, metaphorically, pulling on his dancing pumps – he was, among so many other things, a dab foot at Spanish dancing – in preparation for that evening's party. Dr Gilbert Stanley Bogle, aged thirty-eight, born in 1924 in the small New Zealand town of Wanganui, was an outstanding physicist, a near-genius some said. A Rhodes Scholar, he had gone to Oxford, where he obtained his doctorate for his researches into atom crystal structure. It was while he was at Oxford that he had met there again a girl whom he had known in his undergraduate days back home, Vivienne Rich, MA, daughter of Archdeacon E. J. Rich, later Anglican Bishop of Auckland. They returned to New Zealand together and married. Before joining the CSIRO in 1956 and coming to Sydney, he had taught at Otago University.

Move the milled wheel of the microscope delicately and bring Dr Bogle into fine focus. What do we see? A top flight scientist. A linguist. An accomplished musician. Favours Bach. Sang in a choir. Plays the clarinet. Likes beer and fine sherry. Fun-loving and gregarious. Enjoys parties. Another turn of the milled wheel. Finer focus. We see a sexual athlete. Dark good looks. Laid back social manner. Laid back ladies. A lot of them. Then. . . like a flaw in the lens. . . the nasty streak. A fickle man, with an insensitive and uncaring way of discarding the used partner who no longer pricks the capricious satyr in him.

Gib Bogle will be a bachelor gay, just for tonight. Vivienne will not be coming with him. She is staying at home with their four children in the fine house behind the copse of tall, straight, slender gum trees. She must miss the party, as, indeed, she has had to miss the CSIRO Christmas party, and for the same reason: the latest baby Bogle, a four-month-old, is still not at all well. Clutching his clarinet, the Picasso-style sketch which he has executed and which is his contribution to the party gimmick – each guest to bring a specimen of his or her own unaided effort at modern art – under his arm, smart, sleek, sweet-smellingly after-shaved, he is ready. A kiss. A merry wave. The 1948 green Ford Prefect noses off like an in-season stoat into the star-hung promissory night.

So Prince Charming went to the ball – *le bal de mort*.

A dozen or so miles south-west of the Nashes' residence in a small, double-fronted, weatherboard cottage on Cromwell Street, in the Sydney suburb of Croydon, live Geoffrey and Margaret Chandler. They are among Ken and Ruth Nash's invited guests. He, aged thirty-three, is a Research Officer, Grade Two, at CSIRO. The son of a Queensland schoolmaster, he came to Sydney to work for the Amalgamated Wireless of Australia, while studying for an engineering degree. He met Margaret Olive Chandler at a party at Bondi about 1957. She was then a nursing sister at Sydney's Royal Prince Alfred Hospital. They had married in 1958. She was now twenty-nine. They had two children, Gareth, aged two, and baby Sean. They had also five vintage cars – a passion for which they shared – and dachshunds were another mutual interest.

Put Mrs Margaret Chandler under the microscope. She will be the one to watch. We see a vivacious woman. Attractive. Extravert. Good mother. Many friends. Apparently happily married. Rather a jolly, good-natured girl. But what does dark-ground illumination reveal? Boredom. She misses the stimuli of her nursing days. Finds unrelieved domesticity and *Kinder*-caring a drag. Zoom in a finer lens. Something else, too. She is harbouring an infatuationary careless enrapturement re the Bogle. She has, allegedly, and this is to be questioned, only met him once before – ten days before, at the CSIRO Christmas barbecue party. But Dr Gib has got to her. Driving to the Nash party that evening, the children safely parked at Margaret's parents' home at Granville – about twelve miles west of Sydney – for the night, Margaret, according to her husband's testimony, made rather an odd remark. 'It would be an interesting experience,' she said, 'to have an affair with the Bogle.' Geoff's reply had been even odder. 'If you want to have Gib as a lover, if it would make you happy, you do it.' Theirs, Chandler would later claim, and there is absolutely no reason to doubt him, had been a 'modern' marriage. They both had affairs.

The victim's husband and the first police suspect.

Now they are getting ready for the party. At least she is. He will turn up in slacks, open-necked sports' shirt, and open-toed sandals; a rig-out that goes with his beard (unusual at that time in Australia) and nonconformist persona. She is decking herself out with pride and care for the occasion: off-white, ballerina-style flared floral dress, narrow shoulder straps, printed with a pattern of brilliant red roses in bud and bloom, flanked by bright green leaves.

So Cinderella went to the ball – the death masque.

The first of the evening's guests to arrive at the house on Waratah Street, shortly after 9pm, was Dr Bogle. Fairly close upon his heels, the Chandlers appeared. So there we are. Now all the necessary ingredients for conventional tragedy are neatly assembled in the persons of these brilliantly unconventional people.

By ten o'clock the party was well under its decorous way. It was a quiet and sober affair, not cast in the traditional wild mould of most Australian shindigaroos. Margaret and Bogle spent a lot of time together. Geoffrey Chandler, circulating amiably aimlessly, appeared unconcerned. At around half-past eleven he suddenly announced to Margaret that he was slipping out to buy some cigarettes, leapt into his vintage Vauxhall and roared off across the harbour bridge to Balmain, where his friend, Ken Buckley, was throwing another New Year's party at his house in Phoebe Street. Chandler's current girlfriend, Pamela Logan, a blonde secretary in her middle twenties whom he had known for some time, was there, and after Auld Langsyne-ing 1963 in, he and Pam had shot out

Margaret Chandler, who bore an extraordinary resemblance to Margaret Fowler.

to her bedsitter at Darlington for a more personal celebration of the year's nativity. Let it be recorded that, in betaking himself thus to Pam's single room, Chandler was nobly and deliberately, of benevolence aforethought, leaving free for the corporate use of Margaret and Bogle, if required, the marital cottage on Cromwell Street. The game of musical beds was fairly widely played among the mature, well-educated, articulate and sophisticated people of the Sydney 'Push' or 'in' set. 'Advanced', restless, faintly radical, strongly adventurous and 'liberated' in that period before the bonds of Aids would bind them to a cringing chastity, they were sexual revolutionaries to a man – and woman.

It was *circa* 2.30am when the free-wheeling Chandler wheeled his way back to the Nash party. All innocence to the last tooth of his zip, he joined his wife and Gib, who were talking demurely, well separated, on a green sofa. Supper was being served as the emotional triangle chatted amicably, exchanging three-way pleasantries. As the clock struck four, Chandler, a tardy Cinderella in drag, as it were, yawning, excused himself, bade thank you and goodbye to his hosts, headed for his vintage pumpkin, and drove unobtrusively off into the impending sunrise.

No sooner had his exhaust-pipe vanished across the horizon, than Gib and Margaret took to wheels. It was done with subtlety. Bogle left on his own, flourishing a flamboyant farewell toot on his horn. But Mrs Nash, watching from cover, saw Margaret Chandler. She was standing by herself at the foot of the front steps. She walked slowly, insouciantly, down the garden path, out through the main gateway, took a studiedly casual ten or twelve paces to the left, then . . . darted off, to join, of course, the Bogle, waiting for her just out of sight. An early morning motorist saw the green Ford Prefect turn into Lane Cove River Park, and cruise down its secluded Lovers' Lane. At 5am an inquisitive passer-by, glancing, sharp-eyed, into the car parked near the Lane Cove River's slimy east bank, saw the couple, and noticed that Bogle looked pale.

It was à good three hours later, around 8am when Michael McCormick, aged sixteen, and his friend, seventeen-year-old Dennis Wheway, arrived at the park to search for golf balls lost from the adjoining Chatswood Golf Course. Foraging through the clumps of bush and undergrowth young Mike spotted a man lying face down on the sloping riverbank. He did not take any notice. He thought it was a tramp who had been drinking, sleeping off his premature greeting to the newly dawned year. However, when, passing the same spot an hour later, he saw that the man had not moved, was lying in the identical pose and position, he felt uneasy. He shouted to Wheway and the two lads went over to the man. His face was deep purple. There was a small trickle of blood coming from his nose, and another from the corner of his mouth. Luckily, the little refreshment kiosk beside nearby Fuller's Bridge was open. They fetched its proprietor, Mr Little, to have a look. He knew at once that the man in the bush was dead, and immediately called the police.

It was 10.45am before they arrived. Chatswood police station was undermanned and its one patrol car was out on call. First on the scene was Sergeant Arthur S. 'Andy' Andrews, soon followed by Constables Wright and Jackson, who were set to work searching the surrounding marshland; an uninviting place, covered with an ill assortment of litter, broken bottles, old cans, cardboard cartons and rotting newspapers, mouldering among the rank weeds. Andrews was immediately struck by the odd state of the body. The man was wearing a shirt and tie, and shoes and socks, but no strides, under-strides, or jacket. He was lying flat on his stomach, arms spreadeagled, legs fully stretched out, and from neck to buttocks he was covered with a piece of grimy carpet. On top of the carpet were neatly draped his jacket and trousers, sleeves following the lines of his outstretched arms, trouser legs following the line of his legs, so positioned as to give the impression that the man was fully dressed.

Mrs Margaret Fowler. Dr Gib's passionate friend.

Wright, a motorcycle constable who had wandered about 150 feet further up the dirt track, suddenly called out: 'Sarge, I can see part of a leg here.' It was protruding from under three torn, but joined together, flattened sheets of a mouldy beer carton. Beneath them was concealed the body of a young woman. She was lying on her back in a slight hollow, one hand carelessly across her stomach, as if she were fast asleep. Her rose-floral dress was open down the front and pulled off the shoulders, and her strapless bra, still fastened at the back, had been tugged down to expose her breasts. The lower part of her dress and her half-slip were bunched up around her waist. She was nude from there down. A pair of men's underpants was scrunched into a bundle and had been placed between her ankles. Her missing white underwear was later found, together with her brown shoes and Bogle's trouser belt, on a dry part of the river bed below the high-water mark. The underwear was wet, as if it had been washed out in the river.

Constable Wright subsequently testified: 'I took hold of her left wrist, but could not detect a pulse. I felt the body and it was warm. *Rigor mortis* had not set in, but there was no sign of breathing.' In the case of the man, *rigor mortis* was well advanced. He must have died before she did. Sergeant Andrews noticed that the man's shoes were partly covered with mud. This led him to take a look further down the riverbank, where the ground was soft. There he observed fresh human excrement. And, returning to the body, keeping an eye on the ground, he now saw in its vicinity a small amount of vomit. The man, and as it later transpired the woman also, had obviously crawled around vomiting and defecating before death supervened.

In the dead man's pocket the sergeant found a wallet. He was no hobo full of plonk. She was no vagrant OD'd on New

Year's booze. The wallet identified him as Dr Gilbert Bogle, of the CSIRO and Turramurra. Sergeant Andrews promptly contacted Sydney Criminal Investigation Bureau. A squad of CIB detectives, forensic experts and photographers descended, locustian, upon the east bank. They quartered the ground for clues. Turned up nothing of significance. The bodies were removed to the old Sydney morgue, down near the Sydney Harbour Bridge.

Because of the public holiday, it was not until at least thirty-six hours after their deaths that the autopsies on Bogle and Mrs Chandler were carried out. When they were, the results of those post-mortem examinations were a total puzzlement. All forms of violence and virtually all kinds of disease were excluded as causes of death. Inspection for injuries – such as ruptured eardrums – resulting from high-frequency soundwaves or supersonic waves, produced nothing. Checks for radiation poisoning and residual radioactivity proved likewise negative.

The next logical step for the pathologists was to proceed to chemical analysis in quest of poisons. New South Wales Government Analyst, E. Samuel Ogg, examined specimens of the couple's brains, hearts, livers, spleens, kidneys and blood. Hair was tested for arsenic. Other tissues were searched for traces of aconite, atropine, cocaine, henbane, mercury, nicotine, opium, phenol, phosphorus, santonin, strychnine, and dozens of other poisons, including even the venom of the Queensland cone fish.

Nothing.

Geoff Chandler's prized vintage model outside the cottage on Cromwell Street, in the Sydney suburb of Croydon.

Tests were performed for the use of fluorides. Ionizing influences were sought with rays ultra-violet and infra-red and radiation monitors. Signs of food poisoning were looked for. So was the presence of alcohol, sedatives and carbon monoxide.

Nothing.

Officers of the police scientific squad went to the Nash house and took away samples of every remaining item of food and drink from the party night. They tested them all.

Nothing.

Bogle's car was examined, dust from the pockets of his clothes was analysed, and so was the clothing itself, and Margaret Chandler's.

Nothing.

The pathologists went back to the dissecting table and carefully scanned the cadavers for marks of hypodermic needles, signs of pinpricks and animal or insect bites.

Nothing.

The Lane Cove River Park killing ground.

Although blood tests had more or less certainly eliminated snake or spider bite, at the request of the police, Australian Museum arachnologist, Mr McAlpine, went with them to the Fuller's Bridge area of Lane Cove River Park on a poison spider hunt. He looked for trap-door, red-back, and funnel-web spiders. He found no sign of any of them.

Dr John Laing, Director of the New South Wales Division of Forensic Medicine, said: 'There are many cases of fatal heart attacks without autopsy signs, and it is not inconceivable that two such cases should occur together.' Not *inconceivable*, perhaps, but highly unlikely.

Professor Roland H. Thorp, Professor of Pharmacology at Sydney University, plumped, despite all the tests having proved negative, for poisoning. His suggestion was that the poison might have dissipated, or have been an unusual one, available only to research workers. Certainly a possibility, for, as Ogg was at pains to point out: 'There are about forty thousand new chemical substances created every year. The majority of them are toxic in varying degrees. No one can say that these substances can be detected. No one can say of any one of them that, if it had been used to poison someone, it could be detected in the body.'

Thus, the entire causal spectrum seemingly exhausted, the pathologists had, reluctantly, to put both deaths down to acute cardiac failure associated with anoxia and pulmonary oedema. *Vulgatim*: Heart failure. Lack of oxygen. Lungs filled with fluid. It was a description: not a diagnosis. It said no more than that they both died because their hearts stopped beating and they stopped breathing, or because they stopped breathing and their hearts stopped beating!

And that, after fifteen days of hearing at an inquest – opened on 21 March, adjourned until 7 May and again until 21 May, and completed on 29 May – listening to more than fifty witnesses and viewing sixty-three exhibits, and an investigation which Dr Laing described to Coroner J. J. Loomes as equipped with every facility known to modern science for determining the cause of death, was the best they could do.

To sum up. It had been demonstrated that:

1 Both dead persons had sweated profusely.
2 There had been no ante-mortem sexual intercourse, although traces of semen were found on Bogle's suit jacket.
3 Bogle had probably died soon after 5am and Mrs Chandler very possibly as much as an hour or so later.

And that was all it came to . . .
Nothing.
Simply that two people died of acute circulatory failure.

Unofficially, of course, there was no shortage of theories. They, and their accompanying rumours, buzzed busily around Sydney like bonnet-fleeing bees.

The first, and most popular, was that Bogle had been working on some sort of 'death ray'. Actually, as a Senior Research Officer at the National Standards Laboratory of CSIRO, he had been developing the maser (Microwave Amplification by Stimulated Emission of Radiation); and masers, later developed as lasers, had already been used to control the Nike-Ajax guided missile. But, and this was emphasised both by the CSIRO authorities and the coroner, there was no security aspect to his work. Perhaps not, said the wiseacres, but wasn't it a fact that he was off soon to the United States to take up a research fellowship position with the Bell Telephone Company in New York? That was where many US Defense Department contracts had gone, wasn't it? Work on anti-ballistic missile systems, anti-satellite programmes and suchlike. Wasn't his work in their laboratories going to involve him in expensive, highly complex scientific and secret research of great military importance, vital, indeed, to the defence of the US? No denying that. Well, wasn't it likely that he'd been murdered by enemy agents? What about Mrs Chandler? Oh, she'd just been unlucky, happening to be with him when the killers struck. She'd had to be silenced, too.

Wilder speculations embraced witchcraft and the influence of demons in Outer Space. As to *how* they were killed, nominations ranged from sci-fi death rays and capsules of neuro-toxic gas, placed to be crushed under the brake pedal of Bogle's car, to the more feasible theory privately held by analyst Samuel Ogg. He believed that the couple had died of an overdose of LSD. Was it possible that someone at the Nash party who had access to LSD – not difficult for people in the medical and scientific world – had slipped some into Bogle and Margaret Chandler's coffee? Little was known about LSD at that time. Had someone *accidentally* given them an overdose? And had toxicological tests failed to discover LSD in the corpses because it was not there; because it had been dissipated during those hours of delay before the medical examiners got to work?

Detective-Sergeant Jack Bateman, one of the best CIB detectives in the New South Wales force, nicknamed the 'Father Confessor' because so many murderers had felt compelled to 'cough' to him, was convinced that the couple died as the result of a stupid practical joke that went tragically wrong. He believed that someone, one of the guests most likely, had slipped something – he did not specify LSD – into their coffee. What's more, he was sure that he knew who it was. It *could* have been Bogle himself. It has been suggested that, his reputation as a lady-killer notwithstanding, he had sexual problems. It may be that his endless questing for new sexual partners was a symptom of his own inadequacy. According to some psychiatrists of the time, LSD was to be regarded as a true aphrodisiac, and Bogle, who could, if anyone in Sydney could, undoubtedly have obtained a supply of the drug, may well have been experimenting with it as a cure for impotence. No one at that stage of the drug's development knew what constituted a lethal dose. The usual – *c.*600 micrograms – dose, barely covers a pinhead. Bogle, thinking to stimulate himself and Margaret Chandler to better performance, may have tipped what was in truth a fatal overdose into their coffee cups.

For most people, Geoffrey Chandler was an obvious target of suspicion. He was 'the bearded man'. He was a member of the 'Push'. He dressed and thought unconventionally. He aired unpopular views on sex, marriage and politics. In him Nature had obligingly provided a ready-made murderer. Sydney split into two camps: those who believed that Chandler was the killer, and those who thought that he was being made a suspect only because of his weirdo lifestyle. The man himself made small contribution to the coffers of either party. He told the coroner's court no more than he absolutely had to. He played hide-and-seek with increasingly resentful newspaper men. He was later to write his own strange book about the case, *So You Think I Did It*. He claimed to care only that Margaret was 'a

Chatswood, the Sydney suburb where the Nash homestead was located.

good mother to the children and a good wife'. He 'did not like underhand things', was 'broad-minded' and preferred her to 'do it openly'. He knew all about the affairs she had been involved in, and testified that she was 'fed up with a closed-in domestic existence'.

Initially, he *was* regarded by the police as a prime suspect.

At one o'clock in the afternoon of New Year's day, asleep at his house, he was awakened by the police.

'Is your wife at home?'

'No.'

'When did you last see her?'

He told them she had left him at a New Year's Eve party. They did not react. They said only that they were from Burwood, and had instructions to take him over to Chatswood. He dressed the children and they sat in the back of the police car with him. To his anxious question, 'Has there been an accident?' they returned a stolid, 'No, no accident.' He read about what had been found on the riverbank when the police sergeant at Chatswood handed him the afternoon paper. His first interrogation lasted ten hours. He had one other – on 11 January. Neither produced anything which, however morally shocking his narrative, enabled the police to proceed further.

Chandler told them that after leaving the party at nearly 4am, he drove to his girlfriend Pamela Logan's place. She was sound asleep and not precisely overjoyed when he woke her up at that hour, but, good sport, agreed to go with him on the drive to Granville to collect the children from his mother-in-law's. Pam waited tactfully down the street while he picked up Gareth and Sean. Then all four of them drove back to Pam's room in Darlington. They arrived there at 6.30am. He and his children left there at around 10am and then went straight home to Cromwell Street.

The bridge over the Lane Cove River, beside which the bodies were found.

Not only did Pamela Logan corroborate, which, cynics might say, was only to be expected, but Chandler's distinctive 1924 vintage Vauxhall, with its gleaming silver aluminium body, was seen on the Parramatta Road, near Burwood Road, between 4.45 and 5am by a photographer, John Sherry, on his way to early morning Mass. It was also seen shortly after by Leo Powning, an engineer who knew Chandler slightly, travelling in the direction of Granville. Thus was Geoff Chandler demonstrated to have been in the right place at the right time – just as, if his theory was correct, Mrs Chandler was in the wrong place at the wrong time.

For a while, a calumnious jingle, 'I'm in Love with Miss Logan', went the rounds of the Sydney night clubs, a sort of ongoing reverberation of the original scepticism regarding his innocence, but gradually suspicion withered and died. Chandler was to stay on at the CSIRO, a further five years after the tragedy, the object of un-understanding pity rather than misunderstanding hostility.

Chandler's own theory, more than a theory really, was: 'It is clear to me – and I choose the words carefully – that his death was due to the offices of some quasi-governmental agency. My wife, Margaret, was an innocent victim.' He wrote:

> Gilbert Bogle, you must understand, was more than a brilliant CSIRO scientist with a happy-go-lucky approach to social life. He was involved in undercover activities, the full extent of which no one, including myself, publicly knows. But he was involved. This is undeniable.

Chandler said that in May 1969 he received the first of a series of anonymous telephone calls extending over a period of six months, from a man who had told him that Mrs Chandler had been the victim of a vast international conspiracy organised by an alliance of Russian Jews, the CIA, and rogue security officers from various countries. Bogle had been killed to prevent his impending departure for the United States. Mrs Chandler had to die because she was with him. Chandler also said:

> I believe that the agent used to kill Gib and Margaret was from the extensive armoury of chemical-biological warfare, because the symptoms are consistent with those assessed and described in several scientific reports. An agent of this type kills in minutes and leaves no trace, the effect being to produce those two simple causes of death – cardiac arrest and respiratory failure. . . . As the appearance of mace at the Chicago riots showed, mixtures which come in aerosol cans can be sprayed on the person or inside the car to have a cumulative effect inducing nausea and death.

The Sydney police did not believe that Bogle's death

Gib's artistic contribution to the party.

had anything to do with his work. Two senior detectives, for instance, were totally satisfied that the motives for the murders were personal, and that the killings were carried out by two men, blood relations, specifically hired for the purpose. They posed as private detectives, engaged, they said, to further divorce proceedings, and, just to show that there were 'no hard feelings', they persuaded their quarry couple to have a drink with them. That sporting gesture cost Bogle and Chandler their lives, for the drink was laced with a poison of an unacceptable kind.

Was it, then, death in a heat of human passions? Or was it extermination in the cold blood of the politics of dispassion? There stood the choice. It might well have been that the Australian Security Intelligence Organisation had recruited Bogle as a part-time agent. Did they perhaps hope that, because of the nature of his work, he would sooner or later be approached by a KGB agent? Alternatively, had he been recruited by the AISO to keep a big brotherly eye for them on his CSIRO colleagues? Or did they see *him* as an up and coming security risk? Admittedly, it had been stated loudly and clearly that Bogle's CSIRO work had no security implications, however . . . there was at that time a sub-committee that had been looking at developments in chemical and biological warfare, and representatives of CSIRO sat on that committee. Not Bogle, true. That was not his field. But he would be bound to have known who was representing CSIRO, and, just a small point for the pot, Australian defence laboratories were collaborating with the US in the refining of shellfish toxins for inclusion in the weaponry of the CIA – and government analysts tested the bodies of Bogle and Chandler for shellfish toxin. On the other hand, it has been the fate of more than one lady-killer to be killed by a lady.

The majority of the detectives would, bless their romantic hearts, choose the human alternative. Actually, they would probably have accepted Ogg's LSD theory – the chivalrous male trying to make sure for his lady – if it had not been for the *other* Margaret.

Her name was Margaret Fowler. Married to a Sydney chemical engineer, she was young, vivacious and eye-catchingly well dressed. She was also highly intelligent, holding a London University degree in physics and mathematics. She was working in the library of the CSIRO when, in 1956, she met Bogle. By 1959 they were lovers. She became obsessed with him. True to form, he would eventually treat her callously and try to dump her. As their turbulent affair progressed – or, rather, didn't – Mrs Fowler made valiant efforts to keep away from Bogle. She took a new job in north Sydney, but could not resist pathetically seeking news of him from a friend of the family, Jenny Newbold. And when she heard that he was to leave Australia, she became hysterical, telling Jenny Newbold that she was in love with him, and had been for a long, long time. 'I should have taken the poison I had. I can't live without him,' she added. And, later, she confided to her friend Jenny: 'The police asked me if I had wanted to do away with myself, and I told them that I had on dozens of occasions. Anyway, it was only phenobarb that I had.'

Interviewed by the police – on 7 January and four subsequent occasions – Mrs Fowler was understandably quick to point out that she had an alibi for the night of the murder. She had been attending another party at Turramurra with her husband. They had not left the party until 3.45am, and then they had driven home. She had not, she said, gone to the Nash party – although the police are said to have received one report early in their investigations of her having been seen outside the Nash home some time after midnight. There was a persistent theory that she had followed Bogle's car to the park, and waited there, intending to confront her lover *in flagrante* with his new woman, but she had instead found them both unconscious, or already dead. It was she who had then arranged the bodies in the extraordinary manner in which they were found.

Sydney psychiatrists stated an opinion that the arrangement of Bogle's body suggested that whoever had done it had wanted to give him a semblance of dignity. The dressing of a corpse had been beyond that person, but the draping of the clothes so as to make him look as if he were clad suggests that the person felt sorry for, and cared about, him. Whereas, the indecent way in which Mrs Chandler's body had been disposed and displayed was suggestive of disapproval and contempt. Everything, they said, pointed to the fact that the person who had done this to the two bodies was a woman who knew them both.

Geoff, Margaret and baby Gareth in happier pre-Bogle days.

That conclusion was echoed by at least one senior detective on the case. Convinced that Mrs Fowler was the murderess, he was very much against her being permitted to leave the country after the inquest, but since there was no evidence upon which he or anyone else could hold her, there was nothing he could do about it. Other detectives felt that she was innocent, but neurotic.

Mrs Fowler claimed: 'Dr Bogle called on me after he had been to the American Consulate about his trip to America. He said, "We'll have a flat together in London." I told him that I could not live without him.'

Then came the CSIRO Christmas party, at which Bogle first met Margaret Chandler. Margaret Fowler was at that barbecue too – and noticed Bogle's reaction to Mrs Chandler. She told her husband, 'I pity that Bogle if he's going to get mixed up with the Chandlers.'

The truth may be that Gib and Margaret had met several times, secretly, after the Christmas party and before the fatal New Year's party, and that Margaret Fowler, in a frenzy of jealousy, found out about it. Certainly Vivienne Bogle suspected nothing awry. She seems to have remained in tranquil ignorance of the great romantic storms blowing themselves out about the house of Bogle – 'Ours was a very happy family. I have done a lot of thinking about it, and Gilbert's behaviour in the past two weeks was the same as always. He was very happy and seemed content.' And, in reply to what she regarded as a most peculiar question, 'I have absolutely no reason to think my husband would kill himself.'

Margaret Fowler remarked, purely speculatively, that Bogle could have taken a 'sex drug'. A strange thing to say, you may think, unless she had evidence of previous indulgence with some such substance. Had he perhaps played that game with her? Perchance we need not after all relinquish the heartening image of the determinedly chivalric male, the knight indeed errant, struggling to resurrect himself, for the damsel threatened with distress, from the desiccated scientist.

That drug need not have been LSD. And this is where the Cheung clue may fit comfortably in. Two years after the mysterious Bogle–Chandler deaths, Dr Pang Teng Cheung, Director of Forensic Medicine for the Hong Kong Police, reported two deaths which showed precisely the same symptoms. They occurred after the taking of yohimbine. Yohimbine, sometimes called 'Japanese chocolate', is an illegal Asian sex drug. It is said to be used by breeders for getting certain animals on heat.

A colleague of Margaret Fowler's, Graham Carlton, has testified that at the time of the Bogle-Chandler tragedy he found her in a state of great distress. She kept repeating, 'It's all going to come out.' He asked her what she meant. 'You'll soon know,' was all she would reply. And then she began to talk about the deaths of Bogle and Chandler, giving Carlton

The Father Confessor, Detective-Sergeant Jack Bateman. He was sure he knew who did it.

the impression that she was somehow involved in them. 'My life is ruined,' she said. And again, 'They were going to cop it.' On another occasion she discussed poisoning someone on a dance-floor by pressing a ring containing a toxic substance into the victim's back. Carlton did not believe anything that she said. He thought that she was a very bright woman, but that she had problems, and was 'very scatty'.

It has been put forward that Margaret Fowler's worry that it was 'all going to come out' did not refer to its coming out that she had killed Bogle and Chandler, but that she had, of her own jealousy, been on the scene of the deaths at the approximate time of the deaths, and that that would make her a prime suspect in the police investigation. As it turned out, she need not have worried. The coroner permitted her to talk to him in private. She was the 'Mystery Witness' who was never publicly called in the case. No sooner was the inquest over than she left Australia. In 1967 she was divorced. On 18 June 1977, she died in a London hospital, following an illness.

Before her death she read a book, *Without Hardware*, privately published in 1970. It was written by Catherine R. Dalton, daughter of the poet, Robert Graves, and widow of Dr George Clifford Dalton, the scientist who played an important part in the invention of the fast breeder atomic reactor. He died in 1961 after a mysterious and protracted illness. *Without Hardware* fuelled the theory that Dr Dalton had been murdered by intelligence agents, and that Bogle, who had been a close friend of his, had shared a like fate. Mrs Dalton said in terms that the AISO had killed Bogle by spraying nerve gas in his face. They had eliminated him because he had intended on arrival in America to report on a plot between the rightist National Security Council and the Australian and British communists for interfering with the affairs of the Australian Energy Commission. His death was, she said, to be viewed in the light of the rivalry between the right-wing and moderate branches of the American security services.

A significant pointer, an inescapable factor in evaluating the equation, is that, even today, a quarter of a century on, Bogle's FBI file is still classified. *Something* in it constitutes a danger to US security.

Speaking, shortly before she died, of Catherine Dalton's book, Margaret Fowler told a friend: 'I've been puzzled for years, but this book has finally supplied the answer.'
Did it?
The answer?
Or a loophole?

ANNIVERSARY NOTE
Exactly thirteen years later, on New Year's Day 1976, Kenneth Nash, the man who hosted the fateful New Year's Eve party, died with a .22 calibre semi-automatic rifle between his knees. His body was found on a vacant lot near his home in Robinson Street. Police said there were no suspicious circumstances. Depressed since his wife's death two years earlier, he had become a recluse. He left a note for his neighbours apologising for the inconvenience of finding his body. It was obvious that he had planned to kill himself.

Sweet Fanny Adams

Baker beheads Sweet Fanny.

On the warm, sunny afternoon of Saturday, 24 August 1867, eight-year-old Fanny Adams, her seven-year-old sister, Lizzie, and their friend, Minnie Warner, aged eight, were playing in Flood Meadow, a field four hundred yards from their homes in Tan House Lane, Alton, Hampshire, when they were joined by Frederick Baker, a twenty-nine-year-old solicitor's clerk. After helping them to pick blackberries, he handed little Minnie three ha'pence, and told her to take Lizzie off with her to buy some sweets. He then picked Fanny up and carried her away. By four o'clock Fanny had still not returned home. Her worried mother and neighbours began a search for her.

At seven o'clock that evening a labourer came upon a pool of blood in a hopfield. Close by was the severed head of a child laid on two poles. Both eyes were missing. The right ear had been sliced off. Yards away lay a leg, a thigh, and the dismembered torso. It had been cut open and practically all its internal organs removed. The police subsequently found the child's heart and an arm. Most gruesome of all, two eyes were seen floating in the river Wey. Baker, who had been spotted in the meadow by a local woman, was questioned. Then arrested. There was blood on his clothes and two small knives in his pocket. Also a diary, in which, under 24 August, he had written: 'Killed a young girl. It was fine and hot.' Tried and found guilty, he was hanged on Christmas eve at Winchester prison. A crowd of five thousand cheered his Yuletide exit. The poor little child's brief existence is commemorated by the phrase 'Sweet Fanny Adams' meaning 'nothing at all' – which was what was left of her after Baker's butchery. With typical sailor's grisly humour, the Royal Navy christened the tinned mutton, first issued at this time, 'Fanny Adams'.

Victorian Bogey Woman No. 1

Kate Webster: She-Devil with a Cleaver

Some account of the curious circumstances encompassing an Irish witch's brew in the copper of a Richmond kitchen and the far-flung voyage over Richmond water of the cook-general's anatomised employer.

Kate Webster, the cook-general.

'I little thought when Kate came in and I chatted with her that she had left her mistress boiling in the copper!' said Mrs Hayhoe, landlady of the Hole in the Wall public house, on the corner of Park Road, in Richmond, Surrey.

When thirty-year-old Kate Webster had taken up her new situation as cook-general with Mrs Julia Martha Thomas, a fussy widow in her fifties, at 2 Mayfield Villas, Park Road, Richmond, on 27 January 1879, there is small doubt that murder was *not* then her intention. She was just an Irish con-woman, down on her luck. Although she had 'form' as long as her sinewy arm, it was all for crimes against property. True, she had a nasty temper, but there were no warning signs that it would inevitably lead her to homicide.

Light-fingered Kate, strong-fingered Kate, was tall and dark, with good white teeth that gleamed gypsyish in a sudden smile. There was something rugged and elemental about her, a whiff of peat bogs and standing stones. Her rebarbative effigy, sallow and slant-eyed, scowling and pitiless, used to be a real crowd-puller in Madame Tussaud's Chamber of Horrors, and such was the terror aroused by the case, that women living on their own took to checking their servants' references more carefully. Many a lonely widow cast a queasy look at cook as she filleted a joint of mutton for supper.

Kate Webster, the cause of all this consternation, was born Catherine Lawler in the village of Killane, in the County of Wexford, in about 1849. Her native land soon became too hot for young, jackdaw Kate, and after serving a term of imprisonment for larceny, she took the boat across the Irish Sea to Liverpool, where it did not take her long to find a pitch among the seething criminal dens.

Although glib and quick-witted, she was not quite smart enough to keep out of trouble, and more convictions under a series of aliases began to notch up. Her speciality was lodging-house theft; she would talk a landlady into letting her a room, and then decamp with all the goodies she could lay her sticky fingers on, a burdened jackdaw. In 1867 four years' penal servitude somewhat clipped her wings, and it was a hardened, embittered woman who made London her next port of call. For some three years, she claimed, she then went straight, slaving as a domestic.

An illegitimate son was born to her on 19 April 1874, at 5 Acre Road, Kingston, Surrey, and he was, henceforth, the centre of her life. Her constant devotion to Johnny was a redeeming feature in her savage psychology. She paid Sarah Crease, a charwoman and wife of a shoeblack, to look after him from time to time, when she was presumed to be in service. Childbirth and parenthood pushed her right back into crime (if she had ever been out of it) and she spent as much of her life inside as out during the next five years.

In January 1879, she surfaced with her little boy, lodging at Sarah Crease's humble Richmond home. Regularly every Saturday Sarah did cleaning for a Miss Lucy Loder, at No 2 The Crescent, Richmond, and on several occasions Kate Webster filled in for her. It was Miss Loder who unwittingly made the fatal connection between killer and victim. To be fair to her, she did not actually *recommend* the servant who had done occasional charring for her. When her friend, Mrs Julia Thomas, told her that she was, yet again, looking for a resident cook-general, she merely said that she knew of Kate Webster who was free.

Mrs Thomas was frantic for some help; she was known locally as an eccentric and a tartar, and could not keep a servant. She jumped at the chance of a new skivvy, and after a cursory interview engaged her on the spot, without a 'Character'. Probably Kate concocted some plausible tale to explain the want of that vital Victorian chit, and Mrs Thomas must have reasoned that she had performed adequately at Miss Loder's.

Such, then, was the collision between the fluttery widow and the flinty, gaol-coarsened predator, desperate to provide

for her child. All might yet have been well, except for an unfortunate coincidence: Mrs Thomas, too, was possessed of a famous temper. She had a tendency to epileptic fits, and an epileptic's short fuse.

We can be sure that when Kate arrived at the grey stone semi-detached villa in Park Road, and humped her few belongings up the stairs to the servant's bare, charity-cold room, her practised eye cased the joint with considerable interest. There was a piquancy in living alone and on terms of some intimacy with a genteel lady who was rumoured to be wealthy, wore tempting jewellery, and had a fine taste in furniture. The jackdaw's eye glittered, but then hooded. She must have intended either to play it straight for a while, to glean the regular pittance, or to carry out her customary flit when the time was ripe.

At first Kate was on her best behaviour, bridling her wicked tongue and leaping to the commands of her taskmistress. All

The Hole in the Wall.

the housework was done the hard way, boiling up the washing in the copper and scrubbing the floors with blue, chapped hands – while Mrs Thomas tinkled on her pianoforte in the parlour. Kate's particular resentment was that 'When I had finished my work in my rooms, she used to go over it again after me, and point out places where she said I did not clean, showing a nasty spirit towards me.'

Within a fortnight, the uneasy paragon became defiant and rebellious, and Mrs Thomas gave Kate notice to quit at the end of the month, on Friday, 28 February. Her maid very definitely did not suit. As the tense days of the period of notice dragged past, with the widow avoiding the louring gaze of her unwelcome incumbent, we know that she must have had a premonition of trouble, because she asked around at her church if anyone would come to stay with her. When all refused, she managed to find a mother and daughter to lodge with her for two weeks, also leaving on 28 February.

Thus supported and emboldened, she sat out the last days of her siege. Kate's workload was trebled, and her sense of injury festered. She had no future to look forward to. A scheme began to simmer and bubble in her mind. On Shrove Tuesday, 25 February, she visited Mary Durden, a straw-bonnet maker, at her home in London Street, Kingston. She was in an excited state, and did not sit down for the whole hour that she stayed, a not entirely welcome guest.

This was no idle call upon a friend, but rather in the nature of a rehearsal or a dry run for a notion which was still half-formed, and might never ripen into a deed. Kate told Mary Durden that she was living in Richmond and was about to go to Birmingham to see to some property which her aunt had left her there. She said that she had had a letter from her aunt, telling her where to find her gold watch and her chain and her jewels; everything her aunt owned was to come to her. The will was in a drawer. She was planning to sell the furniture.

The final Friday of release came. The two lodgers left. But Kate Webster stayed on. She tackled Mrs Thomas about her notice when they were alone and eyeball to eyeball again. Glibly, she spun one of her spidery stories and wrung from her employer the concession that she could remain, some say for a month, others just until the following Monday, 3 March.

Mrs Thomas made what was to be her last entry in her diary – a note that Kate was to stay on – and spent the next afternoon, Saturday, planting spring flowers in her garden. Alas, she never saw them bloom. It was as if she sought, in that small act of creation, to stave off her own extinction. She was, by then, a doomed woman.

Sunday 2 March dawned, and Mrs Thomas took her last Sacrament at the Presbyterian service in the Lecture Hall, Hill Street, Richmond. Kate spent her afternoon in a public house. When she stormed back to Mayfield Villas she was late, and had held up Mrs Thomas' departure to evening church. There was a rebuke, and Kate flew into a terrible passion.

Trembling and agitated, the widow made her escape and walked shakily to the Lecture Hall, where she sank down into a seat just inside the door, instead of her usual, prominent place. Also present was Julia Nicholls, of 10 Whitechurch Villas, Richmond, general servant to Miss Emma Roberts, who was on visiting terms with Mrs Thomas. She noticed that Mrs Thomas was flushed and vexed about something, and that her bonnet had slipped right off her head.

The widow left the service ten minutes early, at 7.35pm, and marched home, a Christian soldier to the battlefield. What a lonely figure she is as we see her now, making her last half-mile journey through the dark streets to a cruel fate.

We arrive next at a silent area, like a layer of deep ocean in which a submarine glides out of radar range. Only the startled mice in the wainscotting and the mute sentinel of Mrs Thomas' favourite rubber plant witnessed the death scene within that vile villa. Our single, independent testimony comes from Mrs Jane Ives, who was sitting peaceably next door at No 1 Mayfield Villas, minding her own business. Between 8 and 9pm she heard a noise in the next house, a thump as if a heavy chair had fallen. It seemed to come from the region of the hall.

If Kate Webster were on trial for murder today, no doubt her counsel would argue that this was a case of 'diminished responsibility' under the Homicide Act 1957, and that his client (inter alia) acted under an 'irresistible impulse'.

The burden of Kate's treacly words in her last 'confession' after all hope of reprieve was abandoned was precisely 'irresistible impulse':

I did not murder Mrs Thomas from any premeditation. I was enraged and in a passion, and I cannot now recollect why I did it; something seemed to seize me at the time. I threw her downstairs in the heat of passion and strong impulse.

Bringing Mrs Thomas to the simmer.

Excellent! – except for the vital testimony of Mary Durden, the straw-bonnet maker, which goes towards premeditation. It might be put that the Birmingham aunt story shows only an intent to steal, but there is an ominous reliance upon the *demise* of the 'aunt'.

As for the acts which make up the killing, let us turn first to Kate's own account:

> Upon her return from church, before her usual hour, she came in and went upstairs. I went up after her, and we had an argument which ripened into a quarrel, and in the height of my anger and rage I threw her from the top of the stairs to the ground floor. She had a heavy fall. I felt that she was seriously injured, and I became agitated at what had occurred, lost all control of myself, and, to prevent her from screaming or getting me into trouble, I caught her by the throat, and in the struggle she was choked.

Popular legend, and most commentators, will not accept this (comparatively) tame scenario. Kate is thought to have been pre-armed with a heavy weapon – a meat axe for preference – and to have felled her victim with one deadly blow, which would explain the absence of a scream. Incidentally, Mrs Jane Ives admitted that her hearing was not very good.

The method of disposal of Mrs Thomas' body by fire and water is no mystery. It is the fine detail of the preparation for disposal which is, perhaps mercifully, not so clear as it might be. Elliot O'Donnell, the editor of the *Notable British Trials* volume on the case, ever a vivid writer with a lively Celtic imagination, thought that Mrs Thomas was still alive when Kate began her feat of dismemberment – and that Kate enjoyed it.

This is how Kate remembered the occasion:

> I then became entirely lost and without any control over myself, and looking on what had happened, and the fear of being discovered, I determined to do away with the body as best I could. I chopped the head from the body with the assistance of a razor which I used to cut through the flesh afterwards. I also used the meat saw and the carving knife to cut the body up with. I prepared the copper with water to boil the body to prevent identity; and as soon as I had succeeded in cutting it up I placed it in the copper and boiled it. I opened the stomach with the carving knife, and burned up as much of the parts as I could.

One knows intuitively that Kate tackled the cadaver as if it were the carcass of a plucked chicken, but did not manage to dissociate herself from the ghastly reality of what she was intent upon; her sense of horror, filtered through the prose of her solicitor, in her 'confession', rings true – 'I was greatly overcome, both from the horrible sight before me and the smell, and I failed several times in my strength and determination, but was helped on by the devil.'

Inside her devil's kitchen, Kate fed her steaming cauldron, while, outside, the world of Richmond rolled on and guessed not. The following morning, Monday, 3 March, at six o'clock, Mrs Jane Ives, bearing a candle, went out to turn the water on at the area steps at the back of No 1 Mayfield Villas. She noticed that there was a light in one of the back bedrooms of No 2. At seven o'clock, she heard a sound of washing and brushing in the next-door scullery. The copper fire was poked and rattled. At eleven o'clock, she monitored a line-full of washing – underclothing, towels, sheets and other things – hanging out in the back garden.

So far, so domestic and normal – except for the smell, which, all that morning, coiled and wreathed over the chimneypots of Park Road, and, no doubt, drifted as far as the Hole in the Wall, whither Kate wended her wan way at least once in the day for a fortifying neat gin or rum. There were interruptions. At 12.30pm William Thomas Deane, a coal merchant, called for his payment. Kate opened the door about eighteen inches, and said that her mistress was not at home. She seemed abrupt and excited (a favourite Victorian adjective in this case). Mrs Thomas' friend, Miss Emma Roberts, was not so favoured; when she paid a visit at about 6pm the door remained firmly closed, although she stood her ground for half an hour. There was a strong light in the hall, the basement and the drawing room.

That afternoon, Mrs Ives' daughter Elizabeth, a dressmaker, and incidentally Mrs Thomas' landlady, who lived with her mother at No 1, was pottering about on their rockery. From that vantage point she was able to spot that the breakfast things

The Rising Sun.

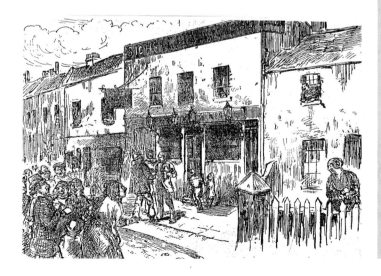

'I thought I saw the wicked
old witch in
    The richest gallipot in the
kitchen!'
    A lolloping galloping candle
confesses.
    'Outside in the passage are
wildernesses
    Of darkness rustling like witches'
dresses.'

Edith Sitwell
from *Façade* I. 'The Drum'

were still on Mrs Thomas' table. And there they remained, scandalously, until the next evening.

On Tuesday, 4 March, Kate was again disturbed at her infernal housework. Young Mary Roberts, apprenticed to Elizabeth Ives from eight in the morning until eight at night, was dispatched next door with the ill-received news that some men would soon be going round to repair a leak in the roof. Kate, speaking from a window above the front door, scotched all that: it had only been snow melting. By mid-afternoon, tired and aching, Kate was satisfied that the villa was shipshape again: even the brickwork around the copper was freshly whitened.

Gleefully, she tugged on to her bony frame one of Mrs Thomas' best silk gowns, crammed several of her gold rings on her own knobbly, work-calloused fingers, and snatched up her watch and chain. Thus incongruously apparelled, she sailed in unaccustomed style to 10 Brightwell Cottages, Rose Gardens, Hammersmith. Her plan was in progress. In her hand was a black American-cloth bag, and back at the villa there was a heavy, corded box.

'Hullo, Father, here you are,' she accosted Mr Henry Porter, who was considerably taken aback by this apparition. He and his wife, Ann, knew her only as Kate, and had not clapped eyes on her for six years. However, they brightened remarkably when she told them an uplifting story: her name was Mrs Thomas, and an aunt had died and left her a very comfortable home in Richmond. She wanted to sell the furniture, because her father had written to ask her to go back to Ireland to look after him. Perhaps Henry could recommend a buyer, since she did not know the Richmond people very well?

It was a masterly performance. Kate produced whisky and sent out for gin. Tea was partaken of. A neighbour, James Thurlow, of 42 Rose Gardens, dropped in and noticed that the sparkling visitor kept the black bag close by her feet under the tea table. As well she might, because it contained the severed head of Mrs Thomas.

At 7.30pm conversation flagged, and Kate, as always a great user of acquaintances, asked young Robert Porter, aged fifteen, to accompany her to Hammersmith Bridge. Henry Porter decided to join the expedition, and shared with his son the gallant task of carrying the black bag. It was heavy – about 20lb in weight. After an hour or so's walk, via the Angel public house, the lights of the Oxford and Cambridge near Hammersmith Bridge were welcoming. All three went inside for a restorative drink, after which Kate announced that she wanted to go over the bridge to see a friend in Barnes. This time, she refused offers of help with the bag, and when she returned after twenty minutes, she was empty-handed.

For her next trick, she asked if Robert could go on to Richmond with her. Eager to oblige, his father agreed, on condition that he returned home the same night. Back at Mayfield Villas, after a trip on the new District Line train,

Kate plied the boy with rum, and persuaded him to help her carry the corded box – to Richmond Bridge this time – to meet a friend. Robert seems to have been a most compliant lad; the box was again, like the American-cloth bag, uncommonly heavy, and the handle on his side was broken, so that his knuckles were chafed.

It was after 11pm by now, and the Thames ran soft and black beneath them. At the last alcove on the bridge, Kate said, 'Put the box down, and you go on; my friend will be here directly. I'll catch you up.' The boy heard a slight splash as he walked away.

Thus happily disencumbered of her embarrassing luggage – it had been a good night's work – Kate took her porter-boy home with her. It was too late for him to catch a train back to Hammersmith, of course. She put him to bed in the same room with her. He lay on the floor: she queened it in Mrs Thomas' best bed. The next morning, she gave Robert some breakfast – cooked in her devil's kitchen.

At the same time, shortly before seven o'clock on the morning of Wednesday, 5 March, the corded box popped up again. The tide had carried it, twirling and clunking, some five miles down-river, to Barnes Bridge. There it wallowed, half-beached on the strand like a lurking mine. When Henry Wheatley, a coal porter, found the piece of flotsam, he hoped for treasure-trove. He cut the cords, and gave the sodden box a good kick. It broke into pieces, and what looked at first – except for the foot – like chunks of cooked meat, spilled out over his boots.

Dr James Adams, summoned post-haste to the scene, soon affirmed that the remains were human, and those of one body only. There was no head, and one foot was missing. Identification appeared to be impossible, and, as is usual in similar discoveries, prankish medical students were blamed.

Blandly shocked by the 'Barnes Mystery', for the rest of the week Kate scuttled to and fro between Richmond and Hammersmith, fearful of sleeping at the villa, and intent on the sale of Mrs Thomas' effects. *That* was when she should have fled, but, buoyed up by an almost convalescent optimism, she was enjoying the new affluence, the conviviality, and the respect of her friends.

According to Mrs Hayhoe, of the Hole in the Wall, some said, it was about this time that Kate jauntily hawked around Park Road two gallipots of meat dripping, rich and creamy, marbled with veins of goodness – rendered down from Mrs Thomas' poor, boiled body. No neighbour ever confessed to involuntary cannibalism! This is the kind of grisly rumour that persists, like the story current in 1970 that Mrs Muriel McKay's body had been fed to pigs by her kidnappers. Elliot O'Donnell thought it worth mentioning, and he noted that there were traces of fat still clinging to the copper when the police examined the premises on 27 March. However, if we turn

Mrs Julia Martha Thomas.

Henry Porter, Kate's innocent go-between, selling the murdered woman's teeth to Niblett, the Hammersmith jeweller. Kate gave him a shilling for his trouble.

to the forensic evidence of Dr Thomas Bond, of Westminster Hospital, he states that the fat produced to him by the police was only black grease – which is not a saleable commodity! The devil, master of that kitchen, would probably like to point out that there was another source of dripping – the range fire on which some parts were roasted.

The next player in the Richmond melodrama was John Church, publican of the Rising Sun, Rose Gardens, Hammersmith – obviously the Porters' local. Foxy-faced and tradesman-like in appearance, he sported a deerstalker hat, but proved to be only a tardy Sherlock Holmes. Introduced to him by the Porters, Kate so thoroughly duped him that he almost ransomed his life for the alluring furniture which he fancied to improve his own home, and for which he offered Kate the sum of £68. She swore, later, that *he* had committed the murder, and his alibi for the night of the carnage had to be exhaustively investigated before he was cleared.

Church found the inspection of the goods so fascinating that he spent many hours at No 2 Mayfield Villas with Kate 'Thomas'. There were noggins and banter and who knows what else. On Monday, 10 March, there was another grim discovery. George William Court was wheeling manure from a heap on an allotment at Copthall, in the Twickenham area, when he dug out a human foot and ankle. It had been recently sawn off, and it seemed reasonable to add it to the hotch-potch of remains at Barnes mortuary. The head, incidentally, was never found; as Dr Thomas Bond gave in his expert evidence, the head will not float in water by itself.

Undeterred Kate carried on with her picnic. On Sunday, 16 March, there was, of all things, a boating party. Kate, Church *en famille*, another Porter son, William, and friend, took to the River Thames, the Thames which runs sweetly through the whole story, while somewhere below on the murky bed a black American-cloth bag rocked gently in the currents. Church was captivated by strong, bold Kate as she flashed her rings and jingled her keys. Why did she dally? She should have left the furniture and fled with the trinkets.

Monday was packing day. Tuesday was removal day. And the party was over for Kate. The arrival of furniture vans is always a source of interest to neighbours, but Miss Elizabeth Ives was more than intrigued – she was extremely disturbed when two vans rumbled up to Mrs Thomas' gate. Her tenant had not given notice to quit. She ran out and asked the driver, Henry Weston, where he was taking the furniture.

Kate had, perhaps, gambled that Miss Ives would not interfere. Reluctantly, she shuffled forward and muttered, 'Mrs Thomas has sold the furniture; the man here can show the receipts. Mr Weston is going to take it to Hammersmith.'

'Where *is* Mrs Thomas?' Elizabeth Ives persisted.

'I do not know,' Kate said lamely, and turned away. She knew then that it was finished. Her face was contorted, and

2 Mayfield Villas, the house of death.

she could hardly speak.

Church and Porter, who were looking on, did not catch the words of this conversation, but they had sensed enough to smell a minor kind of rat. Obviously, there was some impediment to the sale of the furniture, and they wanted out! 'You have deceived me,' Church exclaimed. 'I will have nothing to do with the goods: put them back again.'

Before the empty vans trundled away, Kate threw into the back of one of them a bundle of Mrs Thomas' dresses – sure, she was not the eejit to be going off with nothing! Then she sped over to Hammersmith by hansom cab, collected her son from the Porters, crossed to Ireland by coal boat, and went to earth at her uncle's farm at Killane. The black sheep had come home. But not for long.

In the pocket of one of those dresses, which had been taken to the Rising Sun, Church's wife Maria found a letter to the real Mrs Julia Thomas signed 'Menhennick, 45 Ambler Road, Finsbury Park.' Thither Church made his way, deerstalker firmly planted on his puzzled head. It soon became painfully apparent that the Menhennicks' Mrs Thomas was not the aunt of Church's 'Mrs Thomas'. The police took over. Young Robert Porter identified the corded box, mainly by the missing handle. And thirteen-year-old Edith Menhennick, who had stayed with Mrs Thomas, also identified it.

Kate Webster was not difficult to trace. In a dress which she had left behind at the villa, a letter from her uncle in Ireland was found, and she was arrested at Killane on 28 March. Nor was that all that was discovered at Mayfield Villas. Inspector John Pearman searched the ashes under the kitchen grate and sifted out 'a quantity of charred bones, dress buttons, and two pieces of house flannel'. There were charred bones under the copper grate, too, and Kate had missed some bloodstains on the walls. Under the sink in the scullery there was a handle which fitted the corded box – and some of the cord! In fact, the villa was bursting with clues. It was crying out for vengeance.

The night before she was hanged at Wandsworth Prison, on 30 July 1879, Kate Webster made a final confession to her priest, Father M'Enery, which, it was said, shocked him so terribly that he was never the same man again.

The Kensal Rise Trunk Fiend

What especial quality of homicidal magic is it that catapults some murderers up into enduring headlines, while others, just as villainous, fade away in unremembered silence? Few people have ever heard of George Albert Crossman, but he was quite a criminous character. A gentleman of no fixed employment, bigamy was his hobby. He had stood, matrimonially button-holed, next to seven brides by the time he was thirty-two. In 1898, with three marriages under his belt, he was sentenced at the Old Bailey to five years. Released on licence in December 1902, he celebrated by 'marrying', early in January 1903, at Holy Trinity, Brondesbury, London, a woman bearing the loaded name, Edith Thompson. And a week after that, still in nuptial mood, he gave himself at the altar to Mrs Ellen Sampson, a widowed professional nurse. Ellen's honeymoon lasted twenty-four hours. She was then packed away, in cement, in a tin trunk, and the trunk installed in a cupboard under the stairs at No 43 Ladysmith Road, Kensal Rise, where George and Edith, and the two children of George's previous 'marriages', all lived happily – but not for ever after. The crunch came when, in the first months of 1904, the tenants of the ground-floor flat at Number 43 complained of a horrible smell emanating from the tin trunk, and threatened that if the offending and offensive object were not removed, the sanitary authorities would be summoned forthwith. On a bright March morning in 1904, Crossman was in the very act of removing the trunk when the police – to whom Crossman's tenants had communicated 'certain suspicions' about the sinister-smelling object – turned up. Crossman panicked. Pursued through three-quarters of a mile of North London streets by an athletic constable named Reeves, and caught up with in Hanover Road, he turned, at bay, cut his throat with a razor, and died on the pavement. Since 'marrying' Edith he had not been idle. Mrs Crossmans Nos 6 and 7 were found set up in separate establishments in different parts of London. Strange that altar-hopping Gentleman George is not remembered – if only for marital valour!

Victorian Bogey Woman No. 2

Mary Eleanor Pearcey: She-Devil with a Perambulator

A cautionary tale in which is demonstrated the impossibility of squaring the infernal triangle, the futility of lust, and the lethal consequence of giving the green light to jealousy.

The love of Mrs Mary Eleanor Pearcey for Frank Samuel Hogg may not have been pure, but it was cruelly true. And it was in the name of love – that tender force which should beget and cherish life – that she perpetrated a savagery so severe that it set the nape of Victorian London tingling with the fear that Jack the Ripper was back at work.

A russet woman. Compelling russet-coloured hair, thick and soft as antler-velvet, parted in the middle, tumbling in mossy loops above her ears, an overflowing russet stream which seemed somehow to drown out the imperfections of a nose too large, a mouth too wide, teeth too prominent, a chin too weak and recedent, and lasciviously to complement fine blue eyes, bold against russet and delicate sallowish skin. The face is long. So is the neck, very long and very thin. The figure is full and tall – 5 feet 6 inches – powerful to the verge of masculinity. Hands feminine, small and shapely.

But this is no ordinary woman. She is only twenty-four now, but she has been different from all others from the beginning. She has, since birth, been reported subject to epileptic fits. Her father died when she was fifteen. Her grief was extreme. She was found in the garden, suspended by a rope about that long, thin neck. She had stood upon a basket and kicked it away. She was black in the face. Her mother finds her a puzzlement. Flesh of – and not of – her flesh. She has siblings, a brother, a sister, apparently of the coinage of normalcy. She has early perceived the red alert of sexuality and attended it. But has never married, although pretended it, having borne both the title and status of marriage. There was one Pearcey, John Charles Pearcey, a young carpenter, with whom in her late teens she had shared pseudo-marital domesticity, shedding for him her given name of Mary Eleanor Wheeler. After a year or two the

Mary Eleanor Pearcey, the reality modelled by Madame Tussaud's. Madame Tussaud's Archives, London.

The terrible perambulator, dark corpse-carrier, spindly wheels whirring through the stone forest of North London streets. Madame Tussaud's Archives, London.

Mary Eleanor Pearcey (an idealised portrait).

Victim Mrs Phoebe Hogg.

loose partnership grew looser. Pearcey, it has been said, left her, becoming tired of her infidelities. For whatever reason, the relationship palled, and ended in pseudo-divorce. With pride, and, as it transpired, cunning purpose, she continued however to bear the label of her whilom illicit connubiality, Mrs Pearcey.

Pearcey flown, others came, attracted by the moth-lamp of sexual magic that burnt in her bedroom window, and went. Of different ilk, less nectar-sipping flighty, was more mature visiting fireman from Northfleet, Gravesend, Kent, Mr Charles Crichton. Well-heeled and well-satisfied enough to pay his key money – the rent of Mrs Pearcey's North London premises, No 2 Priory Street, Kentish Town, and of its mistress – he called punctiliously once a week to inspect both pieces of his property. Instalments kept up, her body, all but her heart, belonged to (sugar) daddy. But *she* and her *cor cordis* were reserved for another, who, seen through the distorting lens of her own lonely need, she held more precious than life itself.

This other, doing absolutely nothing to deserve it, but accepting the irrational, obsessional, unearned devotion which he inspired as his woman-given right, the unworthy object of all this misbegotten, mis-shapen love, was middle-aged, bearded, amoral, self-centred, self-pitying, lachrymose Frank Samuel Hogg. Hogg by name and nature, he was a feckless fellow, but dowered with that syrup of sentimentality which so often does bastard service for genuine sympathy. He was selfish, conceited, opinionated and apologetically arrogant, these qualities being compounded within him in just the right quantity and combination to produce the standard irresistible psychopath.

His marriage to Phoebe Styles, in November 1888, was the early fruit of his psychopathy. Having impregnated her, he was induced, but not without the weight of her hefty brothers' muscular logic, to see the social desirability of matrimony as prooemium to parenthood. The ensuant marriage fell, not perhaps surprisingly, short of idyllic. Even the arrival, six months later, of bouncing baby Phoebe failed to inject rejuvenescence, if that is the correct word to apply to something which does not seem to have been joyfully juvenscent in the first place. In fact, Hogg greeted the nativity of Phoebe Hanslope with outbursts of hot male tears upon Mary Eleanor's shoulder and hysterical threats of suicide. Nor was it only verbal comfort which, undoubtedly encouraged by his sister, Clara, he sought of Mary Eleanor. Such, indeed, is the intricacy of the most peculiar tripartite situation obtaining between the three females in the life of this odious caliph of Kentish Town, that it seems neccessary at this juncture to submit it to some scrutiny.

First, there was Phoebe, wife and mother of his baby daughter. A large, plain woman of thirty-one. Rather sickly and on the thin side. Redeemed by a head of striking black wavy hair and lovely violet-blue eyes. He had taken her after their exigent marriage to live in rooms at his mother and sister's house at 141 Prince of Wales Road, Kentish Town.

Secondly, there was Mary Eleanor Pearcey or Wheeler. He had known her, most likely in all the graduated significances of that term, for two or three years before his circumstantially enforced alliance with Phoebe – although he vehemently denied having been, as he so delicately put it, 'criminally intimate' with her before December 1888. However, living with his family thus conveniently just around the corner from Priory Street, he continued to 'know' her after his marriage – several times a week, acquaintance being facilitated by his being supplied with his own latchkey to No 2.

Thirdly, there was Clara Hogg, his sister. She and Phoebe do not seem to have got along too well. Reportedly, they quarrelled frequently. On the other hand, Clara was friendly with Mary Eleanor and seems to have given tacit encouragement to brother Frank in his dalliance with her.

Oddly, a much less fraught relationship prospered between Phoebe and her husband's mistress than existed between the sisters-in-law. When, in the February of 1890, Phoebe had been taken ill – the result, claimed the Hogg clan, of a miscarriage; the product, countered the aggrieved Styles tribe (Phoebe's sister, Martha, a domestic at Egham, Surrey, and her niece, Elizabeth, in service in St John's Wood), of undernourishment, neglect and ill-treatment – Mary Eleanor it was who beat a path to her bedside, laden with delicacies and bearing charity's basket-load of sympathetic understanding.

Actually, Phoebe and Clara had been frequent friendly visi-

Mary Eleanor Pearcey was not an educated woman. Her story is one of low life. She was nothing more than a 'call on' girl, entertaining a regular succession of paying lovers. You would expect her letters to be, if not actually depraved, those of ignorance – whining, selfishly demanding and self-indulgent. They are not like that at all. They are not, perhaps, epistolary masterpieces, but they have a simple beauty, a natural grace, and breathe a sincerity and intensity of pure love which transcends not only such quibbles as correct spelling, grammar, and punctuation, but even the shifts for a living to which the woman who penned them was driven.

2 October 1888
My Dear F,
Do not think of going away, for my heart will break if you do. Don't go dear. I won't ask too much, only to see you for 5 minutes when you can get away. But if you go quite away, how do you think I can live? I would see you married 50 times over – yes, I could bear that far better than parting with you for ever and that is what it would be if you went out of England. My dear loving F, you was so down-hearted today that your words give me much pain, for I have only one true friend I can trust to, and that is yourself. Don't take that from me. What good would your friendship be then, with you so far away? No, no, you must not go away. My heart throbs with pain to only think about it. What would it be if you went? I should die. And if you love me as you say you do, you will stay. Write or come soon, dear. Have I asked too much?
From your loving
M.E.

18 October 1888
Dearest Frank,
    I cannot sleep, so am going to write you a long letter. When you read this I hope your head will be much better dear. I can't bear to see you like you were this evening. Try not to give way. Try to be brave, dear, for things will come right in the end. I know things look dark now, but it is always the darkest hour before the dawn. You said this evening, 'I don't know what I ask.' But I do know. Why should you want to take your life because you want to have everything your own way? So you think you will take that which you cannot give – you will not if you love me as you say you do. Oh, Frank, I should not like to think I was the cause of all your troubles, and yet you make me think so. What can I do? I love you with all my heart, and I will love *her* because she will belong to you. Yes I will come and see you both if you wish it. So dear, try and be strong, as strong as me, for a man should be stronger than a woman. Shall I see you on Wednesday, about 2 o'clock? Try and get away too, on Friday, as I want to know if you are off on Sunday until 7 o'clock. Write me a little note in answer to this. I shall be down on Monday or Tuesday in the morning about 9am.
    So believe me to remain your most loving

M.E.

tors to Mary Eleanor's home long before Phoebe's ascension into the branches of the Hogg family tree. And, a later quiddit this, there were even to be quarrels between Frank and Phoebe because of secret notes written by Mary Eleanor *to Phoebe*. Notes which Phoebe would not allow Frank to read!

In lugubrious Kentish and Camden Towns, across the mounting months, life inexorably shaped its pattern towards its pre-ordained grand climacteric. Frank, formerly manager of his mother's provision shop, sometime dealer in furniture, moved lethargically on to work, sporadically, for his brother, who was in a good way of business as a furniture remover. Phoebe attended to the domestic needs and demands of her slothish spouse. Mary Eleanor, receiving in regular clandestine ecstasy the wayward and perfidious Frank in her back-parlour bedroom, arrived at the conclusion that not only was Frank Hogg essential to her happiness, but the realization of *his* happiness must henceforth be her sacred duty. Clara, watching, knowing and sharp-eyed, saw her pampered brother join the phalanx of visitors, all others of whom paid for the privilege, passing into Mary Eleanor's arachnoidal parlour.

So tripped by the months for wife, mistress and sister. Perhaps, ignorance on the one side maintained and yearning on the other subdued, they might have lengthened into innocent and happy hypocritical years, but it came to pass in the precarious balance of Mary Eleanor's incessantly brooding mind and epilepsy-tainted thinking that the resolution of her consuming emotional dilemma must be the killing of Phoebe.

Assembled now are all the essential ingredients of Greek tragedy come to Kentish Town. Hellenic horror in Hampstead. The backstreet Venus of Camden Town has resolved to snap her fly-trap.

Thursday, 23 October 1890.

'D' for 'Do It Day'.

The plan goes into operation. Mary Eleanor scribbles one of those little secret notes . . .

Dearest,
Come round this afternoon and bring our little darling. Don't fail.

Phoebe did fail. She could not make it. Mary Eleanor was standing, spider awaiting fly, at the door of her ugly yellow brick house, when, by long flexure of the arm of startling coincidence, her ex-lover Pearcey passed. Why, he asked her, were all the blinds drawn. Her fourteen-year-old brother had died, she said, and the funeral was to be on Tuesday. It was not true. Pearcey offered his condolences and, for the second and last time, passed out of her life.

No Phoebe. Teatime came and went.

Operation aborted.

Friday, 24 October 1890.

'A' for 'Achieve It Day'.

The plan succeeds.

Mary Eleanor, frustrated and hungry for blood, was abroad in good time this morning. At about 11am, in the street where the Hoggs lived, she gave a small boy, little Willie Holmes, a penny to deliver a note to Mrs Phoebe Hogg at No 141. And at half-past three that afternoon, Phoebe, watched by sister-in-law Clara, left Prince of Wales Road without telling a soul where she was going. She took baby Phoebe, best-dressed in brown pelisse and beaver bonnet tied with spick blue ribbons, with her in her bassinette.

Advantaged with the clear signposting of hindsight, it is possible to trace that last pilgrimage of the lost. Down Kentish Town Road, large hooped, spiky pram wheels spinning merrily, smartly into Royal College Street, sharp right, branch off into the drab street – then Priory Street, since renamed Ivor Street – where, by Priory Place, a railway arch spans, dark Titanic, the exit, and then those last few free yards to the flat-faced, three-storey, no basement house where, all unknowing, she and her little child have a rendezvous to keep with all eternity. Pull the bassinette up the steps, park it in the narrow dark entrance hall . . .

What comes now can only be dreadful conjecture. One living witness alone emerges from the carnage to tell, and she, the assassin, had sealed the compact of blood with silence. But it must have been that the tall, plain woman, her eighteen-month toddler clutched in her arms, blind both to all sign or scent of danger, strangers, too, in those comfortably familiar environs to fear, followed the younger, smaller woman, her friend, trustingly into either the front parlour or the poky kitchen at the hall's end. Was there, one wonders, the refinement of some prelude? Did china wink and tea steam upon a neat-laid table, with thin-cut bread and butter and strawberry jam and scones? There is no knowing. There may or may not have been the charade of afternoon tea.

But what happened before the tea-hour had run its disrupted course, is written in splashes of blood on kitchen walls and ceiling – the mute and harrowing tale of a terrifying struggle which frothed and spurted back and forth across that tiny claustrophobic arena. The broken window panes, the shattered chinaware, the dented, splintered wood, tell plainly: Phoebe Hogg was not easy to kill. Neighbours heard noise. Bangs. Crashes. A child's screamings. And good neighbour-like ignored them. 'I keep myself to myself. Never interfere.' What the 'banging and hammering' noises heard around 4pm were, was the plying of poker and knife to the fracturing of a skull and the cutting of a throat – so deep and true as almost to hack the head clean from the body, leaving it attached there only by a fragile anchorage of torn skin flap and shredded strands of muscle. 'I make it my business to mind my own business.'

2 Priory Street – the spider's parlour.

2 Priory Street, Camden Town.
19 October 1888
Frank Dear,
    You said 'if you thought I loved you'. What did you mean by that? Don't you know that I do? How can I prove to you that I do love you dearly? If there is anything I can do to prove it, I promise you it shall be done. You have more power over me that anyone on earth. When I say that I say all. Do have a wee note for me when I come tomorrow. I hope you did not get into any bother. Good night Dear.

Where Mrs Hogg's body was found in Crossfield Road. The circle with the 'X' marks the spot

25 October 1888
Dear Frank,
    Thanks so much for the letter. It was so good of you to send it. I am thinking how selfish I am for asking you to come here to see me. Of course you don't want to be bothered with me, but if you can come on Friday, I shall be very glad to see you, as I am afraid to come to the shop. I might make mischief, so to prevent it, I had better not come. People say ugly things sometimes, not nice to hear. So when I come into the shop again I shall be very careful and especially if an inquisitive lady should come in – you know who I mean. Dear Frank, the time has been so long today, every minute an hour of waiting for you. Do try and come on Friday. So good-bye till then, with good wishes from M.E. In this false world we do not always know who are our friends and who our enemies, and all need friends.

The entrance to Newgate. 'In that dream I see a great archway . . .'

Slaughter over. Mopping-up operations. The washing of blood. The sponging of rugs. The wiping of walls. The packing away of bodies, mother and child, in the bassinette. Neatly covered. A shroud of freshly-laundered, starch-crisp antimacassar. All cleaned clean away. Washed Pilate hands.

Mary Eleanor was not, as we have said, as other women. Her crime was literally insane jealousy. This epileptic Venus consummated her passion with a killing – two killings – of the innocent. She moved isolate, alone, in a big wind, under the quivering wing of madness.

Still, motionless, crouched at web's centre like a taut-poised black widow spider, corpses trussed secure as spider's larder flies, Mary Eleanor, a murderess now, awaits the friendly passport of darkness before putting on her bonnet and starting forth with her perambulator's load of carcasses.

Bump the weighty pram down the front door steps. Out into dark and cold October night. Did the moon perhaps ride high in the North London sky that night? Did Selene set the animals howling in Regent's Park Zoo? Did Artemis-Phoebe set up an echoing howling through the bone mazes of Mary Eleanor's skull and soul?

The doleful odyssey is well begun. The bassinette wheels whirr and blur – faster, faster, spokes invisibly revolving, eating up mile after mile of London paving stones. Anonymous streets whisk by. A bent, pale-faced, puffing woman, diminutive with head drooped right over the pram's high white china handlebar, is glimpsed battling in and out of successive gas lamp pools of light, pushing and straining, back braced, up the inclines her overloaded pramful of – washing?

Screw eyes against the darkness. Peer closer. A little epileptic froth at the corner of Mary Eleanor's mouth. A glazed blue eye deflecting the gaslight's wandering shafts and beams. Up Kentish Town Road she goes . . . Prince of Wales Road. . . . past the Hoggs' very door . . . across where Haverstock Hill meets Chalk Farm Road . . . Adelaide Road . . . Eton Avenue

. . . Crossfield Road, where, hard by Adamson Road, on to the pathway beside a building plot, straddled by its starkly roofless part-built house, her dark voices tell her, tip Phoebe out – the mother, not the child.

On then, on a further mile, to dump the wasted body of plump baby Phoebe in the place of the nettles, wasteland by the Cock and Hoop in Finchley Road. And on, a third mile, to St John's Wood, Hamilton Terrace. There to jettison the blood-sticky baby carriage or hearse. Kick herself free from the perilous basket on wheels. Back to life, this time; not, as once before, forward to death. Then home . . . home . . .home.

But the epic journey is not quite at its end. Disembarrassed of the bassinette and its temporary tenantry, driven by God alone knows what weird buffetings of relief, Mary Eleanor's lightened footsteps pointed her out of the Hampstead darkness to the bright spaces of Great Portland Street. There, at eight o'clock, she was seen and recognized by a girl who worked in a West End drapery house and knew her well. Mrs Pearcey was standing, in the girl's own – innocently symbolic – words, 'on a dark flagstone'. The girl did not approach her. She did not like what she saw. For Mrs Pearcey, whom she knew as normally nice and neat and tidy and ladylike, stood now hat awry, hair rough, gloveless and with what seemed like dark stained hands. Untidy and dejected, she was looking rapidly from one side to the other in a very peculiar and disinhibited sort of way. She might, the girl thought, have had too much to drink, and she decided to give her a wide berth.

When at last she reached home, a note awaited Mary Eleanor. It was from Frank. Arriving back from work latish that Friday evening, he had found neither wife nor baby at Prince of Wales Road, simply a scribbled line on a scrap of paper, 'Look in the saucepan' – meaning that his dinner awaited him there. Typically seizing his chance, that slug-pale, hirsute Lothario had slipped round and into No 2 with his latchkey. But he was out of luck there, too. Mary Eleanor was not at home. He took an envelope from the mantelshelf in the bedroom and wrote upon it, 'Twenty past ten. Cannot stay.' Then he slipped quietly out again. Obviously, he did not go into the disclosive kitchen. Why should he?

No sign still of the two Phoebes when, soon after 6am the following morning, Frank Hogg left his home for work. He was not seriously worried. He assumed that they must have gone to visit Phoebe's sick father at Chorleywood. Frank was back at Prince of Wales Road for breakfast at 8am. After swilling down a last cup of tea, the lethargic Frank bestirred himself and lumbered off to Chorleywood to fetch the missus home. He was flummoxed to find that she was not, had not been, there. Meanwhile, sister Clara was reading with rapidly peaking unease an account in that morning's paper of the discovery of the body of a murdered woman in a street in a part of Hampstead close to the route which Phoebe would have taken had she

Undated (post-1888)
Dear Frank,
You ask me if I was cross with you for coming only for such a little while. If you knew how lonely I am you would not ask. I would be more than happy if I could see you for the same time every day dear. You know I have a lot of time to spare and I cannot help thinking. I think and think till I get so dizzy that I don't know what to do with myself. If it was not for our love, dear, I don't know what I should really do, and I am always afraid you will take that away. Then I should quite give up in despair, for that is the only thing I care for on earth. I cannot live without it now. I have no right to it, but you gave it to me, and I can't give it up. Dear Frank, don't think bad of me for writing this. I do hope your cold will soon go away. Hoping to see you tomorrow, with love from your ever loving and affectionate
M.E.
PS Don't think anyone would know the handwriting.

No dream. The stark reality – the entrance to Newgate.

The condemned cell at Newgate

The execution shed at Newgate – the end of a dream.

been travelling to Chorleywood from Swiss Cottage station. Moreover, the description of the clothes which the murdered woman was wearing seemed to her to tally with Phoebe's.

When Frank returned from his fruitless journey, alarmed now and heedful of his sister's suspicions, he asked her to go round to Priory Street and ask Mary Eleanor if she had seen or heard anything of Phoebe. At first she denied all knowledge, but there must have been something in the way that she answered, perhaps some subtlety in her tone of voice, which left shrewd Clara unconvinced. Choosing her words carefully, phrasing her question differently, she put it to Mary Eleanor again. 'Well,' came the reply, 'as you press me, I'll tell you. Phoebe did come at about five o'clock and asked me if I would mind baby for a little while. I refused, and she then asked me if I would lend her some money. I said I couldn't as I had only a shilling and three halfpence in my purse, but I said she could have the shilling if she liked. I didn't tell you before because Phoebe asked me not to let anybody know she'd been here. That's why I said "No" '. Mary Eleanor added that Phoebe had then left the house. The obvious implication was that Phoebe would not want Frank to learn that she had been obliged to try to borrow, as he would almost certainly think that it reflected badly on him.

This conversation puzzled Clara. It did not ring true. For if there was one thing she knew about Phoebe it was that she was absolutely fanatical about not getting into debt. It amounted to a positive phobia. No way would she ask for a loan – even the most trifling one. No, it just went against everything that she knew of her sister-in-law. But Clara was too street-wise and wily a bird to give anything away. She held her whisht, said nothing; although the wick of a tiny nightlight of suspicion had just been ignited in her mind.

'I'm going,' said Clara, 'to ask to see the body of that woman they found murdered. Just in case. It might be Phoebe. It'll set my mind at rest. Will you come with me?' Pouring scorn on this fancifully premature identification, incredibly, Mary Eleanor agreed to go with Clara Hogg to Hampstead police station. They were taken to Hampstead mortuary. Shrinking together, they peered at the blood-caked mask on the slab. Mary Eleanor, the strong vein cords on either side of her long, thin neck raised and pulsing like prodded white worms under the stress, grew hysterical. 'That's not her. It's not her. It's not her. Let's go. Let's get out of this place,' she kept repeating, plucking like a crazed harpist at Clara's sleeve and torso.

Clara was not so sure. 'They're her clothes,' she said, eyeing the black cashmere dress, the unmistakable imitation astrakhan-trimmed black jacket, the underclothes with their neatly embroidered initials, 'P. H.' in red cotton, and, the clincher, the metal brooch with a true lovers' knot.

Their chaperone, Detective Inspector Thomas Bannister, led them gently out of the room. Dr Thomas Bond, who happened to be in attendance at the mortuary at the time, sponged the crusted blood from the face and matted hair of the thing on the table, made it more stark and whitely presentable. Bannister brought the women back. They looked again. 'It's Phoebe,' said Clara. She stretched her hand out, fingering the corpse's clothing. 'Oh, don't touch her,' Mary Eleanor screamed, trying to pull Clara away. 'Don't drag me,' said Clara sharply. Bannister had been watching all this closely. He spoke up. 'Don't drag her about. She can bear it, if you leave her alone.' In his mind the die was cast. He did not, could not as yet, distil the why and wherefore of it, but the good detective's third eye had snapped open to focus irreversibly on the ruffled russet woman. His poker player's face leaking nothing, he sent the women on with Detective Constable Murray to Portland Town (now called St John's Wood) police station to see the bassinette. It had been seen standing abandoned by some railings on the pavement of Hamilton Terrace, St John's Wood, by Elizabeth Andrews, a cook. That was at 8pm on Friday, 24 October – just about an hour after a young clerk named Macdonald, homeward bound at workday's end for Belsize Park, stumbled upon Phoebe's body. Elizabeth Andrews reported her discovery to PC John Roser, the beat policeman. The pram was still wet with blood and in it lay a pathetic, half-eaten piece of butterscotch, bearing the marks of a child's teeth. Clara duly identified the pram as having belonged to her sister-in-law.

Under a police sergeant's solicitous escort, the women were taken back to 141 Prince of Wales Road, where a questioning of them and of Frank Hogg began, and where, Frank's far from impressive façade rapidly disintegrating, was revealed, with all its implications, nestling in his pocket the key to No 2 with which his ever-ready Mary Eleanor had lovingly equipped him. The cat had been sprung from the bag. Suspicion's crystals were precipitated into a recognisable morphology. The protagonists were courteously requested to accompany the officers to Hampstead police station to assist them in their inquiries.

And there Mary Eleanor gradually emerged as the most significant figure. Would she, asked Detective Inspector Bannister, object to one or two of his men inspecting her apartments? Not at all, she said, 'but I would like to go with them.' So, at about three o'clock that Saturday afternoon, while Bannister, accompanied by Superintendent Beard and Mr Melville Macnaghten, went to the Hoggs' home to make a search, off she went in a cab with Sergeant Nursey and Detective Constable Edward Parsons to Priory Street.

Their arrival was discreet. Mary Eleanor had always done her best to maintain high level discretion on her home ground. The persona which she had laboured to project there was one of refinement and respectability. Sheltering behind the deliberately retained style and status of *Mrs* Pearcey, she had contrived for herself a wholesome bunch of bogus relatives, giving it out that the elderly gentleman – Mr Crichton – who

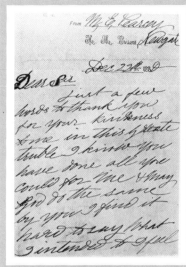

A last letter, written on the eve of her execution.

H.M. Prison, Newgate
Dec 22nd, 1890
Dear Sir,
   Just a few words to thank you for your kindness to me in this greate trouble. I know you have done all you could for me, and may God do the same by you. I find it hard to say what I intended to. I feel I cannot thank you enough for what you have done, but believe me I am truly greatfull for all that as been done. I would much better die now than be in prison all my life. So dear sir, thanking you again for your kindness believe me to remain ever your debtor
M.E.

Dead Man's Walk, Newgate. The bodies of the executed were interred beneath the flag- stones

To Mr F.F Palmer
5.30pm
22-21-90 (sic)
Dear Mr Palmer,
   My last request off you is for you to see Mr Hogg and tell him I received his returned order. I know his handwriting. It is the last kindness he could have done for me on earth. Will you tell him I forgive him as I hope to be forgiven. But he might have made death easier to bare. Also tell him I am justly punished for ever thinking any thing about him.

Dear Mr Palmer,
   You will kindly see him and tell Mr F. S. Hogg what I say. You will do this last kindness for me I know.
M.E.
Monday evening, 5.55
Just had such a kind letter from Miss Hogg.

visited her every Monday was her father, that Frank Hogg was her brother, Phoebe Hogg her sister-in-law, and one of her other regular paying gentlemen callers was made known as her husband. Thus did she endeavour to hide the secrets of her professional life from Mr Walter Butler and his wife, Sarah, to whom she sub-let the two upper storeys of her rented house. Opening, as quietly as possible, the front door with her latchkey, Mary Eleanor ushered her latest two, very out-of-the-ordinary gentlemen visitors into her abode. The rooms were small but attractively furnished. On the left as you came into the entrance hall was the front parlour, its window facing on to Priory Street. In it, much prized, stood an upright piano. A folding door opened to a bedroom overlooking a yard at the rear. There was also at the back a bijou kitchen. Tight-lipped, the police-men took in other, less favourable features of the landscape, and Nursey, excusing himself, departed to dispatch an urgent telegram to Bannister. Parsons stayed with Mary Eleanor in the parlour, doing his best to engage her in conversation. She spoke, misty-eyed, of her 'poor dear dead Phoebe' whom she loved so much, and rambled on in maudlin fashion about the 'dear baby, who was just beginning to prattle, oh, so prettily,' and of whom there was still no sign. Then, suddenly bored, she crossed to the cottage piano, and began to play on it and sing. This could well have been a classic display of *la belle indifférence* of the hysteric, had she been an hysteric; but, weighing all the diagnostic symptoms, the scales seem to come very decidedly down in the territory of true psychosis.

   On receipt of the telegram, Detective Inspector Bannister came hurrying over to Priory Street. Guided by his sergeant, he raked through the blood-spattered kitchen, finding there, in a table drawer, two fearsome carving knives, their handles stained darkly with blood, a recently-washed apron and skirt, and a vermilion-smeared rug, reeking strongly of paraffin. There was also a poker – long, heavy, ring-handled – encrusted with blood and matted hair. The curtains were missing; the window panes broken. The curtains he found, incarnadined, in an outhouse, stowed away with a blood-stiffened tablecloth. And in the dustbin, secreted away but awaiting discovery like the single vital clue in a classic detective story, a button. Dis-tinctively embossed with a Grecian figure playing the lyre, it matched those on Phoebe's jacket, one of which was missing from the sleeve. Face set into the pattern of grim severity elicited by the less pleasing bonuses of his office, he made his way to the parlour, where the notes of music splashed merrily around like jolly goldfish darting in a bowl.

   Mary Eleanor was seated strumming at the piano, fixed and wooden as a fairground automaton; a painted-on smile, an epileptic jerking of hands and head and neck, an alternating intermittent whistling and slightly off-key crooning. There was something eerie and chilling about the set scene. She seemed smilingly distraught: her speech a chuckling incoherence.

Like a pianola possessed, the piano went on automatically chipping out chunks of meaningless melody as, in answer to his solemn questioning about the universal blood-splotchings in the kitchen, she chanted, shudderingly reminiscent of the nursery rhyme's carving-knife-wielding farmer's wife, 'Killing mice. Killing mice. Killing mice.' She struck him as patently mad as a March hare, but he had, of course, no alternative but to arrest her. 'Mrs Pearcey, I am going to arrest you for the wilful murder of Mrs Hogg last night, and also, on suspicion, for the wilful murder of the female child of Mrs Hogg.' Mary Eleanor jumped up from the piano stool. 'You can arrest me if you like. I'm quite willing to go with you. But I think you have made a great mistake.' He led her quietly away to Kentish Town police station. On the way she told him, 'I wouldn't do such a thing. I wouldn't hurt anyone.'

Is it not, as Miss Tennyson Jesse has so astutely descried, a Zolaesque tale? Its whole atmosphere is of sordidness and domestic intrigue, its milieu of lower working class struggle against poverty and failing onslaughts upon the bastions of self-betterment. Is not Mary Eleanor the veritable Thérèse Raquin *britannique*? A woman, 'remorseless, eaten up with her own desires, and with all the persistence of an animal with its nose on the trail.' She was rightly to be feared, and if the word of Phoebe's sister, Martha Styles, is to be relied upon, and there is every reason to believe that it may be, likewise the confirmatory word of her niece, Elizabeth, then Phoebe did in fact experience the warning pricklings of that self-preservatory fear. Some three weeks before her successful dispatchment, Phoebe had received one of Mary Eleanor's mystery notes, this one inviting a rendezvous at a public house. Phoebe went, there to receive a further invitation to accompany Mary Eleanor on an excursion to Southend that very day, in order to look over an empty house which she said that she was thinking of taking. Atrophied, dim out of somewhere in our human primeval past, some premonitory instinct filtered out its caution. Phoebe declined. Afterwards she told Martha, 'If I'd gone to Southend no one would have thought of looking out for me there in an empty house.' An odd remark. Was Phoebe, one wonders, perhaps inclined to be psychic?

It was early on the morning of Sunday 26 October that the body of baby Phoebe was found, face down in the nettles on the ground where he grazed his ponies, by a tinker named Oliver Smith. She was fully clothed, except for a missing shoe and stocking. There were no signs of violence on the little body. Certain marks visible on the child's neck were due to the pressure of its clothing, which was tight on its plump, well-nourished body. Phoebe Hanslope was taken to Hampstead mortuary, where she was formally identified by a very, and genuinely, distressed Frank Hogg. The precise cause of the child's death has never been decided. Dr Augustus Joseph Pepper, that same specialist who, exactly twenty years later, would give evidence

Mr F. Freke Palmer, solicitor. He fought valiantly to save Mary Eleanor.

The Pearcey page from Madame Tussaud's catalogue. Madame Tussaud's Archives, London.

Madame Tussaud & Sons' Catalogue. 51

THE HAMPSTEAD TRAGEDY.

MRS. PEARCEY.

A MODEL OF THE KITCHEN, containing the identical Furniture and Fixtures from No 2, Priory Street, where Mrs. Hogg and her Baby were murdered.

LIST OF FURNITURE, &c.,

TABLE, CHAIRS, OILCLOTH, COOKING UTENSILS, CROCKERY, FIREPLACE, GRATE, WINDOW AND FLOORING.

THE TABLE against which Mrs. Hogg was supposed to have been leaning when the blows were struck.
THE WINDOW supposed to have been smashed by Mrs. Hogg in her death struggles.

All the articles contained in the Kitchen have been removed from No. 2, Priory Street, and are placed in exact relative position as found by the Police when they entered the premises.

Mrs. PEARCEY'S SITTING ROOM, with her identical Furniture, Couch, Chairs, Table, Mirror, Carpet, Piano, Ornaments, Curtains, Blinds, &c.
The Piano is the one on which Mrs. Pearcey played whilst the Police were searching her house.

Mrs. PEARCEY'S BEDSTEAD and FURNITURE.
THE PERAMBULATOR in which the Bodies were carried.
CASTS OF THE HEADS OF Mrs. HOGG AND HER BABY, taken from Nature after death.
THE CLOTHES worn by Mrs. Hogg and Baby when murdered.
Mrs. PEARCEY'S RECEIPT in her own handwriting.
THE TOFFEE found in the Perambulator.

The Figures of Mr. and Mrs. Hogg and their Baby are placed in the Ground Floor Gallery.

Arthur Hutton.

We shall accompany the ever-courteous Mr Arthur Hutton – tall, silvery-voiced, with a large, gentle eye, in one of which is fixed a monocle, without which he scarcely ever appears in court – Mrs Pearcey's defending counsel, to his cosy chambers in quaint, old, restful Pump Court, Temple, where he will tell us some very interesting things, from his own point of view, connected with this strange case.

We enter No 6, in which Mr Hutton's chambers are situated, from the flagged court, with its trees and its pump, by climbing a few stone steps, and then mount a wide, ancient wooden staircase that would figure most appropriately in a Dickens ghost story. Mr Hutton's white-haired old clerk, whose figure is as well known in the Temple as is that of his master, receives us upon the threshold. A few words pass between the two and we are then ushered by Mr Hutton into his private room.

for the prosecution at the trial of Dr Crippen, testified that the cause of death was either smothering, suffocation or exposure to the cold. Pepper did not think that the child could have been carried in the pram at the same time as its mother because 'the perambulator was covered with blood and the child's clothes were not so covered, as they must have been, had it been in the vehicle.' This does not present an especially persuasive argument, for it surely only required that the child's body be separately wrapped for bloodstaining to be entirely avoided. The baby could have suffocated under her mother's corpse in the pram. She could have been smothered beneath a cushion at Priory Street. Or, just possibly, she could have been tossed out alive to die of exposure on the Finchley Road waste ground. There is no way of knowing. Let us pray that, whichever way, it was swiftly merciful.

At Kentish Town police station Mary Eleanor was charged and searched. When she removed her gloves, her hands were seen to have cuts and scratches on them. She was wearing two rings. One was of brass. The other, a broad, gold wedding ring, was at first thought to be the one that had been dragged from Phoebe Hogg's finger. But, although Mrs Hogg's wedding ring was in fact missing, there was sound evidence to show that the rings on Mary Eleanor's fingers were both her own. Her underclothes, apparently unchanged for twenty-four hours, bore quite considerable bloodstaining. They, together with the rest of her clothes, were taken away, and she was supplied with workhouse garments in their place. Sarah Sawhill, who searched female prisoners at Kentish Town police station, subsequently told of a conversation with Mary Eleanor. She stated that the prisoner had remarked to her that she had been affronted by Mrs Hogg, who had apparently cut her in the street, but who had, in response to a note, come round to tea between four and a quarter past. As they were having tea, Mrs Hogg made a remark that Mary Eleanor did not like, and 'one word brought up another. Perhaps I had better not say any more.'

Mary Eleanor Pearcey, still wearing her dark workhouse clothes and a green straw hat with matching ribbon, was arraigned before the magistrates at Marylebone police court on 27 October, and after the usual adjournments and series of remands to Holloway Gaol, was committed, on 18 November, to the Central Criminal Court. Her trial was set down for Monday, 1 December 1890, before Mr Justice Denman, sitting at the Old Bailey. She was defended by Mr Arthur Hutton, instructed by Mr F. Freke Palmer. Mr Forrest Fulton represented the Crown. Mary Eleanor took her place in the dock, wearing now a black dress, over which was a brown buttoned cloak. She looked, with her hair brushed attractively back and her shining blue eyes, pleasing and intelligent, yet she seemed curiously indifferent to everything. The stoic way in which she conducted herself throughout mirrored the correctness of her solicitor's judgement that she had 'as much resolution as twenty ordinary women.' She sat between the wardresses, calm, remote, dignified and enigmatic. Mostly she stared straight in front of her, hands folded in lap, only an occasional slight twitching of her mouth or jumping of the orbicular muscle below her lower eyelid betraying the overwhelming feeling of terror she was masking. Her demeanour was in marked contrast to that of the sobbing hulk, Hogg, in the witness box. He may, as he let it be known, have been a regular church worshipper, she may have been flighty and immoral – amoral is possibly a better word – but there could be no argument as to which was the more sterling character. Her spineless lover cut a shoddy and unpopular figure in, and out of, court. There was something ineluctably antipathetic about him. Judge and jury, seeming to disregard his tragic and bereaved situation, continually referred to him as 'the man Hogg'. Public sympathy ran low, too. His was surely the uniquely unwelcome distinction of being hissed, booed and hooted at as, drenched by pouring rain, he attended the burial of his wife and child in St Pancras Cemetery. There were, of course, those who were convinced that Hogg had had a pudgy hand in the slaying of Phoebe. Physically, he absolutely did not. He had an alibi of police-tested platinum. Throughout the crucial time he had removed himself on a removal job far, far away from the heady purlieus of Camden and Kentish Towns. What is more, Mary Eleanor herself left behind her a letter addressed to Clara Hogg in which she categorically absolved the faithless Frank of all knowledge of, never mind participation in, the slaying of Phoebe. That some other hypnotised male might have rendered assistance in one way or another has always been bruited. There, is not the smallest evidence for it, but many have felt that another should have sat beside Mary Eleanor in the dock and possibly stood beside her on the scaffold.

The trial ended on the fourth day. The judge delivered himself of a two-and-three-quarter-hour summing-up. It did not lean conspicuously to the prisoner's favour, but neither was it unfair. The jury retired at 1.20pm. They were out fifty-two minutes. Their verdict went unanimously against Mary Eleanor. The chaplain, whose face at such times became the face of doom, the face of death itself, shuffled forward, servile to secular authority, to do his Christian duty with the black cap – place it ritually atop the judge's bewigged head. Mary Eleanor heard the old, callously-worded formula of judicial death pronounced upon her with that identical impassivity, lack of affect, which she had most bizarrely displayed the entire trial through. Then she disappeared into the black maw of the prison-house, there to see out her three clear Sundays.

During that ultimate trinity of weeks, as she lay condemned in Newgate, she requested repeatedly to be permitted to see Frank Hogg. At last, as she entered within the very shadow of the noose, all hopes of appeal and clemency drained away, a

When the door is closed behind us we seem to be entirely shut off from the outer world. It is not a very large room, and it is quite plainly furnished. A fire is burning in the old-fashioned grate. On a small office table repose piles of briefs, most of which contain staggering human stories of human depravity. How quiet the place is! So different from the bustle and turmoil of the Old Bailey. What few sounds there are that penetrate from without are muffled and almost inaudible. Occasionally the distant and faint sound of a knocker is heard echoing through the building. All or most of the inner doors are fitted with knockers.

It is in such eyries as these that barristers think out their plans of attack, on the one side or the other, in cases to be heard at the CCC, as the Central Criminal Court is familiarly known. Mr Hutton has kindly introduced cigarettes, and between appreciative exhalations of the fragrant weed he makes his pregnant observations. Let us listen.

'She was certainly a very strange woman,' observes Mr Hutton contemplatively, in a soft, sibilant, persuasive voice – his *professional* voice, one might almost say. 'Yes, one of the most mysterious clients I have ever had . . . I never understood her or quite why she committed the terrible murder, of which she was undoubtedly guilty . . . The line of defence I wanted to adopt was to the effect that a quarrel suddenly arose between the two women, words led to blows, and that in the heat of the combat, Mrs Pearcey struck Mrs Hogg an unlucky blow, which proved fatal. Then, scared at what she had done, she tried to dispose of the body, as most murderers are anxious to do, but found it very difficult, as most murderers usually do. The killing of the child, I maintained was incidental and accidental. And when you come to think of it ' – and here Mr Hutton leans over and gazes steadfastly at us with his large, earnest eyes – 'it is just what might very well have happened!'

Then Mr Hutton leans back in his chair, contemplates us with a look of incubating incredulity, and exclaims

'But, would you believe it, she flatly refused to agree to such a defence! Absolutely refused to consent to my adopting that line at all. She would give no reason for her objection, nor could all the eloquent persuasion I was enabled to bring to bear upon her induce her to alter her mind. Why did she adopt such an attitude? . . . I am quite unable to say. A most mysterious woman, more baffling in fact, than is usual with her mysterious sex. At all events, and much to my regret and chagrin, I had to abandon that line of defence. And as; failing that, there was little or no defence to put forward, the ultimate outcome of the trial was merely the confirmation of a foregone conclusion.'

Mr Hutton remains silent and thoughtful for a few moments, engaged apparently with some perplexing problem, as is indicated by his knitted brows. Then he adds contemplatively and slowly:

'There has always been a vague idea in the minds of many people acquainted with the case that Mrs Pearcey had a male confederate. There was never any definite evidence of it though, nothing in fact beyond vague suggestions. At one time the man Hogg was suspected, but events proved that he was quite clear of it. She herself lent colour to this theory by requesting to have an advertisement inserted in a Continental paper . . . What it meant or what was the object of it I have never been able to discover.'

After a brief pause, Mr Hutton proceeds:

'By the way, while I think of

written order was forthcoming granting permission for him to visit her between two and four o'clock of the last afternoon the law had sanctioned her on earth. Her mother and her sister, Charlotte Amy, came to take their final farewell. They left. She waited, flushed and excited as a bride. No Frank. Time passed. He did not appear. Overcome, crumpling for the first and only time, she slumped upon her bed in the condemned cell, her hands over her face, and wept and wept and wept.

At a few minutes before eight o'clock on the bitterly cold and foggy morning of Tuesday, 23 December 1890, the prisoner's 'passing bell' sounding its heavy tolling upon the frost-steamed air, the knot of death's invigilators came soft-footed to Mary Eleanor's cell door. She met them, as she had all the many tragedies of her short, brave life, face-on, with the courtesy of fortitude. Upright, unflinching, she took the place prescribed for her by protocol, following in procession behind the sheriff and the whey-faced chaplain, moving with dignity to her chalk-marked place. Mr Hangman Berry received her in his shed with great politeness. 'Good morning, Madam,' he said, shaking her hand. Then, with compassionate celerity, pinioned and hooded her, and, ere the last note had shivered from St Sepulchre's clock, Mary Eleanor had flown and the black flag struck from its staff. Later, the heavy-booted warders would hustle her empty shell away beneath those other black flags, that paved Dead Man's Walk.

Mary Eleanor herself is said to have commented to the chaplain, the Reverend Mr Duffield, or somesuch, before they broke her neck: 'The sentence is just, but the evidence was false.' But *was* it? Was she not, if ever there was one, a suitable case for treatment in Broadmoor? Albeit, the defence of epilepsy has become a forensic cliché, but the Pearcey case gives one pause. It is an undisputed fact that Mary Eleanor had actually been subject to severe attacks of epilepsy since birth. Her mother had also suffered from fits before her daughter was born. On three or four occasions, while in a state of epileptic trance, Mary Eleanor had attempted to commit suicide. Once, as we have already seen, by hanging; twice by taking poison. After these epileptic seizures, manifestations of violence invariably ensued, but when the paroxysm had passed she could remember nothing of what had taken place. On the Sunday preceding the murders – Sunday, 19 October – she had complained very much of headaches and said that she felt that she was going out of her mind. It was the opinion of the eminent alienist, Dr L. Forbes Winslow, that the brutality of the murders, together with the violence and strength exhibited, indicated the probability of the crimes having been committed whilst in a condition of acute, violent epileptic trance. This accorded well with the widely felt doubt that a normal woman could have brought to bear the sheer physical force and fury of the attack. Mary Eleanor Pearcey was not a big, powerful woman; from what *normal* source could she have recruited the demonic strength required to wield poker and knife with such devastating savagery, to lift and crush the bigger, heavier woman's dead-weight body into the bassinette – even allowing for the fact that 'folding' it in would be made easier because the head could be doubled back on its broken stalk and loose hinge of hanging skin – and then, on top of all that, to wheel the heavy burden of death at least three miles, much of it uphill?

Mary Eleanor Pearcey's persistent denials of all knowledge of the crimes would, if true, support a diagnosis of epileptic furore. At the very end, all further need of play-acting and pretence evaporated, on the eve of her execution, a day so cold and dark that her last meeting with her mother and sister at Newgate was permitted in the warmth and comfort of the Chief Warden's room, beseeched by her mother to tell her the truth, she said: 'Mother, I knew nothing about it. Oh, Mother, as I expect to meet my Maker in a few hours, I cannot tell a lie. I know nothing whatever about the murder. If I knew, I would willingly say so for my own sake now.'

In this context it is worth recalling the evidence of the Priory Street tenants, the Butlers. They said that they remembered stumbling against a perambulator which was partially blocking the passage of the entrance hall of No 2. That was at about six o'clock on the evening of Friday, 24 October. The hall was in darkness, although a light was generally kept burning there. Mrs Pearcey had called out 'Mind!', and Sarah Butler had answered 'All right.' When Walter Butler, a labourer, returned home from work a little later, Mrs Pearcey had immediately appeared in the hall saying, 'Let me lead you Mr Butler, as there is a perambulator here,' and she took him by the hand and guided him past it. Both the Butlers thought that their landlady was behaving oddly. 'She talked very funny and looked boozed,' said Walter Butler. And that is consistent with a person in an epileptic episode.

It must be said that, by order of the Home Secretary, she was, in fact, on 19 December, medically examined by Drs Gilbert (the Newgate prison doctor), Savage and Bennett. These medical gentlemen, attached to the Home Office, who 'possibly had not the same interest in the case that I had,' writes Dr Forbes Winslow, 'and were not so cognisant of the actual facts, and who had not been visited by her relations and friends, or knew the history of her case, or perused any documents bearing on it . . . were simply sent to form an opinion as to the objective, not the subjective, condition of the prisoner.' They found, after spending one hour with her, no medical reason to interfere with the law's taking its course. Mrs Pearcey's solicitor said, 'I felt very much disappointed with the Home Secretary's decision because of the extraordinary mass of reliable evidence which I had collected to show that the prisoner was insane.'

All her life Mary Eleanor had a dream.

it, let me relate the details of a rather uncanny experience I had in connection with this case before it came to trial at the Old Bailey.

One day, accompanied by the Chief Inspector who had charge of the case, I paid a visit to the house in Priory Street where the murder was committed. It was rather a small house, and we made our way to the kitchen in the rear, where Mrs Hogg met her death. It was in the early evening, at that period of twilight when one is most apt to feel 'nervy.' We stood silently in the half-dark chamber, gazing round at the still evident traces of the desperate deed committed in it, in the shape of blood splashes and stains on walls and ceiling, and the broken panes of glass in the window. The latter looked directly on to the kitchen window of the house next door, which was quite close, only a low fence dividing the two gardens. Suddenly, above this fence, appeared a white, scared face, which gazed curiously and distractedly at us! With one accord we simply jumped! The face was simply ghost-like, and for the moment I went quite cold, my heart beating nineteen to the dozen, as the saying has it. My companion suddenly exclaimed, 'What the —!' and glared back at the face. There was really nothing to be alarmed at, the explanation being quite simple. The face was not that of a ghost, the ghost of the murdered woman, as some hectic-minded people might have supposed, but merely that of the woman next door, who, having heard footsteps and being curious, was looking across from her own house to see what was going on. Of course it was the association of ideas that made it for the moment so startling. Subsequently this woman gave evidence at the trial, and very important evidence it was.'

We smile, nod our heads, and

wait attentively for Mr Hutton to make further comments about his strange client.

'That Mrs Pearcey,' proceeds the distinguished advocate, 'although undoubtedly guilty of this very brutal murder, had a most humane side to her character, was proved, I should think, by her behaviour while in prison. Or, at all events, by one incident alone which occurred during her detention. Birds would daily settle on the sill of her cell window, and she regularly fed them with bread crumbs. It seems almost incongruous, does it not? But there, who is to solve the mysteries of the human heart and mind?'
Hargrave Lee Adam, *Old Days at the Old Bailey*

Ever since I can remember I've been haunted by a queer dream . . . It comes and goes again, but I'm never without it very long. In that dream I see a great archway, and through it I go to darkness, dreadful darkness, that seems to hide something more terrible beyond. I've never seen that arch yet so far as I know, but some day I shall come to it, and then my dream will come true.

Was it that titanic railway arch spanning the end of Priory Street, through which she trundled her terrible pram? Or was it the great frowning entrance arch of Newgate, through which she walked to the gallows? There is no saying for sure. But one thing is certain: Mary Eleanor had found her archway.

A curious codicil.

When, on the eve of her execution, her solicitor came to bid her goodbye, she asked him to insert for her a small notice in a Madrid newspaper.

Asked by him if this message was relevant to the case, she answered, 'Never mind.' Mr Freke Palmer was afterwards to say that he understood it to refer to a marriage which had taken place between Mary Eleanor Wheeler and one M.E.C.P., whose name she had taken an oath never to divulge, and who was to remain for all time the nucleus of enigma around which was wrapped the enduring mystery of Mary Eleanor Pearcey. The keeper of the archway one might almost say. . . .

Victorian Bogey Woman No. 3

Mrs Amelia Dyer: She-Devil with a Carpet-Bag

A devout soldier of the Salvation Army, who was a stickler for red – or any other colour – tape, and a savage shepherd of souls for the Lord of any babes and sucklings she could profitably bag.

Squat as a toad, grey and wrinkled at fifty-seven, Mrs Amelia Elizabeth Dyer, doyenne of the late Victorian baby-farmers, looked more like an ogrish but decent nursery nanny than a swift and deadly slayer. Her neat, bonneted appearance was her stock-in-trade. Weeping governesses and ladies' maids were not going to hand over their carefully swaddled love-children – and a packet of money – to some dishevelled old slattern. Her Salvation Army upbringing, too, gave her a good line in pious sentiments; she was never at a loss for an improving text.

Mrs Dyer had a long run for her packets of blood-money. No one knows how many innocents she coolly snuffed out, but the number probably ran well into double figures, because she operated without detection for fifteen years. Cunningly, she kept on the move, and the police found a hoard of *numerous* letters at her last address, all written by mothers anxious about the fate of their babies.

Finally, in 1896, her wrathful Salvationist God decided to haul her in before the judgement seat. She left a kind of visiting card at one of her crimes. This is how it happened: in March of that year, she was living under the name of 'Mrs Harding' at 45 Kensington Road, Reading, still up to her old tricks, like the old woman who lived in a shoe, the house overflowing with boarded and adopted children. She loved the little mites so.

On 30 March a man who knew her saw her stout figure waddling along the towpath of the Thames. Several times, she stopped and looked into the water. That was the day when the first body was found. A Thames barge was gliding slowly up-river on a stretch between the mouth of the River Kennet and the Caversham Lock, about 400 yards from the Great Western Railway Station at Reading. The river bank there was green, flat and open, made up as it was of a public park, Huntley & Palmer's cricket club ground, and a field belonging to the same firm. The towpath followed the river faithfully.

A brown paper parcel becalmed in the river close by the

Mrs Dyer, the Reading baby-farmer. The only know image, fashioned by Madame Tussaud's
Madame Tussaud's Archives, London

bank was a conspicuous object in all that expanse of level water and greenery. One of the bargemen used his punt-hook to grapple in the parcel, and as he lifted it up, the wet paper tore and disclosed a tiny, baby's leg.

PC Barnett carried the waterlogged bundle to the police station on his back, in a sack. Then, in the mortuary, the many layers were peeled away as gingerly as if it were an Egyptian mummy. The body – it was that of a little girl – had been wrapped in sheets of paper and napkins and other materials. It was not decomposed, nor had it been long in the river, for parts of the core of the parcel were quite dry. It had been weighted with a brick, as if someone had disposed of a surplus kitten.

The cause of death was clear – and beastly. A piece of tape – a lethal ligature – was tied tightly round the baby's neck, with the knot under the left ear. Detective Inspector J. B. Anderson, who had charge of the case, preserved that tape in his own, private, miniature Black Museum, a more piteous relic than blade or bullet. There were no laundry marks or other easy clues, but, incredibly, the very last sheet of paper, the one nearest to the body, bore a name and address: Mrs Harding, 20 Wigott's Road, Caversham.

Mrs Dyer had left her spoor. How could she have been so careless? Had she, after so many undetected infanticides, become cocksure? Had Satan terminated his contract with her? Did she nurse an unconscious desire to be caught and punished? That does not accord with her subsequent conduct.

Suppose that she did not check the wrappings because she was, quite simply, supremely confident: why, then, did she deposit the parcel where it would easily be spotted? Inspector Anderson had an excellent, pragmatic explanation. When Mrs Dyer tossed the body into the river, she did not, until it was too late, realize that there was a shallow, four-foot-wide channel between the towpath and the deep water. Bodies are better jettisoned from bridges or boats. When the parcel failed to submerge, and she cursed her miscalculation, she could not reach it to throw it further out in the mainstream. She was only about five feet tall, and so her arms were short (no one said she was like a gorilla!). Nor could she hang around, acting suspiciously. The towpath was well used.

They did not trace 'Mrs Harding' immediately. It was not *quite* so simple as that – more's the pity, because she killed again in the following few days before her time ran out. To start with, there was no such road as Wigott's Road, but by the evening of 30 March the police had ferreted out that a Mrs Harding had been living at 20 *Pigott's* Road, in Caversham. So far, so satisfying. She was no longer there, of course, but further detective work led the Inspector to her lair at 45 Kensington Road, where she was arrested on 4 April.

Searching the premises was horribly like going through Christie's cupboards at 10 Rillington Place. The cupboard

A gruesome catch.

under the stairs was dark and musty, with a sickening smell of decomposition. It was stacked with baby clothing.

Mrs Dyer ruled over an oddly-assorted household. Mr Dyer had vanished into the woodwork long ago. In his place there was Granny Smith, a strange old woman whom Mrs Dyer had taken out of the workhouse – for reasons never known. Was her rôle to act as a front, or a skivvy, or a mother-figure? The imagination boggles.

Two children – small, knowing waifs straight from the pages of Dickens – also dodged about the dangerous house. Willie Thornton, whose parents were untraceable, and Ellen Oliver, who had arrived from Plymouth in the charge of a railway guard, were miraculously intact – probably because they were aged nine and ten respectively, and too big to fit conveniently into a brown paper parcel.

Removed to Reading police station with, as it were, a pair of tongs, Mrs Dyer tried to stab herself with her tape-cutting scissors. Thwarted in this laudable attempt, she ripped out her bootlaces, tied them together, and, heaving with all her might, began to strangle herself with them, until she was discovered, a ghastly spectacle with bulging eyes and purply, lolling tongue.

45 Kensington Road, Reading. The ogress' lair.

There were further investigations to be made before Mrs Dyer could be exterminated. Her daughter, Polly Palmer, and her gingery husband, Arthur Ernest Palmer, seemed to be implicated. More baby clothing was found at their home at 76 Mayo Road, Willesden, North London, and they had lived with Mrs Dyer at 20 Pigott's Road, Caversham.

Polly, caged, was eager to sing – but it was her mother she incriminated, not herself. Although never convicted of murder, she was always there or thereabouts, at her mother's elbow, or out foraying in the field. Who can doubt that she learnt Mrs Dyer's horrendous trade at her apron-strings, and that Arthur Palmer was their willing apprentice? Only two years later, Polly and Arthur were sentenced to two years' hard labour apiece for abandoning a baby in a railway carriage at Newton Abbot. They had pocketed an adoption fee of £14, stripped the clothing from the three-week-old girl, wrapped her in brown paper, and left her under the seat of a carriage which was shunted to sidings, so that she was not rescued until the following morning.

The story that Polly came out with, back in 1896, was a tissue of half-truths, and her part in the crimes is like a shadow missing from a figure photographed in bright sunlight. Gradually, however, a very worrying sequence of events began to emerge.

On the evening of 31 March, the day after the brown paper parcel was retrieved by the bargemen (Polly sang), her mother had appeared without warning at 76 Mayo Road, clutching a carpet-bag, and a baby. 'I'm just minding it for a neighbour while she's in a shop,' she reassured her daughter – but we know the real identity of that baby girl. She was Doris Marmon,

Mrs Dyer's daughter, Mrs
Polly Palmer. Polly put the
kettle on while mother put the
baby out.

Arthur Ernest Palmer, Mrs
Dyer's shifty son-in-law.

born in Cheltenham, in January 1896, the illegitimate child of
Evelina Edith Marmon, a pretty young barmaid, who loved
her dearly, but could not manage to keep her.

The advertisement in the *Bristol Times and Mirror* had
seemed like a godsend: a childless woman wished, for a small
remuneration, to adopt a baby as her own. Hopefully, Evelina
wrote off for details, and 'Mrs Harding' of 45 Kensington Road,
Reading, wrote back:

> I should be glad to have a dear little baby girl that I
> could bring up and call my own. First of all, I must tell
> you that we are plain, homely people, in fairly good cir-
> cumstances, and that we live in our own house. I have a
> good and comfortable home. We are in the country, and
> sometimes I am alone a great deal. I do not want a child
> for money's sake, but for company and home comfort.

Poor, duped Evelina was consoled by these unctuous words,
and on 31 March 'Mrs Harding', undaunted by the adventures
of the previous day, chugged her way through the heart of the
rolling countryside, on a train to Cheltenham. There, Evelina
was waiting for her with Doris, well wrapped up in clean,
white shawls. The wretched sum of £10 changed hands. The
young mother wept. And Mrs Dyer wept, too – shameless
crocodile tears that oozed down her seamed and treacherous
face. 'Don't worry,' she said 'My neighbours call me "Good
Mrs Harding".'

Before leaving the railway station at Cheltenham, Mrs Dyer
claimed a large carpet-bag which she had deposited there. It
was a tired woman who turned up with a baby and a carpet-
bag late that evening at Mayo Road. Polly fetched some coal,
washed her hands, and put the kettle on for a pot of tea for her
mother. When she went into the sitting room, the baby was
gone, and Mrs Dyer was bending down, puffing, and stuffing
the carpet-bag under the couch.

'It's all right, I've handed the baby back,' she lied through
her rat-trap teeth. She had brought a ham as a present (or
a bribe?), and after gorging a hearty supper, like a snuffling
porker herself, she lay down, bloated, on the couch aforesaid,
and slept the heavy sleep of the damned.

Early next morning, indefatigable, she was about her
business again. This time, at her mother's request, Polly
accompanied her to Paddington Station, where they met a
Mr and Mrs Sergeant, under the clock. Harry Simmons, the
inconvenient issue of a lady's maid who had abandoned him at
the Sergeants', was that day's piece of barter. On his way back
to Mayo Road, baby Harry was restless. *'The little devil!'* Mrs
Dyer exclaimed. *'If it keeps on like this, I shan't stick it for long.'*

No more than one day, to be precise. That evening, as Polly
was leaving her sitting room, her mother told her, 'Don't come
in for a few minutes'. When she returned, the baby was lying

as still as a log on the couch, underneath a shawl.

'Is that the little nipper?' Arthur Palmer asked in an avuncular tone, when he came home. But Mrs Dyer refused to let him dandle her new charge.

That night, Polly and Arthur and Mrs Dyer went off arm-in-arm to the music hall. And the couch doubled as a bed again. Next morning, the baby had vanished. The carpet-bag seemed strangely full, however, and Polly could see a brown paper parcel, as round as a baby's head, sticking out of one end.

'What will the neighbours say?' Polly cried, as her mother heaved up the weighty bag and prepared to go home. 'What will they think, seeing you enter the house with a baby, and leave alone?'

'Never you mind. You must make some excuse or other. It's all right, I tell you.'

Dutifully, the Palmers escorted Mrs Dyer to Paddington, and put her on the 9.15am train, due to arrive at Reading at about ten o'clock. She carried the bulging bag, but Arthur held it for her while she bought some cakes from a shop, to eat on the journey. She had to keep her strength up.

Not surprisingly, on hearing all this from the candid lips of Polly, Inspector Anderson's mind was much occupied by the subject of carpet-bags when he ordered the Thames at Reading to be dragged. Especially since Mrs Dyer had been seen by a warder at Reading Prison coming away from the direction of the river at about 10.50am on the day of her return home from Mayo Road!

And sure enough, on 10 April the river in the region of Caversham Weir Head yielded up the carpet-bag, weighted with a brick, and still holding its two dead babies – Doris Marmon and Harry Simmons. Nor was that the only harvest. *Four more* pitiful water-babies were trawled up from the slow-stirring weeds and mud.

'You'll know mine by the tape around their necks,' said Mrs Dyer, and the whole of Britain went mad with rage – and guilt. Victorian hypocrisy looked in the tarnished mirror, and did not like its reflection. Mrs Dyer's words meant more then than their face value suggests today: they were not a mere boast, but a reference to the truth that unwanted children had a short life-expectancy, and the Thames was the receptacle for who knows how many babies dispatched by other hands.

The first baby – the one found on 30 March – was identified as Helena Fry, aged fifteen months, transferred to Mrs Dyer on 5 March by a Bristol servant girl in trouble, for £15. Another female baby was identified as the child of a barmaid named Elizabeth Goulding. Polly Palmer was the carrier who had taken the train to Gloucester on 23 September 1895, to collect the baby and its valuation of £10. This was probably the body that was stashed away to moulder in the cupboard under the stairs at 45 Kensington Road. Two very young infant

Unmarried mother Evelina Marmon hands over her baby to the detestable Mrs Dyer at Cheltenham railway station.

Granny Smith, mystery figure in the house of death.

Dr Lyttleton Stewart Forbes Winslow. 'A distinguished, if ever so slightly batty-looking figure'.

Mrs Dyer's dream.

boys brought up on 8 and 10 April were never claimed.

'All of 'em against me, poor lone woman,' Mrs Dyer wailed in her prison cell. 'All of 'em a-tryin' to hang me.'

Even her precious daughter, it seemed, because Polly gave evidence against her mother at the trial at the Old Bailey on 21 May with composure, if not with alacrity. Mrs Dyer did not object. She was determined to absolve her own dear child, Polly, and Polly's shady husband, of any guilt whatsoever.

Dr L. Forbes Winslow, who was the most celebrated alienist of his time, did his best to save Mrs Dyer's stubby neck by proving that she was insane at the time of the crimes, but, as in the modern Yorkshire Ripper trial, public revulsion was so strong that his account of the prisoner's delusions and hallucinations was not well received.

The case still rankled when he re-argued it in his volume of memoirs, *Recollections of Forty Years*. He did not, naturally, like to look a fool, and (he claimed) he did not enjoy appearing for the defence in notorious murder trials, although there was, in fact, some quirk in his temperament which inclined him to take the minority view. Since he was also somewhat cranky, egotistic, bombastic, rigid, and blessed, like Sir Bernard Spilsbury, with illusions of omniscience, he was a complicated character. As far as medical facts were concerned, he was sound and expert, but his theoretical constructs, however reliable the footings, tended sometimes to be dubious and flimsy.

It was through his own spontaneous intervention that he entered the cause formally, and it is difficult to doubt that such was his intention:

> It having come to my knowledge that Mrs Dyer had been examined by a physician appointed by the Treasury on 11th May, I thought it only fair that the wretched woman should have the benefit of someone on her behalf, and on the 13th inst I wrote as follows to the press: 'From a long experience in such cases, I desire to express my strong opinion that the defence should also be represented by its own nominee.' I was nominated, and, though I was instructed by the prisoner's solicitor, I received my fee from the Treasury – rather a unique position.

Forbes Winslow's most endearing and praiseworthy characteristic was his paternalistic and compassionate concern for the mentally ill, and his genuine abhorrence of the execution of such people. The Dyer case is puzzling, because he, of all physicians, was competent to assess whether a patient was faking insanity. For, indeed, for many years he had sat gravely, all day long, and listened to the ramblings and rantings of the patients in his care. He was at the height of his powers in 1896, at the age of fifty-two, and he made a distinguished, if ever so slightly batty-looking figure, as he held forth from the witness box.

Impressive in his top hat, he had twice grandly made his entrance into Holloway Prison to interview Mrs Dyer: his descriptive comment does not instil much confidence in the reader, although one knows what he means – 'She gave me the impression of a good old carefully attired monthly nurse, but not of the murderess type.' He kept a record of their two dialogues, and it is extraordinary that he does not appreciate how lame Mrs Dyer's hopeless denials and evasions really are. This is no genuine memory defect:

Q 'What about the two children found in the river?'
A 'I can't recollect anything about it. When I begin to think I get mystified.'
Q 'What were the names of the children?'
A 'I am sure I do not know. I can't tell now.'

The execution of Mrs Dyer – a rope for a tape.

Forbes Winslow based his diagnosis of insanity on delusions (that is, to use a modern definition, incorrigible false beliefs of morbid origin) and hallucinations, elicited by him in interview, and of the same nature as those reported during several previous admissions to asylums. It was powerfully argued by others that those admissions had been engineered by Mrs Dyer when the hue and cry for missing children got too close to home – and he was well aware of this view. He also took into account the known facts that her mother was insane, and that Mrs Dyer had made a number of suicide attempts (we do not have sufficient evidence now to evaluate their seriousness). His diagnosis, in antique terms, was of both 'melancholia' and 'delusional insanity'. He gave little, if any, weight to the other known fact that Mrs Dyer had had the opportunity to watch and copy the behaviour of psychotic inmates of both asylum and workhouse, having herself been thus confined. The medical report for the prosecution notes that she had [additionally] been an asylum attendant.

The most that the prosecution would allow was that 'it is likely that she (the prisoner) is of defective power of self-control, and might be induced to do wrong more readily than the majority as a result of [such] hereditary taint.' In refutation, Forbes Winslow prepared a most fascinating 'Hints for Cross-examination of Medical Experts', of which his two best points seem, today, to be No 2 – 'Have you not frequently known such cases where the patient was perfectly calm and seemingly rational, though entertaining delusions inwardly but not apparent to the outward view?' and No 6 – 'If Mrs Dyer is feigning insanity, would it not be expected that she would have made some efforts to make this visible in some way to the warders or doctors?'

Wrapped in her wooden parcel.

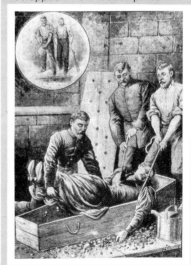

Now Mrs Dyer was a very cunning woman. Is it possible that she was cunning enough to fake insanity only in the presence of the defence doctor? (Dr Scott, of Holloway, sat in during the two interviews.) The prosecution medical report is

Nellie Oliver.

Willie Thornton.

Last Letter of Mrs Dyer, written in Newgate Prison to her daughter, Polly

My child, my dear child, may God Almighty bless you and keep you. It was a great relief to me to know that you would not be prosecuted. I knew it yesterday. Now, my child, for Willie's and Annie's sake, don't go abroad. You will have a letter from our chaplain. I, myself, can say no more now, only God bless and keep you both.
'My hope is built on nothing less
Than Jesus' blood and righteousness.'

MOTHER, A. DYER.

quite sharp! It *is* possible that, as may well happen even now in repellent murders, the prison staff might have recognized abnormal symptoms, but chose not to disclose them. Or is the truth of the matter that only Dr Forbes Winslow was skilled enough to winkle out the words that spelled madness? His questions – with which he has obligingly furnished us – display no particular finesse, but are of the leading nature practised still by psychiatrists all over the world. For example:

Q 'Do you ever see any visions?'
A 'Pray do not ask me (looking very terrified at me).'
Q 'What do you see?'
A 'I can't tell you; that is why I keep awake at night. The sounds I hear and the sights I see are dreadful.'

So, neatly, Mrs Dyer presents the doctor with both auditory and visual hallucinations. Too neatly? She does not over do it, but feeds him her voices and visions grudgingly. Finally, when pressed, she manages an eschatological passage:

A 'I see my poor boy Willie and my mother.'
Q 'Do they ever speak to you?'
A 'Frequently. I hear them talking and telling me to come to them. The spirit of my poor boy, Willie, seems to be with me all night. I fancy I could handle his bones, and that I was picking them out of the ground. When my poor boy enlisted and went away I was very ill for three weeks, and when I came to myself I was beating the rats off, who were all gnawing on my body, and the worms were eating me up.'

Not a bad effort! But is it an artefact of the sights and sounds of genuine patients, with an admixture of the remembered Bible? We are dealing here with a woman astute and dramatic enough to produce tears on demand.

The jury seemed unimpressed by Dr Forbes Winslow's evidence of rats and worms, and he sensed that the sympathy of the court was against him – a feeling painfully reinforced when he overheard a member of the jury snigger to his neighbour, 'Aye, she may have dreamt all that, but it will soon be a reality!'

There was no point in appealing to the Bench, in the person of that ferocious character, Mr Justice Hawkins, who was as cannibalistic as Rumpole's Judge Bullingham, because, Forbes Winslow thought, his lordship was quite as prejudiced as the jury. Anyway, no defence could neutralize the truth that Mrs Dyer knew exactly what she was about when she stretched out her paw for her fee, and kept weeding out her stock of babies to make room for more nice little earners.

Amelia Elizabeth Dyer, was hanged by the neck at Newgate Prison on 10 June 1896. About four years later, the skeletons of four children were dug up from the garden of a house in Bristol which Mrs Dyer had once occupied.

Victorian Bogey Woman No. 4

Christiana Edmunds: She-Devil with a Bagful of Chocolates

The seaside romance of a marcescent spinster whose sweet disposition had lethal effects on cheerful 'Doctor' Brighton.

The Bride, *by Raffaelle Monti – a fantasy for Christiana. The way it should have been.*

An unplucked flower – an overblown rose, drooping and withering on its dry stem – was, in Victorian euphemism, an unmarried woman, and Christiana Edmunds at forty-two, pretending to be thirty-three, fought against the image that she hated. Fair and innocent-looking, with a slenderness that was still graceful, she had lived, all her years, a life of middle-class leisure and moderation, and known none of the world's vices. Her immaculate, crystalline skin, shielded from the suns of Brighton by parasol and becoming millinery, kept her secret well.

There was a modicum of time left to her to bear a child, and Nature cruelly stirred her dwindling hormones into one last, desperate drive for fruition – a drive which, ironically, cancelled out the offspring of another woman, entirely a stranger to her. Christiana's mother noticed a change in her, a new restlessness. Better read than a married woman of her age, whose reading would have been stopped by the customary quiverful of children, she now began to slip romantic novels between the volumes of Tennyson and Ruskin and to pore

Christiana Edmunds, she-devil with a bagful of daydreams on the Esplanade.

over them within the privacy of her be-tasselled bedroom. Across the English Channel, which she skirted on her daily walks, lay the Continent, land of inconceivable adventures, never to be hers.

The elation that she felt in church as the anthems soared above nave and chancel was not the intellectual response that she imagined it to be, but a trick, a goad, to send her out hunting along esplanade and promenade. No suitor had ever climbed the steps of No 16 Gloucester Place and entreated her widowed mother for the hand of fair Christiana, but now, in her final bid to attract, she sought new outfits from the smart dress shops in the arcades of Brighton, and these, together with a certain aura about her, a receptiveness, drew the masculine glances which covertly warmed her.

Anxiously, her mother noted the evanescent flushes, the hectic pulse ticking at her throat. She had sheltered Christiana more, perhaps, than her daughter realized, because, in the unpleasant thinking of the Victorians, the family was 'tainted' with hereditary madness and epilepsy. With her unusual, fated name, like an icy Ibsen heroine, Christiana must have known something of the family background. The matter was not discussed. Who knows what dread she might have felt as the salt sand of the years sifted through her fingers.

Apart from a bout of 'paralysis' at the age of twenty-one (more likely to have been, in isolation, an hysterical conversion symptom rather than catatonia) and some 'hysteria' in its lay meaning, Christiana had, so far, shown no sign of abnormal behaviour.

The chronicle of this 'family of degenerates', in the offensive words of a commentator, Hargrave Lee Adam, writing in 1912, is a sad saga. Christiana's father had been a gifted architect and engineer, who, in an exalted mood before madness claimed him, when form met light and sky and sea, had designed the lighthouse in Margate where she herself was born in 1828. Allegedly a 'dangerous lunatic', suffering from 'suicidal and homicidal mania', he died in middle age, in 1847, in the Peckham Asylum. One of Christiana's grandfathers was 'perfectly imbecile'. Her brother, Arthur Burn Edmunds, died 'an epileptic idiot' in Earlswood Asylum, in 1866. A sister suffered from 'constant hysteria'; perhaps this was schizophrenia, or mania. It is a mixed picture all round, with the fear of going off your head, like Father, a skeleton at every brown meal at the mahogany dining table.

When widowed Mrs Edmunds, quite well provided for, migrated along the coast to 'Cheerful Dr Brighton' as Thackeray called it, to make a fresh start in life, she hoped, how she hoped, that her remaining sound offspring, her ice-maiden, would prove immune to the family curse. Better if she did not marry – it might tip her over the brink – and suppose her children were not normal . . .

Nature will out, however, and, disagreeing, had decided

The lighthouse at Margate, designed by Christiana's father.

that Christiana was a suitable machine for procreation of the race. Cupid flexed his bow, and wounded her deeply with his arrow of fire. A romantic scenario, a legend, has evolved over the years, that Christiana first encountered the object of her passion on the sea-front. As the band played, and the seagulls swooped with rending cries, the man's gaze penetrated her veil (for she was known to affect a veil) and in a moment of blinding *éclaircissement*, Christiana knew what it was to be in love.

The truth lies, however, in the plain words in evidence of the man's wife – he was married, of course, and Christiana's choice was, at the very least, a neurotic one, null and void, a duff one, since the marriage was inalienable in the Victorian mode, with progeny – 'I have known the prisoner five or six years. She was for some time a patient of Dr Beard's, and for some time I and my family have been on terms of intimacy with her.'

A doctor. *Her* doctor. Dr Beard, general practitioner, of 64 Grand Parade, Brighton, and possibly Bluebeard by secret fantasy of his own. *Gradually*, her whole passionate imagination fastened upon him – *Vénus toute entière à sa proie attachée* – and she summoned him ever more frequently to her chaperoned bedside to assuage her 'headaches'. She positively exuded a yearning for dalliance, and he should have snatched up his stethoscope and run for his life – and his reputation. No Dr Gully, we can be ninety-eight per cent certain that he never dipped so much as a toe within her agitated sheets. The situation cannot have been novel, but he did not handle it well. Unwisely, he allowed, perhaps even encouraged, his interesting patient to address to him a romantic correspondence, which he preserved, and kept from his wife, Emily.

Gradually, while no one, not even her watchful mother, guessed that the balance of her mind was tilting dangerously, Christiana shifted her position from longing for the absence of her 'rival', Emily Beard, to that of taking positive steps to eliminate her. Nothing so unsubtle as a sudden attack – a push over cliff or breakwater – but, hatched in her bedroom at Gloucester Place, a painful and mysterious death by poisoning.

Of the various lethal poisons available to the Victorian lady intent on domestic use, Christiana's unlucky first choice was probably strychnine. Arsenic, which is tasteless, or, if anything, slightly sweetish, would have better served her purpose of swift and total extinction of the hate-object. As for strychnine – 'Its bitter taste is its most prominent physical characteristic. I have verified the statement that one grain of strychnia in a gallon (70,000 grains) of water is distinctly perceptible. One grain in 30,000 is markedly bitter.' (*Reports of Trials for Murder by Poisoning* by G. Lathom Browne and C. G. Stewart, 1883.)

According to the same excellent authority, there was a false assumption abroad, since the trial of Dr William Palmer in 1856, that strychnine was undetectable *post mortem*. Dr Alfred Swaine Taylor, the leading English medical jurist,

Dr Alfred Swaine Taylor. His alleged mistake led to Christiana's deadly error.

Brighton sea-front esplanade and the West Pier.

was represented as the author of that opinion in an interview – obtained by trickery, and afterwards repudiated by him – published in the *Illustrated Times*. His statement during the Palmer trial, in which he gave evidence for the Prosecution, did not improve matters:

> Question – Supposing a minimum dose, which will destroy life, has been given, could you find any strychnine? Answer – No. It is taken up by absorption, and is no longer discoverable in the stomach. The smallest quantity by which I have destroyed an animal is half a grain. There is no process with which I am acquainted by which it can be discovered in the tissue. As far as I know, a small quantity cannot be discovered.

In his later works Dr Taylor retracted this view, but, even supposing that Christiana Edmunds read learned medical journals, that retraction would have come too late for her. At some time during the year 1870, she obtained an unknown quantity of an unknown poison from an unknown source, and in some manner infiltrated it into one or more chocolates bought from an unknown shop: certainties come later. The quantity of the poison was probably small, because she found herself, after its use, in need of replenishments. On the balance of probabilities only, it was strychnine, both because we know from later events that her mind turned upon strychnine, and because, after that first poison's use, she desired to replicate the symptoms suffered by her first victim, in subsequent poisonings proved to have been effected by strychnine.

Against this, however, in her 'Dorothea' letter to Dr Beard (see pages 72–3), she asserts, 'You see there were two poisons. Zinc was in La Sposa's case and mine.' Zinc sulphate, which is poisonous, has a metallic, astringent taste, and was used as an emetic. Thus, obviously, it would have been easier to obtain than strychnine. On the other hand, one would not have expected Mrs Beard to experience such a severe reaction and aftermath as she subsequently did after merely holding the chocolate in her mouth before expelling it after registering, indeed, its metallic flavour.

If it were zinc, then, why did Christiana switch to strychnine for wider use? Perhaps she calculated that strychnine would be more effective. Or perhaps there was an element of viciousness in her thinking: strychnine has always been known as an agonising agent of death. If Mrs Beard's chocolate *were* laced with strychnine, Christiana, seeking to minimise what she had done, might, in effect, have been saying to Dr Beard, 'I didn't do it, of course, but if I *had* done it, it was only silly old zinc, not this dreadful strychnine.'

The gap between priming the chocolate – in itself little more frightening than sticking a pin into a doll – and actually leaving the safety of her bedroom with it secreted in her pocket must have been enormous. It was a September evening as she walked through the decorous crescents to the Beards' house. The doctor was out – perhaps she knew so – but Emily Beard welcomed her in the drawing room. Christiana produced some chocolates from her pocket and said that they were a present for the children, but, as she was well aware, it was too late for the children to be up.

Then, in the ultimate exercise in 'S'cuse fingers' (see the arsenical scone in the Hay Poisoning Case), in a gesture which may have been pre-planned, she popped one of the chocolates into her rival's unsuspecting mouth. Emily Beard reacted quickly; after one bite or suck, or not even that, she said: 'It had a very unpleasant, cold, metallic taste, and I spat it out directly. I experienced very unpleasant feelings after it, and saliva ran from my mouth all night. The next day I had an attack of diarrhoea and felt very unwell.' There is nothing here that could not be consonant with strychnine, except that in a massive dosage vomiting precedes diarrhoea, typically, and is much more significant.

Visibly shaken, and utterly foiled, the venomous visitor scurried away. Either she had not realized that strychnine is bitter, or she had miscalculated the efficacy of the sugar in chocolates as a disguise. Now guilty of attempted murder, but still with feelings unchanged towards Dr Beard, she lay low and hoped that there would be no consequences. For some interesting reason, Emily Beard did not tell her husband about the suspicious chocolate immediately, although she was demonstrably ill – 'I mentioned what had occurred to Dr Beard within a day or two.' Did she sense that there was a delicacy in the relationship between her husband and Christiana Edmunds? Did she fear that poisoning was a preposterous idea? Or did she simply not want the heavens to fall?

When she finally risked telling Dr Beard, he reacted in such a dramatic and positive manner that he must have had some previous misgivings about Christiana's mental state. It was too late to analyse his wife's faecal material, but he was confident enough to deliver a warning at Gloucester Place, where, in the presence of Christiana's mother, he alluded to the chocolate incident, 'as trivially as possible, in order to see what would come of it . . . I had my worst fears in my own mind . . . I then, to prevent any recurrence of the kind, spoke of the great use which had lately been made of the spectroscope for the purpose of detecting the most minute particles of poison. From her answers I quite understood that she denied all intention of anything of the kind on her part and said that she herself had been ill from eating some chocolates.'

The apprehension that he stood in the shadow of a great scandal may have now caused Dr Beard to absent himself from Brighton for three months. He reassured himself that his wife, without his protection, was 'fully on her guard', and, indeed, she suffered no further attack of any kind during that period,

The high tide of seaside fashion in the 1870s.

The main gate to Broadmoor.

but, with hindsight, she was in great danger. Christiana waited for his return, and, in January 1871, called at his house to beg to be reinstated in his regard. He denied her, and told her, in terms, that 'I could not help fearing she had attempted to poison my wife. She was very indignant, and on the following morning she and her mother called to expostulate. I then laughed off the idea, simply because I could prove nothing, and did not wish to lay myself open to an action for libel.'

Absolutely rejected, and shunned, Christiana haunted the streets of Brighton, hoping for a glimpse of the loved one. The brisk little sea waves slapping on the pebbly beach mocked her anguish. She *had* to make Dr Beard recant. Scorned and furious in her private Hell (for there is none so lonely as the solitary poisoner without accomplice) she did not care who felt her sting. He did not believe her story that she, too, had been made ill by chocolates? Very well – she would prove it to him. Others would suffer. She would seed the shops of Brighton with a positive glut of poisoned chocolates until he sank on his knees before her and begged forgiveness. Later, perhaps, she would have another go at Emily Beard.

Replenishment, or augmentation, of her stock of poison was an enterprise which required a certain manner in dealing with shopkeepers. No more tears. She was not so placed that she could flit, unaccompanied and anonymous, around the back-streets of London, and her best option was to have recourse to a chemist – Isaac Garrett, of Queen's Row, Brighton – to whom she had been known for two years by sight, but not by name, as a purchaser of harmless articles.

Disconcertingly, Mr Garrett was (by his own account) a reluctant supplier, when, on 28 March 1871, she first petitioned him for strychnine to kill cats which were raking up seeds in her garden (a cruel lady), but she kept her nerve and did not hurry away. Class prevailed, and he parted with ten grains. A quarter of a grain is sufficient to kill an adult, one-sixteenth to kill a child. He did insist on a witness to her signature of

Broadmoor Criminal Lunatic Asylum at it was then called.

'Mrs Wood, Hill Side, Kingston, Surrey' in his poison book, and Christiana obligingly produced a nearby milliner, Mrs Caroline Stone, her furnisher from henceforth of fine Shetland 'falls' or veils, to perform that function.

On 15 April, 'Mrs Wood' repeated the entire procedure, complaining that the cats had flourished and multiplied: if she had allowed Mrs Stone to chat too freely in the chemist's, Mr Garrett would have been fascinated to learn that Mrs Wood had just told her that she needed poison for stuffing birds. The chemist must have overcome all his scruples, because on 11 May (presumably without having compared notes with Mrs Stone, whose shop was only three doors away from his) he did not demand a witness when relinquishing a further ten grains, this time to kill an old, diseased dog (still a cruel lady).

Swollen as she was with success, when, later, Christiana found herself in pressing need of more strychnine, even she did not dare to repeat her 'Mrs Wood' impersonation. Instead, on 8 June, she sent a small boy into Mr Garrett's shop with a note purporting to be signed by another Brighton chemist's, Glaisyer and Kemp, of North Street, requesting the favour of a small amount of strychnine, since their own stock had run out. Mr Garrett duly obliged, and the boy bore off one drachm – to the veiled lady hovering in the street.

The long view of Broadmoor from the back.

It is difficult not to believe that she gloated over her fabulous hoard of strychnine, secreted in some maid-proof receptacle, such as a needlework basket, nor that her original, single purpose had become magnified into a grander design. How stealthily she paced out the intervals between her garnering trips to Mr Garrett, with what self-control did she construct her edifice!

Dissemination of the poison carried less risk. A troupe of errand boys were to be her unknowing accomplices – not the street urchins that some have pictured, but respectable lads (one, Adam May, asked his mother's permission) who could be trusted not to abscond, and who would make a good impression as they stood before a shop counter. Having selected a likely lad, she bribed him to buy for her sixpennyworth of large chocolate creams from Maynard's confectioners, and then, when he trotted back with them to the veiled lady waiting on the corner, she put into operation one of two alternatives. By Method A, she sped home with the chocolates and doctored them with strychnine, and then, a day or two later, bribed another lad to return them to Maynard's, saying they were the wrong sort, and to exchange them for another bagful. By Method B, when the first boy brought the chocolates to her, she objected there and then that they were the wrong sort, and sent him straight back to the shop with a secretly substituted bag of chocolates which she had previously treated. The chocolate creams were sold loose, and the returned chocolates were merely tumbled out into the open tray, so that Maynard's entire stock of loose chocolates was infiltered with Christiana's chocolate bombs.

The ballroom at Broadmoor, where Christiana once upon a time waltzed.

For all she cared, the beaches of Brighton could have been strewn with people writing in their last agony. Perhaps the thought was not without its satisfaction. A number of chocolate eaters were quietly ill at home, and then came the public outcry for which she had long schemed. Death stepped forward. On 12 June 1871, Sidney Albert Barker, aged four, died in convulsions within twenty minutes of eating a chocolate from a bagful bought for him at Maynard's by his uncle, Charles David Miller. A post-mortem, and an analysis of the chocolates at the shop, revealed strychnine.

There was a great deal of publicity. Christiana was in her element. The inquest at the Carpenter's Arms, West Street, was her finest hour. Triumphantly thrusting herself into the case, she gave evidence that she had felt ill after buying chocolates at Maynard's – 'It tasted like copper. I felt a burning sensation and tightness in my throat; saliva kept coming into my mouth . . .' The *ratio* of her oration was for Dr Beard's attention only – 'I bought some in September last, which I fancied made me ill. I ate two and gave some to a friend, who was also ill. I did not notice any bad taste in them. I had violent internal pains and a burning in my throat, which came on about an hour afterwards.' At the face value of her words Dr Beard would have protested that she should not have offered chocolates first to his children and then to his wife in the belief that they had made her ill; but she must have intended to convey that she *afterwards* fancied they had made her ill, that she had eaten them just before her visit to the Beards', and that her symptoms had begun on her return home.

The verdict of 'Accidental Death' did not satisfy her. She wanted a stern finger of guilt to be pointed at Mr Maynard. *Then* she would be truly exonerated and restored to the bosom of Dr Beard. To this end, she wrote three anonymous letters to little Sidney Barker's father, urging him to take proceedings against the confectioner for his gross negligence. Poison pen letters, indeed! They are strongly and rationally written, and one of them, outrageously, refers to herself – 'I feel sure the young lady will willingly come forward, as I know, from good authority, she was very dissatisfied with Mr Maynard's conduct.'

Perhaps Christiana would have gone no further if she had at this stage received from Dr Beard the apology for which she craved. But he still kept his distance. She spread her lethal net wider, to demonstrate, she thought, that there was a wholesale poisoner at large in the town: in reality, her actions now acquire a wildness which suggests that her disappointed mind was losing its fine precision. Forsaking her errand boys, she turned to Her Majesty's mail, and entrusted to the postman a series of gift-parcels, containing poisoned cakes, fruit and sweets. Several recipients, prostrate, called out their doctors, having sampled the delicacies with no misgivings, because they came with a cordial letter, unsigned, but showing an intimate knowledge of their circumstances.

Emily Beard herself was, on 10 August, favoured with a special parcel bearing one of the beguiling letters:

> A few home-made cakes for the children, those done up are flavoured on purpose for *yourself* to enjoy. You will guess who this is from; I can't mystify you I fear. I hope this will arrive for you in time while the eatables are fresh.

Dr Beard's judgement that his wife was on her guard was proved to be faulty, because she actually ate some of the contents! She was unaffected, but her servants were not so lucky. Cutting into a plum cake the size of a teacup, which was different from the others, merely intent on its consumption, not on investigation, she did not like the look of a piece of 'unbaked flour'. Instead of recoiling with a scream, she told her maid that it looked bad, and asked her to take it away. Below stairs, famished, no doubt, two Mary Janes scoffed the manna from above. They did not die.

There was one week of freedom left to Christiana. Inspector Gibbs, of the Brighton police, had, for some time, suspected the loquacious lady who had made such a spectacular intervention at the inquest. Someone who fitted her description had been 'losing' bags of bitter chocolate creams at grocers', stationers', shops all over town. The chemist, Mr Garrett, had offered information about 'Mrs Wood' and her penchant for strychnine. He also remembered a curious incident when a boy brought him a letter, purporting to come from the Borough Coroner, requesting him to let him see his poison book, to assist him in certain enquiries. Mr Garrett surrendered the book, and a few days after its return, discovered that a page

Female inmates at recreation.

had been torn out. It was the page *before* the entries of sale to 'Mrs Wood'. In haste, or agitation, Christiana had removed the wrong one.

Well might Christiana fear documentary evidence, because Inspector Gibbs had, by now, a veritable portfolio of written material for comparison – the 'Mrs Wood' signature, the Glaisyer and Kemp note, the bogus coroner's letter, the three anonymous letters to Sidney Barker's father, and a letter from Christiana Edmunds in her own person, replying to a fishing letter from the police. For good measure – since Dr Beard now betrayed her – there was her pathetically revealing, oleaginous and affected missive sent after the inquest to 'Caro Mio' from the desk of 'Dorothea', with a 'long, long bacio'. A modern reader may fairly smile at the intimation that Dr Beard was asking her for the return of his etchings . . .

CARO MIO,

I have been so miserable since my last letter to you. I can't go on without ever speaking to you. What made me write so! I thought, perhaps, it would be better for both of us, but I have not strength of mind to bear it.

We met La Sposa the day after her return and were glad to see her back again. La Madre thought she looked very thin and careworn; I hope she will feel the good now from her change. You must have missed her. I didn't enter on the poisoning case in the street, but I called and told her that I was obliged to appear at the inquest in a few days, and I hoped she would send you a paper and let you know, but she said No, she did not wish to unsettle you. However, dear, I mean you to know about this dreadful poisoning case, especially as I had to give evidence; and I know how interested you would be in it as you told me you would give anything to know what La Sposa swallowed. I sent you the analysis and have no means of knowing if it was sent you. Yes, through my analysis the police found me out and cited me to appear. You can fancy what I felt; such an array of gentlemen; and that clever Dr Letheby, looking so ugly and terrific, frightened me more than anyone; for, if I gave wrong symptoms, of course he would have known. You can fancy my feelings, standing before the public, looking very rosy and frightened as I was. When I saw the reporters' pens going and taking down all I uttered, Burn's (sic) lines rushed to my memory: 'The chiel's amang them taking notes and faith he'll prent it.'

I did the best I could, thankful when I had finished. It seemed so long and my evidence was useful. As the jury had nothing to say, my heart was thankful. When Mr Gell and Penfold attacked me – Mr G: 'Why didn't I show Maynard the analysis?' – it was so sudden, my ideas all left me, and I merely said, because I found Mr Maynard so sceptical and prejudiced, and I thought I had done sufficient. Oh! Why didn't I say as I meant. Because, I suppose Mr M would take the same steps as I had done or else destroy his stock, and that, if those sold to Mr Miller were from the same stock, I had warned him against *these* – he was answerable.

If I had only said that, *for I had no friendly feelings towards Mr M*. That man's chocolates have been the cause of great suffering to me. The Inspector said he wished I had spoken as I felt and as I did to him when he came to me, earnestly and energetically. But La Madre told me I should be thought *flippant, so you see I was subdued*. It was unfortunate the woman Cole's case was dropped. The Inspector told me Dr Letheby took one of the chocolates from the bag and said, 'Good God! this is filled with strychnine'. He felt the effects of it all day: it was rash of him. You see there were two poisons. Zinc was in La Sposa's case and mine. I was troubled to describe the taste. The reporters smiled when I said castor oil and brandy. The Coroner said, 'Ah! Your usual remedy'. I was stupid. He is so deaf. I was told to stand close to him. I took care to turn my back on the jury and on all I could. They were all very polite to me, even that fierce Mr Penfold. Dr Letheby's evidence was so interesting, and showed the different sweets in one glass tube, yet separated. His physique is large and grand, like his mind. Now, darling, rest assured through the whole affair I never mention *your name* or La Sposa's, and if I had been asked to mention a friend I should say Mrs Dix. She is very kind and fond of me, and would have come forward had they wanted her, to help me. No, the rack shouldn't have torn your name from me, and the only reason I said September was, that you might see I had concealed nothing. My dear boy, do esteem me now. I am sure you must. What trial it was to go through, that inquest! La Madre was angry I ever had the analysis; but you know *why* I had it – to clear myself in *my dear friend's eye*. She always says nothing was meant by you. No, darling; you wanted an excuse for my being so slighted. I never think of it; it was all a mistake. I called on La Sposa and told her how I got on. She said my evidence was very nice. She didn't ask me to come; but perhaps she mustn't. *Now there is no reason*. La Madre says if you were at home, she is sure you would ask me just the same as ever.

Come and see us, darling, you have time now. La Madre and I have been looking forward to your holiday to see you. She wants to know how you get on and like the North. Don't be biassed by any relatives: act as your kind heart tells you, and make a poor little thing happy, and fancy a long, long bacio from

DOROTHEA

I haven't taken back your etchings yet, and I'll not call while you are not here, as I have just been and it will be better and right for you to come to us.

Today, the more interesting aspect of the 'Dorothea' letter is no longer, as it used to be, its revelation of motive and guilt, but rather, its indication of the tone of the relationship. If the

The old cemetery at Broadmoor. Christiana would have been buried there.

A day room at Broadmoor (Female Wing).

expressions used, and the intimacy implied, are grossly inappropriate to the real nature of the acquaintanceship, then it is, indeed, the effusion of a very sick woman. On the other hand, in many ways it reads quite naturally, and may demonstrate at least a measure of that which Dr Beard denied to his thin and careworn wife. It is also interesting, if true, that Christiana's personality was so compellant that she was able to suborn a witness, Mrs Dix (however ignorant of the attempted murder), to perjury, in the cause of 'reputation'.

The arrest – for attempting to administer poison to Mrs Beard – took place at Christiana's home on 17 August. 'I poison Mrs Beard!' she fluted. 'Who can say so? I've been nearly poisoned myself.'

At her trial at the Old Bailey on 15 January 1872, she was indicted for the murder of Sidney Albert Baker. The defence was that of insanity, and the only time the fascinating prisoner in the dock lost her glacial composure was when her mother, also in a storm of tears, sobbed forth the catalogue of family madness. The shame was searing. Concurring with the acid dictum of the robust trial judge, Baron Martin, that there was method in her madness, the jury, unimpressed, brought in a verdict of guilty.

The embarrassment of Dr Beard was consummated by the ice-maiden's wishful claim to be pregnant by him. If this were true, she would be spared the death penalty. In the quaint fashion of the time, a jury of matrons, empanelled on the spot from spectators at the trial, assisted by two doctors, examined the prisoner – and found her to be empty . . . The mind shies away from this indelicate scene – the shrinking, untouched, fragile girl-woman, the unplucked flower, beside herself with grief and rage, observed to be in a 'paroxysm of insanity' when pronounced not with quick child.

Compassion prevailed in the heart of the Home Secretary

and, reprieved, she was confined in Broadmoor Criminal Lunatic Asylum until she died there, in 1907, at the age of seventy-nine. Against all the rich characters who twined and gibbered and posed and told their convoluted tales, Christiana Edmunds was a celebrated and imperious relic. A legend has come down to us that she used to write letters – edicts – to famous people, inviting them to come and take tea with her. They were invitations which went unanswered!

Preferable and more telling, is a story reported by the writer H. M. Walbrook to have been recounted by Wilhelm Kuhe, pianist and concert impresario:

A year or two ago, I spent part of the Christmas holiday with some friends whose house was in the neighbourhood of a great criminal lunatic asylum. On the evening of my arrival my host and hostess mentioned that it was their custom to go to the Christmas ball at this institution. They asked me if I would care to accompany them, and I replied that it would much interest me to do so. The experience proved extremely curious, and I brought away with me a host of unforgettable impressions. The figure I most vividly remember was that of one of the inmates, a tall woman of more than middle age, who, while dancing, suddenly caught sight of me, and stared hard at me again and again as she waltzed with her partner round the ballroom. When the dance was finished she came straight up to me 'You are Mr William Kuhe,' she said. 'I am,' I replied, looking into her face, and observing that it was powdered and painted to an extent that was disgusting. 'You don't remember me?' she said with a ghastly smile: her mouth appeared to have been contorted as if by paralysis. I had to admit that I did not. 'Have you forgotten all the excitement there was over Christiana Edmunds?' she asked.

The inmates paced their lives away up and down the Broadmoor exercise terraces.

Although this may be, in fact, a clever fabrication, it has a ring, a peal of truth, even if one would have wished for the account not to be in *oratio recta*, since Walbrook is remembering the story as told as part of a speech delivered by Wilhelm Kuhe in his office as President of the Brighton Musical Fraternity at a meeting some thirty years earlier, in the late 'nineties. William Kuhe proves, on investigation, to have been born in Prague in 1823, and to have died in London in 1912. He enjoyed a European reputation as a pianist, lived in London and Brighton, and organised annual musical festivals in Brighton from 1870 to 1882.

The ballroom would have been the splendid theatre hall, still proudly shown, and the drop-scene of the stage would have been decorated with an apocalyptic painting of the Temple of Fame, the work of Richard Dadd, the parricide, who did not waltz. Christiana Edmunds, one feels, would have gladly waltzed. The lurid make-up also figures! The manner, the approach to the visitor, the hint of irony, they all match the well-preserved personality which one would expect. It would not have been in character for her to crumble away, nor to have saved one last bitter-sweet chocolate for herself.

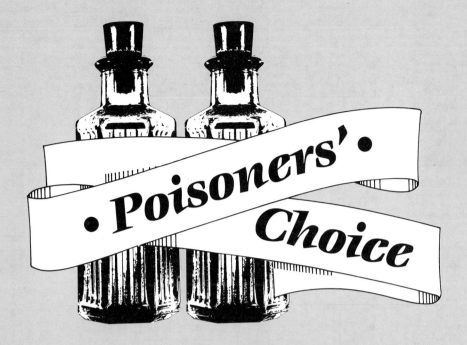

Poisoners' Choice

The baneful alchemy of the poison-cup has over the centuries changed the course of love – and of history. But it was never quite the homicidal commonplace that fiction's fiction made it out to be. Prosaic statistics indicate less than six of every hundred criminal killings as attributable to causes venefic, and in the span of the last half-century murder by poison – the so-called coward's weapon, whilom favourite of the ladies and the medical fraternity – has declined to almost nothing in this country. But let us look back in anguish to the painful choices manifest by the Great Artists of Venenation in the more refined times before the day of the shotgun, bludgeon, flick knife and chopper.

Arsenic

Top of the poisoners' top ten pops. A metallic poison. A virtually tasteless, odourless white powder. First produced *c.*1,200 years ago by an Arab alchemist. Used in Imperial Rome. Became an 'art form' in the hands of the Borgias. Known in France as *poudre de succession* or 'inheritance powder'.

Fatal dose
2-3 grains.
Symptoms
Burning throat, thirst, stomach pain, profuse vomiting, diarrhoea, tenesmus, leg cramps, convulsive twitchings, dermatitis, skin discoloration.
Death
Occurs on average in acute cases in 12-14 hours. Usually due to sudden collapse as result of circulatory failure.

1. **Madeleine Smith, 1857**. Glasgow. Gave it to her otiose lover in a cup of cocoa.
2. **Mary Ann Cotton, 1873**. West Auckland, County Durham. Thrice married, forty-year-old former Sunday school teacher and nurse. With a dead certain score of between 14 and 21, she rates as Britain's champion mass murderer.
3. **Florence Elizabeth Maybrick, 1889**. Liverpool. Gave it to her odious husband in Revalenta Arabica and Valentine's Meat Juice.
4. **Frederick Seddon, 1912**. Islington, London. Gave it, of avarice aforethought, distilled from fly-papers and added to Valentine's Meat Juice, to his lodger Miss Eliza Barrow.
5. **Major Herbert Rowse Armstrong, 1922**. Hay, Powys. Deprived the dandelions and gave it – in the form of weed-killer – to his nagging lady wife.

Antimony

A metallic poison. Usually employed criminally in the form of tartar emetic, an odourless, white, crystalline salt, with a faint, sweetish metallic taste. Soluble in water. Like arsenic tends to preserve the body. More easily excreted than arsenic.
Fatal dose
Smallest known 2 grains.
Symptoms
Astringent, metallic taste in the mouth, burning pain in the throat and feeling of constriction, great thirst, violent vomiting, abdominal pain and cramps, diarrhoea, giddiness, profound depression, spasms in legs and arms, sub-normal temperature.
Death
Depresses the heart and breathing action. Fatal collapse likely to be precipitated by circulatory failure. Death supervenes from exhaustion.

1. **Dr Thomas Smethurst, 1859**. Richmond, Surrey. Gave it to his bigamous wife, probably in doctored medicine, with the motives of loss (of her) and gain (of her fortune).
2. **Dr Edward William Pritchard, 1865**. Glasgow. Prescribed lethal dosings of antimony for his mother-in-law and wife.
3. **George Chapman otherwise Severin Antoniovich Klosowski, 1903.** The Borough, Southwark, London. In the cases of a trio of consorts he found antimonial poisoning the thrice-blessed antimatrimonial specific.
4. **Florence Bravo, 1876**. Balham, London. Wife of Charles Bravo and prime suspect as prescriber of antimony to fight parsimony and vanquish unwelcome passion.

Strychnine

A particularly violent poison. An alkaloid present in the dried, ripe, disk-shaped seeds of the small orange-like fruit of the tree *Strychnos nux-vomica*. A colourless, inodorous crystalline powder with an exceptionally bitter taste.

Fatal dose
¼-½ grain.

Symptoms
Absorbed very quickly. Enters the blood stream and rapidly affects the nervous system, producing a sense of suffocation, breathing difficulties and convulsions, and a feeling of dread. The spine arches dramatically as its motor areas react. The muscles become stiff and rigid, drawing the body back sharply into an arch or bow, so that only the head and heels touch the ground. This condition is known as opisthonotus and is a spasm which lasts for up to two minutes, the victim being conscious and in extreme pain throughout. The contraction subsides, the muscles relax before the onset of another spasm. This pattern may be repeated several times, producing a tetanic spasm in which the chest is fixed, the neck stiffens, the face is set in a sardonic grin, the *risus sardonicus*, which is accompanied by a wild-eyed, staring expression.

Death
Usually after four or five spasms. Intervals between spasms, 5-15 minutes. Cause: respiratory paralysis – asphyxia and exhaustion.

1. **Dr William Palmer, 1856**. Rugeley. Dispatches his fellow turf gambler, John Parsons Cook, with strychnine on a preternaturally rapid gallop along the home stretch to the last post.
2. **Dr Thomas Neill Cream, 1892**. Lambeth, London. Developed the lethal habit of handing out pink pills for pale prostitutes – with fatal results.
3. **Jean Pierre Vaquier, 1924**. Byfleet, Surrey. Transformed the health salts of mine host at the Blue Anchor into highly unhealthy salts by lacing with strychnine – for love of mine hostess.

Morphine

A narcotic alkaloid derived from opium – the dried and inspissated dark-brown juice of the unripe capsule of the poppy, *Papaver somniferum*.

Fatal dose
Probably 3 grains.

Symptoms
Produces narcosis and then deep coma. Pulse slows down. Temperature drops. Respiration becomes less frequent. Sweating and reduced reflexes. Convulsions may occur. Pin-point eye pupils. Sometimes opium may be smelled in the breath.

Death
From central respiratory depression and failure.

1. **Nurse Dorothea Waddingham, 1936.** Nottingham. She believed, wrongly as it turned out, that a mouthful of morphine helped the overdraft go down.
2. **Dr Robert George Clements, 1947**. Southport. The constant inconstant husband who found morphine the best agent of inexpensive divorce.
3. **Dr John Bodkin Adams, 1957**. Eastbourne. 'Eased the passing' of a number of his patients by judiciously injudicious use of morphia and heroin. Acquitted of murder.

Phosphorous

A non-metallic irritant poison. Yellow phosphorus is a luminous, waxy substance, once used for match-heads, but now prohibited for that purpose. Much used in rat paste poisons. Soluble in oil and alcohol. Insoluble in water.

Fatal dose

$c.1^1/_2$–2 grains.

Symptoms

Garlicky taste in the mouth, accompanied by intense thirst. Burning sensations in the throat and gullet. Nausea. Eructations flavoured as of garlic. Vomiting. The vomit is darkened by blood, has a garlic odour, and is usually luminous in the dark. Diarrhoea, also blood-darkened and glowing luminous. Intermissions of several days' duration are characteristic. The original symptoms then return, with increasing uraemia, jaundice, significant nervous restlessness.

Death

Follows hepatic and renal insufficiency – generally within about one week after taking the poison.

1. **Mrs Louisa Merrifield, 1953**. Blackpool. Live-in housekeeper who would not let her mistress live out her days. Used Rodine rat poison as 'inheritance paste'. Her victim had willed her her bungalow.

2. **Mrs Mary Elizabeth Wilson, 1958**. Windynook, Felling, Durham. Still marrying at sixty-six, but seems to have preferred widowhood, for she poisoned her last two husbands. She joked at the wedding feast: 'Keep any cakes and sandwiches over, for the funeral.'

Aconitine

One of the fastest-acting poisons known. Death may occur within eight minutes. Vegetable alkaloid poison, the active principle of aconite, derived from the root and leaves of the monks-hood plant, *Aconitum napellus*. A white crystalline powder. Earthy, bitter taste.

Fatal dose

Probably about $^1/_{16}$–$^1/_{20}$ of a grain.

Symptoms

Tingling and numbness in mouth. Feeling of constriction in throat. Pain in the stomach. Vomiting. Heavy salivation. Visual disturb-ances. Giddiness. Deafness. Rising temperature. Feeble, slow, irregular pulse. Loss of power in all voluntary muscles. Arms, legs, speech, breath-ing all become embarrassed. Mind generally remains clear.

Death

Depresses the central nervous system. Death from respiratory or heart failure.

Dr George Henry Lamson, 1882. Wimbledon, London. Motivated by greed for a larger slice of family legacy money, gave aconitine-spiced slice of Dundee cake to his crippled schoolboy brother-in-law.

Cyanide

One of the most rapidly fatal poisons. Has been known to kill in ten seconds. Formerly most commonly used poison in detective stories. Occurs as a natural vegetable acid in many fruits and leaves, especially those of the cherry, peach and almond, and also in their stone kernels. In its isolated natural form it is harmless, but it is usually found in association with the enzyme emulsin, which reacts with it in the presence of water to release deadly hydrocyanic or prussic acid. Cyanide crystals carried round in small vials used for rapid suicide.

Fatal dose

50-100mg.

Symptoms

Rapid loss of consciousness. Pulse weakens. Convulsions. Coldness of the extremities. Pupils of the eyes dilated and do not react to light. There may be a fine froth at the mouth. Characteristic odour of bitter almonds.

Death

Interferes with the oxygen-carrying capacity of the blood and paralyses the respiratory centre of the brain. Death usually occurs well within five minutes.

Richard Brinkley, 1907. Croydon, Surrey. He tried, unsuccessfully, to prove the old adage that where there's a (favourable) will there's a way – by treating an unwilling witness to a cyanide brewed bottle of oatmeal stout.

Chloroform

A colourless, sweet-tasting, volatile liquid, giving off dense vapour, and presenting a characteristic agreeable odour. When used for anaesthesia, vapour in a 1-2 per cent concentration. Only slightly soluble in water.

Fatal dose

When swallowed, 1-2 ounces.

Symptoms

Nausea. Vomiting. Later, jaundice. Oliguria. Liver necrosis.

Death

Result of heart failure and liver damage. Generally occurs within 5-6 hours.

Adelaide Bartlett, 1886. Pimlico, London. French wife of English grocer who celebrated the New Year by shutting up shop on him in her volatile way.

Hyoscine

Also known as scopolamine. Found in the leaves and seeds of henbane, *Hyocyamus niger*, a botanical relative of the deadly nightshade (*Belladonna*).

Fatal dose

$^1/_4$–$^1/_2$ grain.

Symptoms

Depresses the central nervous system. Slows down reflexes. Convulsions. Hallucinations. Impairs judgement - hence the use of scopolamine as a truth drug. Ultimately produces unconsciousness.

Death

Through respiratory failure.

Dr Hawley Harvey Crippen, 1910. Kentish Town, North London. Having cut down his overblown wife in her prime with an overdose of the truth drug, cut her up, laid her down in the cellar, and tried to lie his way out of the running noose of retribution.

Thallium

A heavy metal, similar to lead and mercury. Extremely poisonous. Found in ant bait and rat poison. Practically tasteless.

Fatal dose

3–15 grains.

Symptoms

Indistinguishable from those of a number of ordinary diseases. Influenza-like aches and pains. Loss of energy and weight. Blurred vision. Stomach pains. Vomiting. Inflammation of the mouth. Peripheral neuritis. Possibly diarrhoea. Numbness in the legs. Loss of hair.

Death

Once ingested, thallium is quickly taken up by most of the body tissues and organs and begins to interfere with metabolism, particularly affecting the nerve cells and upsetting the calcium balance. The poison is excreted only very slowly, so that repeated doses have a cumulative toxicity. Death supervenes from respiratory failure.

Graham Young, 1972. Bovingdon, Hertfordshire. Broadmoor dischargee who distributed tea, sympathy and thallium to his workmates at the factory where he was employed. Two had died of the 'Bovingdon Bug' before the likely lad at the tea-trolley was identified as their 'friendly neighbourhood Frankenstein.'

The Rest of the Best Choices

Kenneth Barlow	1957	Insulin
Edith Bingham case	1911	Arsenic
Charlotte Bryant	1936	Arsenic
Dr Philip Cross	1887	Arsenic
Arthur Devereux	1905	Morphine
Christina Edmunds	1872	Strychnine
Christiana Gilmour	1844	Arsenic
Harold Greenwood Case	1920	Arsenic
Sarah Ann Hearn Case	1931	Arsenic
Ethel Lillie Major	1934	Strychnine
Beatrice Annie Pace Case	1928	Arsenic
John Tawell	1845	Prussic Acid
Thomas Griffiths Wainewright	1831	Strychnine
Thomas Winslow	1860	Antimony

The Half-Hanging of James O'Connor

Being an eye-witness account of a gallows tragedy at Kirkdale Prison, Liverpool, in the year 1873. . .

A warder admitted me, in company with five other press men, and we were shown into a yard, at one corner of which stood the gallows. In the cold we waited, shivering, fearing to witness the very tragedy we had come to see. Presently we heard a gate swing back with a sudden clang, the sound of footsteps, and a voice intoning the opening passages of the Roman Catholic service for the dead. Nearer and nearer came the sounds, the steady tramp of footsteps being mingled with the piteous prayer . . . Then a little procession emerged from the doorway. The robed priest walked directly in front of the condemned, a bound figure. Next hobbled an aged, palsied, trembling man – Calcraft, the official executioner. At the foot of the fatal tree, Father Bonté offered O'Connor a crucifix to kiss, which he did with evident devotion. I shuddered as Calcraft placed the rope round the victim's throat and drew it tight. The white-robed priest – last friend of the dying man on earth – read on. A crash! A thud! The end has come! No; the rope flies loosely in the air! What has happened? With a vault Father Bonté sprang into the pit, his priestly vestments flying in the wind. I followed him. Propped up against the wooden partition lay O'Connor, the broken rope around his neck, and the white cap over his eyes. The good cleric at once drew off the cap and loosened the noose, while he whispered words of consolation into the wretched felon's ear. But it was not to him that the condemned man turned. It was to me. Seizing my arm with his two pinioned hands he exclaimed: 'I stood it bravely, didn't I? You will let me off now, won't you? Let me off, do!' Think of the horror of that appeal! 'You will let me off, won't you?' And there was no power to do so. 'There to be hanged by the neck until you are dead,' was the dread sentence, and the Law must be obeyed. The half-hanged man was supported by warders and taken behind the scaffold, while the other officials hurriedly procured a new rope, and then again he was placed in position. Calcraft pulled the lever, the drop fell, and James O'Connor was dead.

Killer Pictures in a Dead Man's Eyes

The legend of the Dead Man's Tell-Tale Eyes goes back a long way in the folklore of murder.

It is more than a hundred years ago now since a German professor looked into a dead frog's eyes and, quite by chance, spotted reflected in their depths the bunsen burner flame which would ignite a mysterious and controversial fire in the minds of murderers and their hunters.

The scientist was Professor Willi Kühne. The Place, Heidelberg University. The year, 1881.

The frog, a freshly killed victim of Science, had, poor creature, been staring, hypnotised, at the flame for fourteen hours. Amazed at its – the flame's – perpetuation, Professor Kühne proceeded with characteristically ruthless Teutonic dedication to slay experimental batteries of further frogs, to reach the triumphant conclusion that the images of very bright objects with a high level of contrast remain registered on ranarian retinas for half an hour after death, then fade away. In a state of some excitement, he then escalated his experiments to the mammalian optic, sacrificing a rabbit. He placed the animal in front of a bright window, permitted it a lettuce leaf or two, then killed it in a dark corner, sliced the retinas out of its eyes, and found etched in each of them a bright rectangle. Eureka!

Somehow the news of the weird experiments being conducted in Hunnish laboratories filtered down to the criminal world – perhaps via the police – and the superstitious notion that dead retinas retain the photographic – or 'optographic' – images of what they last beheld passed into current belief. And when, in 1888, the London police found themselves really up against it in the Jack the Ripper murders, they hopefully ordered a photographer to take pictures of the eyes of four of Jack's victims. They yielded nothing.

Scene of the shooting of PC Gutteridge. A remote stretch of the Romford to Ongar road in Essex.

The murdered PC George William Gutteridge. The killers shot out both his eyes.

Frederick Guy Browne
and William Henry Kennedy,
the killers of PC Gutteridge.

Thirty-nine years later, September 1927, all Britain shuddered with horror at the murder of Police Constable George William Gutteridge. He had been gunned down on a remote stretch of the Romford–Ongar Road, about a mile from Stapleford Abbotts, in Essex. The killing was brutal enough, but what set a final macabre seal upon it was that, as the thirty-eight-year-old policeman lay dying on the ground, both his eyes had been shot out at point-blank range.

Two professional villains, Frederick Guy Browne and William Henry Kennedy, were subsequently charged with his murder, tried at the Old Bailey, and hanged. It was said that they had put the bullets through his eyes because they were convinced that, locked and frozen in them, would be an embalmed likeness of their faces.

The optographic myth had its votaries in America, too. When, early one June morning in 1920, Mr Joseph Bowne Elwell, the 'Wizard of Whist', was discovered, red-pyjamed, sans toupée and teeth, barefoot, sitting in his regal chair in the reception room of his West 70th Street, Manhattan, home, holding court with death, a neat bullet hole marking the spot where in his pre-depilated days a widow's peak had sprouted, the pixilated police found themselves over-faced by what proved to be an enduring classic murder mystery of New York. Officialdom's beleaguered puzzlement was no wise relieved by the optographic enthusiasm of an elderly medic, one Dr Roland Cook, who forthrightly declared that Dr Charles Norris,

Joseph Bowne Elwell, the New York Wizard of Whist. Dr Roland Cook, optographic enthusiast, pondering the identity of the mystery slayer, was convinced that the eyes had the answer.

An American photographer wanted the murdered Black Dahlia's eyeballs.

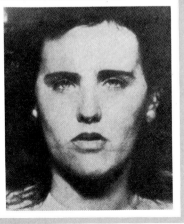

august Chief Medical Examiner of New York City, ought to be sacked. Why? For goodness sakes, for having neglected to do *the* most important thing that should be done at an autopsy – photograph Elwell's eyeballs. Dr Cook argued that, as Elwell had clearly been shot by someone standing directly in front of him, a pair of pictures of the murderer was right there awaiting photographing and developing. Just possibly, it was still not too late to redeem Norris' incompetence. The body must be exhumed *instanter*, preferably at dead of night, as it was impossible to hazard whether or not eyeballs grown accustomed to the fine and private intra-coffin darkness might have their retinas wiped clean of images by incursion of alien, unexpected light.

A cry for optographs went up again, as late as 1947, in the case of the Los Angeles Black Dahlia murder. A photographer tried to convince the coroner that he should hand over Elizabeth Short's eyeballs, so that he could photograph them and record the last image seen by the dead girl.

Although the experts at the New York City Medical Examiner's Office – who have looked and looked in vain into the blank eyes of their 'clients' – pooh-pooh the retinal-retention notion, research carried out in Europe in the last decade seems to indicate the possibility that there may be some truth in the hoary old legend of the 'talking eyes'.

Professors Gustav Sandheim and Evangelios Alexandridis, of old Heidelberg, and criminologist, Hermann Rother, of Bielefeld, West Germany, have claimed that corpses' eyes are a dead give-away. They say that a 'photograph' of the last thing seen *does* remain imprinted on the retina. The search now is for a chemical that can develop and fix poor exposures.

Professor Alexandridis says: 'One has to work quickly. I have developed an image in red on a pale yellow background some considerable time after death, but in thirty minutes the picture becomes muddied by blood passing through the eye.' Using a computerised image intensifier might, he thinks, provide the answer.

Theoretically, a strangler who faced his victim for five minutes in bright sunshine would be identifiable if the optogram could be developed within half an hour.

Practically, the experiments go on . . .

Almanach de Meurtre

Published by a 'Foreign Criminologist' in the earlier years of this century.

Murder *Many cases of this crime occur in August, January, and June; few in February, November, and December.*

Infanticide *Dangerous periods are February and May; very few cases occur in September and December.*

Poisoning *May is the favourite month for criminals of this type; during September, as a rule, they remain absolutely idle.*

Threats of Death *Many such threats are made in August, and few in February, May, and November.*

Murder in the Shadow of the Witches' Hill

Deep in the shadow of witch-haunted Pendle Hill, lies the Lancashire-Yorkshire border hamlet of Bashall Eaves. On the night of Monday, 19 March 1934, farmer John (or James) Dawson, walking home from the village pub, heard a click and felt a light blow on his back. He ate a good supper, slept soundly, and woke up in a blood-saturated bed. Two days later he was dead. A post-mortem revealed a homemade bullet lodged beneath his liver. Perhaps the weapon was a 'poacher's arm' or 'naturalist's gun' – an air cane, in which the propellant is compressed air.

Forty-four years passed. Then journalist Barry Shaw found an old lady living in Salford. She had been Nancy Simpson, seventeen, unmarried, pregnant, at the time of the killing. Shaw found, too, old Tom Kenyon, suspected by Nancy's father, Tommy Simpson, of doing her wrong. Old Tom was sure the bullet had been intended for him. Simpson had shot the wrong man in the dark. A week after Farmer Dawson's death, Tommy Simpson hanged himself.

The hanging of Andrew Carr at Richmond Prison, Dublin, on 28 July 1870. Carr had been found guilty of the infamous Bull Lane murder. In a fit of jealousy he cut the throat of prostitute Margaret Murphy with whom he was living. To the horror of those present at the execution, one of whom was Crown Pathologist Dr Richard Whittington-Egan, the headless trunk of the executed man continued quivering with life for a full three minutes.

The Black Dahlia

How a fine flower of New England young womanhood was plucked, withered and wasted by the Hollywood dream factory, and her jet-tressed corpse was found among the weeds, bearing the stigmata of some very nasty sado-maso chicanery.

Lie back between the black silk sheets, my dears. This is a tale of Tinsel Town. A Hollywood Special. Not a pretty one. From the Hollywood (sick) Bowl. That is, the back-lot Hollywood. Over the Beverly Hills and far away. Beyond the candy floss horizon.

Forget the swish hotels, the American Express and Diner's Card belt, the film stars' mansions, moated with blue-blue swimming pools and guarded by gruff Dobermann Pinschers. Consider not the Brown Derby, Grauman's Chinese Theatre, Ciro's or Sardi's. Off with the paint and the powder, on to the motley back streets, far from the Klieg lights, where the make-believe façades of luxury are architected of hardboard; where tawdriness screams its wares in garish neon, the paper peels, the cardboard rucks, the lath and plaster crack, all under their patinas of ingrained dirt; where cheapjack success rapidly festers into drug or alcohol defeat; where hope is born . . . and dies, hideously.

Ghosts of the greats – the Garbos, Grables, Pickfords, Swansons, Harlows, Crawfords and Monroes – may stalk the Sunset Strip and other celluloid sidewalks, but so do the spectres of the failed, the sacrifices at the shrine of a glamorous myth; those who came, stars of the Hollywood fairy-tale in their eyes, to find fame and fortune, and found only the hard-centre, jagged flint of reality, below the balloons and ballyhoo. Nobody cared. Nobody even noticed. In Hollywood a pretty girl was like a picture – an expendable commodity. They came, they saw, they were conquered; over the golden decades of the Hollywood heyday, a thousand thousand girls just like Beth Short. No, not *just* like Beth. She, the Black Dahlia, was, thank God, unique. Something different . . .

The *thing* – half amid the weeds on the vacant lot beside the local lovers' lane, half on the pavement of Los Angeles' South Norton Avenue, between 39th and Coliseum Streets, a block east of Crenshaw Boulevard – facing queasy-stomached radio patrol car officers, W. E. Fitzgerald and F. S. Perkins

Elizabeth Ann Short, The Black Dahlia. Hollywood-struck and Hollywood struck down.

Vine Street looking towards Hollywood Boulevard.

that bleak and windy Wednesday morning, 15 January 1947, was something different too. A naked female body, flesh pock-marked with cigarette burns, trussed up with rope, cut clean in half at the waist, bisected with a finicky precision which ensured that not a single vital organ had been perforated or damaged; this in horrendous contrast to what had been done to the rest of the body.

The head had been beaten to a pulpy mush of brain and bone fragments. The mouth, once prettily shaped and sexily pouting, had been viciously slashed across into a gaping, scar-let death-grin. The breasts, always the ravager-with-a-knife's prime target, had been tooth-edgingly mutilated, their white half-moon mounds ringed about between the burns with lots of little fetish nicks, tell-tales of a sadist's pleasure, taken in small pinches. And the sweet knife had been further plied to the slicing open of the lower torso and to the signing of the bladesman artist's handiwork, 'B. D.', the initials carved deep into the round, inviting haunch-flesh of the thigh. So neat and tidy an artificer this, that, torturous work terminated by the ultimate anaesthesia of death, the twin palettes of his divisive artistry – head, neck, chest and upper limbs, and abdomen and lower limbs – were meticulously washed, scrubbed even, like a slaughtered pig. And nowhere was a drop of blood. The body had been totally exsanguinated, drained of all blood and liquids.

Horrifying enough. More horrid still was the news to come from the post-mortem room. The pathologist reported that it had been forensically established that most of the injuries had indeed been inflicted before death. Further evidence, rope burns on the limbs and impress marks across the jaw, sug-gested that the woman had been gagged, her wrists and ankles bound with rope or wire, and that she had been hanging head downwards, alive and fully conscious, while her captor made long sadistic sport with her. When found, she had been dead an estimated 8-14 hours. That would put her death as occur-ring at any time between 2.45am on 15 January and 8.45pm on the evening of Tuesday, 14 January. She was described as a once-beautiful girl: weight about 8st 6lbs: height 5ft 3in. High forehead. Small turned-up nose. Ears with almost no lobes. Grey-green eyes. Dark hair, recently hennaed. These were, of course, the calm, scientific calculations and reconstructions of the mortuary; for the two police officers standing out there on the grey, windswept street at a few minutes before 11am, doing their best to view with official detachment that gruesome sight, God knows it was hard enough to see these divided hunks of what looked like kosher butcher's white-bled meat as human, let alone as the remnants of a lovely young woman. It called for a gigantic effort of imagination to reassemble them into anything remotely approaching that guise. But that was what they were going to have to do. That was exactly what the men of the Los Angeles Homicide Squad stood challenged with now. They had to endow this anonymous and already putrifying bipartite carcass with identity and warmth; literally bring it back to life, a breathing, beautiful, desirable young girl, that it might mutely reveal the circumstances, the joys and sorrows, the modes of its living, and the manner of its dying. And – if they were very clever and very, very lucky – persuade this carrion flesh to speak the name of its torturer and destroyer.

It had been at about 10.45am that mid-January morning that Mrs Betty Bersinger, walking with her three-year-old daughter, Anne, turned into the 3900 block on South Norton and beheld the sight that jolted her into a state of near-hysteria. They were heading for the Leimert Park section, where she was going to have Anne's shoes repaired. Going south, between Bronson and Grayburn Avenues, they came abruptly on the body. It was lying face up. Mrs Bersinger could see that it had been sawn in two. Shocked, scared, but above all worried at her little girl seeing such a sight, she scooped the child up and raced off in search of the first house with a telephone. Not wishing to become involved, she avoided any reference to murder, simply telling the police, 'I think a drunken man is lying in the weeds in a lot on Norton Avenue.' Then she hung up. It was not until eight days later – 23 January – that she decided that she had better make her identity known to the Los Angeles Police Department. She was twenty-five-year-old Mrs John Bersinger, of 3705 Norton Avenue.

Three minutes after receiving the flash that morning of 15 January, the radio car had arrived at the scene and confronted the grisly riddle. And it was not long after that that Captain Jack A. Donahoe of the Los Angeles Homicide detail sent in two of his best men, Sergeant Harry 'Red' Hansen and Sergeant Finis Arthur Brown. They were joined by police chemist Ray Pinker and Lee Jones of the Police Crime Laboratory. Practised eyes scanned the terrain for clues. There was nothing, absolutely nothing; not a scrap of clothing, a footprint, a cigarette end, not even a match, to provide a hint as to the identity of either killed or killer. The one, very faint, hope of possibly useful information was that some tyre marks showing up on the little-travelled roadway suggested that a car might have been used to transport the body from the scene of the murder. The car had come from the south. Had the body been dragged from it and left on the lot? If so, the person who had dumped it had then driven off in a northerly direction. Interesting so far as it went, which was, unhappily, not very far, for there was nothing to distinguish the tyre marks from millions of others. However, Mr Walter A. Johnson, resident at No 3815 of adjacent Welland Avenue, came up with the interesting story of the thin man who lurked by the weed-webbed lot in lovers' lane at about 9pm on Tuesday, 14 January. Mr Johnson said that the area was known as a haven for smoochers and trash haulers, and he went there with a car load of shrub cuttings. He was burning rubbish at a lot across the street. He saw parked over on the west side of Norton, directly opposite the

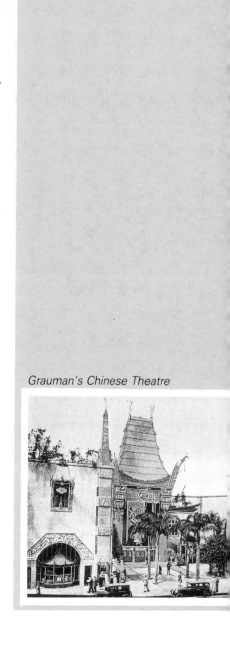

Grauman's Chinese Theatre

Ciro's – 8333 Sunset Boulevard.

fire plug by the lot where the body was found next morning, an old, battered, four-door sedan, 'about a 1935 model'. It was a light, or tan, or cream-coloured car and its right rear door was open. Standing near it was a thin man. He was about 5ft 8in tall, aged about forty-five, and was wearing a tan topcoat and a dark hat, pulled low. As Johnson slowed his car to a stop, the thin man looked up, startled. He walked a little way up the street. Then he came back, crossed the street and walked slowly past, his hands in his pockets. He scrutinized Mr Johnson thoroughly and craned to look into his car. At this point, Johnson, fearing that the man might be a bandit, drove off. He circled the block and returned to the same spot. This time the door of the light sedan was closed and the thin man was at the wheel. As soon as he saw the glare of Johnson's headlights, he sped away with grinding gears and burning tyres.

Rather confusingly, another local resident, Bob Meyer, of 3900 South Bronson Avenue, reported that he, too, had seen a sedan – a 1936 or 1937 Ford, this one – on the morning of 15 January. He had been looking out of his window at about 6.30 or 7am and saw it stop at the curb near the place where the body was later found, linger for a short while and then move off. The tall weeds unfortunately prevented his getting a better view of what was going on. Subsequently, there was endorsement of the likelihood of the body's having been brought to the spot by car in a forensic laboratory report of the finding of a few small bristles on the surface of the body, which could as well have come from a car's floor-mat as from a brush used to scrub the cadaver halves clean. Radio cars were notified to keep an eye open for sedans of appropriate date and colours, but nothing came of it.

Another lead, a bundle of woman's clothes found behind a used car lot at 1600 West Adams Boulevard, not far from the scene, set police pulses racing. They slowed back to normal when, after diligent pursuit of the give-away laundry mark, it was revealed that they had been stolen a few days before from the car of their owner, Cora Bryant, parked near her home at 951 East 46th Street. Police were to check every last possible hiding place for the naked cadaver's missing clothes; the sewers, the storm drains and gullies, the vacant lots, and pretty well every motel in the Los Angeles area. Later, much later, Bob Hyman, manager of a café at 1136 Crenshaw Boulevard, about a mile from South Norton Avenue, would tell them of seeing a pair of black suede shoes stuffed into a black plastic hand-bag in a trash can in front of his premises on the morning of Thursday, 23 January. He could not say who had put the stuff there. By that night, the trash collectors had taken it away. The handbag and one of the shoes were, however, recovered by police combing a trash dump at 1819 East 25th Street, and both were identified by Robert Manley – of whom we shall hear more later – at University police station as having been the property of the dead woman.

Now came the first lucky break.

The prints of the corpse had, as a matter of routine, been taken. As a matter of routine, they had been sent off, apathetically, without expectation, without the enthusiasm of much hope, to be run through the massive, multi-million FBI fingerprint files in Washington. They were unlikely to be recorded there, unless, that is, she had been a criminal, an alien, or had had a job in a government department.

Back came a reply:

Elizabeth Ann Short. Born: 29 July 1924, in Hyde Park, Boston, Massachusetts. Last known address: Santa Barbara, California.

Some claim that it had been a chance in a million. That the victim had had her fingerprints taken *voluntarily*, while working during the war as a government employee, a clerk in the United States Post Exchange. There is, as we shall see presently, another, less chance romantic, explanation. The identification was confirmed by the victim's mother, Mrs Phoebe Short, and her sister, Mrs Virginia West.

Inspired by this modicum of success, Police Captain Donahoe's detectives buckled on their shoulder-holsters, patted smooth their jackets, donned their raincoats and snap-brim hats, and got to work. Out went the call. Check all persons acquainted with Elizabeth Short. Track her every last movement. In came the answers. A trickle at first. Then a flood. Now life *was* breathed back into what proved to have been indeed a very desirable, and much desired, young woman.

Her story, as it came gradually together, proved to be virtually a type-specimen of the same sorry story that could be told of a certain kind of teenager to be found, not just in America, but in their millions the sad world over. Often, as in her case, they are the tragic products of their background – a broken, or severely fractured, home. Starved of love, cold for lack of understanding, they hungrily seek love's counterfeit in the pseudo-warmth of casual sexuality. Having no home worthy of the name, they become foot-loose in their compulsive search for one; wandering, globe-trotting sociopaths – but the 'path' should stand for pathetic.

Elizabeth's parents separated in 1931, when Betty, as she was called at home, was rising seven. At that time, the family – father, Cleo Short, mother, Phoebe, and their five daughters – were living in Medford, the residential suburb on the Mystic River, five miles north of Boston. When he left, her father took the eldest girl, Virginia, to live with him on the West Coast. Those were the bottoming years of the Great American Depression, bad for most people, especially bad for an abandoned mother with four little girls to support. Not a lot of time left over from working, worrying and scrimping for the bestowal of the loving attention which the growing Betty obviously felt was

Mrs Phoebe Short, The Black Dahlia's mother.

Miami, the scene of the Dahlia's earliest blooming – a heady, romantic time.

her need and should have been her meed. Her resentment of deprival expressed itself in the classic manner of the neglected attention-seeker – tantrums, bitten fingernails, and asthma.

In 1942, by now a seventeen-year-old, willowy, tense, delicate, but provocatively blossoming girl, with midnight-black hair and dawn-white skin, superb green eyes, irresistible smile and dangerously attractive figure, she sat down and quietly totted up what assets she had to invest in life. It was not immodest of her to catalogue to her own satisfaction her seductive niceties of face and figure. Other than these physical attributes she is poor. They are her only slender capital, and must be used before cruel Time has spent them all, leaving her not just poor as before, but bankrupt. Decision unsentimentally made, she hung up her shabbying school satchel, clawed together a thin handful of best-clothes finery, turned her back gladly enough on Mom and Medford, and headed on the job hunt for Florida.

She very soon found one. The war was on. Miami had been transformed into one vast Army Air Force Centre. She took her place there as a waitress. The situation suited her well. In this new-found freedom she found herself. She also found others. Men, of course. Servicemen of all ranks, interested in the sort of service that the pretty young waitress, her stern New England background notwithstanding, was only too willing to supply.

It was a heady, romantic time. Stolen kisses beneath a bomber's moon. Vows and avowals. Alarms and excursions. Gains and losses. Hi's and goodbyes. Wings away into the sunset. Briefly tear-wetted pillows. Letters with lots of love and overseas frankings. Promises and betrayals – on both sides. And, finally, wisdom and withdrawal.

Another letter. This one to her father, working now in the Navy Yard at Richmond, California, humbly asking him for help. Give him his due, Cleo Short did not fail her. He sent her two hundred dollars and invited her to come and live with him in Vallejo, twenty-five miles out of San Francisco. He wanted her to keep house for him, the way her sister, Virginia, had before she married an engineer, Adrian C. West, and went off to live with him in Berkeley. Betty arrived, brimful of gratitude and good intentions. She did her best, she really did. But it did not work out. You cannot keep a bird caged once it has known the sweets of the wild wood. Her chagrined father saw it as an undeserved let-down.

Here and now is where the *curriculum vitae* chaos begins, the sequence of places and events shuffled out of order as thoroughly as a Mississippi gambler's deck of cards. The few short years of life remaining add place names to the itinerary of her ill-starred voyagings. After her earlier stop-over stays in Miami, Florida, there were visits to Chicago, on one of which she worked as a cocktail waitress, and on another, later, as a model, and sporadic home flits to Medford; but the map of her dwindling days is mainly spangled with locations in California, her Eldorado, where she flickered nomadically to and fro, squandering what was left in the upturned glass between Santa Barbara, Los Angeles, especially the Hollywood section, Long Beach and San Diego.

It was in Santa Barbara, one eventful day in late September 1943, that she was discovered in the course of a police raid on the El Paseo Restaurant – a somewhat dubious café suspected of selling hard liquor to minors – quaffing a drop or two of the hard stuff amid a group of the licentious soldiery. She claimed that one of them was her husband. It did not take the police long to nail that lie, and she was booked as a juvenile delinquent. And that, runs the less than romantic version, is how her fingerprints conveniently happened to be on record. The Californian authorities put her on a train back home to mother in Medford. Somewhere along the 3,000 mile route she skipped off, and returned to Santa Barbara.

She got work there as a civilian employee in the US Post Exchange – the PX, roughly the equivalent of the British NAAFI – at Camp Cooke. Her job was to act as a sort of hostess, handing out coffee, sympathy and doughnuts to doughboys and lonely GIs. She was popular and decorative. Once, she was elected 'Cutie of the Week'. Her immediate superior at the Camp, Mrs Inez Keeling, said that she was 'one of the loveliest and most shy girls working for me,' and added that she never dated soldiers.

Elizabeth Short stayed at Camp Cooke a long while for her. Right into 1944. It was another romantic interlude. A succession of lighter loves. She lived for a time as the wife of an army supply sergeant. They jointly purchased a car and some furniture and settled in together in Santa Maria. Before long, things began to go awry. Probably she was caught out 'playing around'. Anyway, her sergeant 'husband' cut up pretty rough and threatened to kill her. So alarmed was she by this outburst, that she is said to have reported all to the sergeant's commanding officer, and he was shortly afterwards posted overseas. A most effective divorce!

And then she met – or is said to have met, for one can never be quite sure when dealing with the alleged facts of the life of one so devious and economic with the truth as Elizabeth Short – the love of her life. He was Air Force Major Matthew Gordon, Jr, of Pueblo, Colorado. Elizabeth claimed that they got engaged. Perhaps they did. Came the day Major Matt received his overseas drafting orders, and vanished beyond the blue horizon. To India, actually. All the old familiar insecurity flooded tumultuously back. What if Matt were killed? What if he came home safely, but no longer wanted her? The catalyst of war had quickened Elizabeth Short's street-wise wisdom. A girl must insure. She had. Lieutenant Joseph Fickling, a pilot, had looked good as insurance. She had been investing a modest premium in him even while Matt was still around. But now he, too, seemed somehow to drift away from her.

The Short trail becomes misty. She left Camp Cooke. She

The Dahlia dines out with her dream man, Major Matt Gordon.

moved to Pismo Beach. After that, down-and-out, she lived for a bit with Mrs Mary Stradder, a sergeant in the Women's Army Corps, at Casmalia, eighteen miles from Santa Maria. The trail peters out. A big spaceful of question marks. You expect that in the case of girls like Elizabeth Short.

The next firm point investigation has uncovered is February 1946. Betty is back home at 115 Salem Street, Medford, paying a long-put-off visit to her mother. While she was there, into the post-box flopped a letter from Lieutenant Fickling – 'I have always remembered you. I can't deny that I get awfully lonesome sometimes and wonder if we haven't been very foolish and childish about the whole affair. Have we?' He suggested that she should return to the coast. 'No one will be happier to see you than a certain lieutenant in Long Beach.' But Betty vacillated in Medford. By the time she got back to California, Lieutenant Fickling had long spread those pilot's wings of his and departed for Texas and his discharge.

She moved on. Again, we cannot precisely chart her down the labyrinthine way of her decay. The next sure location is Los Angeles. The West Coast was always the lode-stone of her compass, a sun-and-fun magnet. Not that there is much fun there right now. She has become Beth Short, and she is finding the going rough. She is living – existing – in a theatrical rooming-house on North Orange Drive with a tungsten teenager, fifteen-year-old blonde singer Lynn Martin, whose tender years are out-balanced by a tough core of preternatural practicality and hardness on the subjects of men and money. Lynn has set her rock-crystal sights on the big silver screen. Beth caught a renewed dose of the movies fever. No star was born: only an alluring, sparkling, available creature, christened, because of her high-piled mass of magnificent glossy black hair, often set off by a white gardenia or some such flower, and manifest stock-in-trade fondness for things black, silky and kinky – skin-tight black dresses, foaming lacy black underclothes, sheer sheeny black stockings and shiny black high-heeled court shoes, a jet ring on her pale white hand – the Black Dahlia.

Lynn persuaded her that the swiftest, surest way into pictures was through the door marked 'Sex'. She moved with the easy acquiescent obligingness of a call-girl among the film capital's moguls, magnates and tycoons – real and pretended – of the casting couch. But accommodating emotion did not lead to a motion picture career. Her contacts brought no contracts. Promises, promises. A very occasional, very tiny, part as an extra.

A small-town girl's dazzle still in her eyes where the magic land of movies was concerned, she adored being taken to the nightclubs frequented by the film stars, seeing in the paint and powdered flesh the faces, giant-sized in black and white, at which she had gazed up moonstruck on the screens of the Medford Picture Palais and Plazas. It is doubtful that she ever achieved real closeness to any of the Hollywood stars, but she did for a while play off-screen parts among the lusty buckos of the film colony.

Then, suddenly weary of the hassle and the hustling, the mooching about the Hollywood streets and bars and cafés, picking up this man, being dropped by that, the fading chimaera of silver screen success – preluded so frequently by the proffered carrot of a fun frolic in the movie big shot's king-size bed, coming to nothing: seeing momentarily, as through the mascara clearly, temporarily beaten, she bought her a railroad ticket home to Mom and Medford.

It was, of course, only an impulse buy; only the outward and visible measure of an inner crisis of desperation. Had she been in her normal abnormal state of mind, she would have known that the promise of home was, so far as she was concerned, no more substantial than that of the latest Moviesville little Caesar. Back among her milch cow siblings, she soon realized that the quiet home-town design of their days did not, and never would, do anything but clash impossibly with the extravagant pattern which she had chosen for her own. Not without sadness, she kissed Momma and sisters three farewell.

One more firm point. From 12 July to 3 August 1946, she was living at the Washington Hotel, 53 Linden Avenue, Long Beach, California. Five months later, reporter Bevo Means of the Los Angeles *Herald-Express*, interviewed her former landlady. She sent him to a Long Beach drugstore where Beth had been a regular, meeting men at the soda fountain. The druggist recalled her vividly. 'Sure I remember her. Who could forget a beautiful girl like that? Always in black. The fellows coming in here called her the Black Dahlia.' It was in Bevo Means' story that the sobriquet of the Black Dahlia was first mentioned.

On 22 August 1946, a telegram from Pueblo, Colorado:

Just received word from War Department that Matt was killed in a crash. Our deepest sympathy is with you.

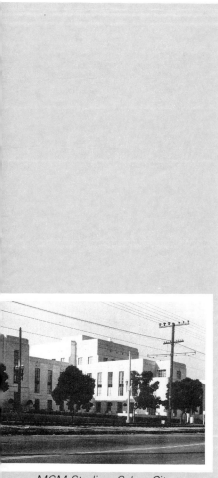

*MGM Studios, Culver City.
For Elizabeth Short, the
Promised Land.*

It was from Major Gordon's mother. At last Beth had a rôle: the bravely grieving war widow. Drifting aimlessly on the floodtide of her tears, she sought life-belts of sympathy. She broadcast to friends and acquaintances far and wide that her Air Force major husband had been killed, and that the baby son that she had borne him had also died. Their displays of honest grief on her behalf were substitute for applause. After she had repeated the lines of her tragic self-written script often enough, she, too, came genuinely to believe in her war non-substantive husband and the dead fruit of her phantom pregnancy. Still playing the part, a widow-virgin now, she broke, for the time being, with the abrasively realist Lynn Martin, and sundry others of that ilk, and went to live, as fragile relicts should, sedately by herself.

But *la ronde* had stopped for only a very brief space. As long as it took tears to dry. No more. Stout-pursed, middle-aged theatre owner, Mark M. Hansen, set it turning again for her. She was introduced to him by an attractive twenty-two-year-old brunette whom she had met in her wanderings around the verges of the studios, Anne Toth – a film extra who seemed to be making it, to the extent that she had landed a bit part in the Tyrone Power and Gene Tierney film that 20th Century Fox was making of Somerset Maugham's *The Razor's Edge*. The Black Dahlia, in that persona, went to live with Anne Toth and other Hollywood hopefuls in one of the rooms made at a nominal rent available to them in Hansen's Grand Panjandrum-style apartment at 6024 Carlos Avenue – and by so doing swelled her list of masculine playmates to such proportion that she could truly be said to have graduated into the profession.

On 2 November 1946, mail from a male once again took a fist in her ineluctably shaping destiny. It was a letter penned by Lieutenant Fickling, now poised upon the springboard of discharge into civvy street. He wrote, apparently in answer to a letter, followed by a telegram, which he had received from her, and in which she seems to have indicated that she wanted to carry on from where she had not taken up earlier in the year: 'You say in your letter that you want us to be good friends, but from your wire you seem to want more than that. Are you really sure what you want? Why not pause and consider just what your coming out here would amount to? You've got to be just a little more practical these days.' Fickling let her have it straight from the shoulder; marriage, or even an engagement, was not on the cards. 'When I get out of the army my plans are very indefinite and uncertain.' Fickling by name, fickle by nature. Her wartime insurance policy had lapsed.

In a strange, bitter state of mind, she moved out of Hansen's apartment and in to share a place on North Cherokee Avenue, way down in the South Gate area, with eight other young women, Anne Toth and Lynn Martin among them. Each paid the apartment manager, Mrs Juanita Ringo, a dollar a day. That entitled you to the questionable comfort of a place in a double-decker bunk and a space of wardrobe in the crowded double apartment. Although the girls laid claim to such unexceptionable employments as telephone operator, cocktail lounge waitress, rouge-room worker at the Max Factor make-up studios, struggling songstress and resting actress, it has been suggested that what they, or some of them at any rate, were really working were the streets of the vicinity.

Whatever, Beth was soon out on the solo tramp once more: a Hollywood drifter again. Things in the dream factory – least ways on its southern outskirts – had not improved. Her friend, Anne Toth, her fleeting moment of filmic glory forgotten, was now on, instead of in, the razor's edge, growing thin on slim pickings as a crowd-scener. Her friend, Marjorie Graham, had thrown in her hand at trying to make it into the movies, and was grafting as a waitress at a drive-in restaurant. Undeterred, Beth donned with determination her Black Dahlia regalia and, like Auden and MacNeice's poetic adventurers, took things as she found them, and looked for pickings where the pickings were. And that was in such beds and bedrooms as she might, clad *à la* Dahlia, be invited to occupy. Or, failing that, in the cafés and cocktail lounges, where she put on a waitress' apron. Or in seedy photographers' studios, where she took it, and everything else, off, to make a few handfuls of much-needed dollars, posing for nude photographs. The nearest she came to a picture career, as one cynic put it.

The Dahlia bloomed among the Cherokee girls for only a very short period – 13 November to 5 December 1946. On that last date she took off, telling Anne Toth that she was going to visit her sister, Virginia, in Berkeley. She never arrived there. It has been reported that what she in fact did, was move in with a mannish woman who introduced her to the Hollywood lesbian community, but she found that it was not her scene.

R-K-O Studios at Gower and Melrose.

The next definite sighting of the Dahlia was a hundred miles south, in the booming seaport town of San Diego. It was there, on Sunday, 8 December, in an all-night movie house, that she fell into conversation with the cashier-cum-usherette, Dorothy French. In character as the *ci-devant* Mrs Betty Gordon, she poured into her sympathetic ear the heartbreak tale of a widow whose Air Force major husband died in the war, whose baby son had followed his daddy to the grave, and who was now herself a helpless, homeless, penniless flotsam, cast up on the stony beach of life.

Miss French, that rare being, one who translates 'feeling sorry' into actually doing something about it, took the life-battered widow back to spend the night with her and her mother, Mrs Elvera French, in their home at 2750 Camino Praderno, the Bayview Terrace Housing Project, Pacific Beach. She stayed for a month. 'In the end we had to ask her to move because our home was so crowded.' Dorothy French was later to tell the police: 'Betty showed me a newspaper clipping she'd been keeping in her purse. She said it told about her and the major.

But I read the clipping and it definitely said they had not been married. Betty had crossed out the 'not'. She told me the newspaper had made a mistake.' The charity guest had been there barely a week, when she appeared on the doorstep with a fine, red-haired six-footer in tow. 'A business associate,' she introduced him. True!

8 January 1947. Betty has now enjoyed a Bayview Terrace Christmas and New Year, been living with, and off, the French family for four weeks. This Wednesday morning a telegram arrives for the destitute widow. It must have been in response to some invitation issuing from her, for it read: 'Wait and I'll be down for you.' It triggered her into a frenzy of packing and feverish expectation. And, at about 7.30pm that evening, as Betty left afoot, carrying her packed suitcases, the Frenches waved 'the *woman* who came to dinner' out of their lives. Neighbours saw her enter a 1940 cream or light tan coupé with a 'Huntington Beach' or 'Huntington Park' sticker on the rear window, with a red-haired man. She and her companion were both in a jolly mood, joking as he loaded the valises into his car. 'Drive me to Los Angeles,' she had ordered mock imperiously. She wanted, she said, to see her sister. He was sorry, he just couldn't oblige. He had business calls to make in San Diego in the morning. OK! OK! She'd take the bus north. That didn't mesh-in with the red-haired man's plans at all. Hell! Business could wait. The business in hand was far and away more delectable. He'd rather risk the sack than miss her in the sack. 'OK, jump in,' he said.

Exactly one week later Mrs Betty Bersinger walking with three-year-old Anne on South Norton Avenue . . .

The hunt for the man who 'plucked' the Black Dahlia was on.

Dorothy French told the detectives that Betty had said that 'Red', as she called the man who had driven her off, was an airlines employee, whose home was in Huntington Park, LA. He had been working in San Diego, and staying at a motel there not far from Bayview Terrace. She also told Dorothy that she first met Red on 16 December. They were frequently together until his departure back to Los Angeles on 23 December.

It was Beth's friend, Marjorie Graham, who told the police about her trunk. It had been shipped to Los Angeles from Chicago by Railway Express and was still lying unredeemed at Los Angeles Union Station. They promptly collected it. It contained an album of men in uniform, democratically representative of all ranks from buck private to lieutenant-general. More promising were the bundles of letters, neatly tied with ribbon.

Their contents turned out to be pretty much what one might expect: love letters written from dozens of different addresses, but all coming from the temporary sojourners, as it were, in one great transit camp of masquerade, situate on a side road off the highway of true love. Here were plastic hearts and artificial flowers . . .

Your devotion is my most precious possession. Darling, how many lips have joined with yours since ours last met? Sometimes I go crazy when I think of such things.

Now someone had gone crazy thinking of – and doing – such things.
Of course there *were* other men and other lips, but, to this ongoing admirer from one of those wartime brief encounters, Beth wrote, in a cloud-cuckooland letter which she would never mail:

It would have been wonderful if we belonged to each other. I'll never regret . . . However, it was nice as long as it lasted.

The postmarks on the ribboned letters which she had received from this once-upon-a-time admirer bear witness that she had pursued him, bret-hot for love and money, in epistollary paroxysms from coast to coast.

Darling, your request is impossible at this time, other obligations have me against the wall. Try to make other arrangements. I'm concerned and sorry, believe me.

and

Honey, I'm terribly sorry about that wire you sent. Couldn't raise the money on that short notice. Glad you managed OK. I want that picture of you very much.

San Diego. One of the last ports of call in a Short life story.

Despite the teaspoon of honey, it was the medicine of brush-off.
'I'll never love any man as I do you,' she wrote persistently to her elusive lover. And then, in that very same letter, 'perhaps Matt was my man, that is why I have been so miserable.'
And here, riffling through the bunch of letters, are a few illustrative lines from another man, another wartime romance, a field casualty, dead, like pretty little Betty herself, beyond resuscitation.
'Your letter,' wrote her long-ago soldier boy toy, 'took me completely by surprise. Yes, I've always had the feeling that we had a lot in common and that we could have meant a lot to each other had we only been together more often.'
Was ever a clearer lament to the twisted vastness of the might-have-been?
Out of the yellowing pages of the Black Dahlia epistles emerged the not markedly heroic figure of the fickle Fickling. He was tracked down to Charlotte, North Carolina, where he had been working since the previous November as co-pilot on the Charlotte-Chicago route for the 20th Century Airlines. He was able to satisfy the police that he had been nowhere near the dead Dahlia since quitting Los Angeles in April 1946. He had, however, received a letter from her, postmarked, 'San

Hollywood. Looking east, Sunset Strip; looking west, Heartbreak Avenue.

Diego. January 8th, 1947.' In it she told him, 'Do not write to me here. I am planning to go to Chicago with Jack, who is from a model agency for a group of Chicago department stores.'

The police decided now to focus the searchlight of intensive investigation upon the last week – 8 January, to Wednesday, 15th January 1947 – of the Black Dahlia's life.

They visited the girl's father. Now sixty-two, working as a refrigerator engineer, and living at 1020 South Kingsley Drive, in Los Angeles, Cleo Short was uncooperative. Not interested. He told the detectives: 'I want nothing to do with this. I broke off with the mother and the family seven years ago.' He had not seen his wayward daughter in four years. Not since 1943. 'She wouldn't stay home, so I told her to go her way and I'd go mine.'

They saw her mother, Mrs Phoebe M. Short. 'I'll do everything possible to see the fiend who killed my little girl is caught,' she said. 'He can't be human.' And she told them that, after leaving Hollywood, her daughter had written to her from San Diego, saying that she had found work there in an Army hospital, or, she was vague, in some connection or other with the armed forces.

Fifty men scoured San Diego, Los Angeles, Hollywood and Santa Barbara cocktail lounges for anyone who might have seen or heard anything. They visited motels, hotels, cafés and all the likeliest, and some of the unlikeliest, pick-up joints and watering holes. Everybody who had been in the girl's company, and even those who just remembered seeing her, was questioned. A great many people had known the Black Dahlia, but nobody knew very much *about* her. Scores had seen and talked with her in the last dark days of her wilting; none of them could say what she had been doing or where she was going. But all told the same story, presented the same picture: a lost soul, plainly sick in heart and mind, wandering the town aimlessly, and scared, scared, scared . . .

The leads began to come pouring in. Almost too many of them. It was looking good. Based on all this buzz of two-way activity, the detectives were able to put together a kind of skeleton diary of Beth Short's seven days to eternity.

Wednesday, 8 January Beth leaves Mrs Elvera French's at San Diego in car with red-haired man. Supposed destination, Los Angeles.

Thursday, 9 January *Evening*. A girl who worked as a dancer in Hollywood night spots saw Beth sitting alone in the Gay Way bar on South Main Street. Either later that same evening, or on the following evening, she could not be sure which, another girl who knew Beth saw her sitting in the lobby of the Chancellor Apartments embracing a young man 'dressed like a gas station attendant.'

Friday, 10 January *Around 9 or 10pm*. The head bartender of the 4-Star Grill, Hollywood Boulevard saw Beth with two girls of – as he put it – 'dubious reputation'. He testified:

When she came in that last time she looked seedy, as if she'd slept in her clothes for days. The black sheer dress was stained and otherwise soiled and crumpled. I'd seen her many times before and always she wore the best nylons. But this time she had no stockings on. Her hair was straggly and some lipstick had been smeared hit-and-miss on her lips. The powder on her face was caked. Another thing I noticed about her: she was cowed instead of being gay and excited, the way I'd seen her before.

Saturday, 11 January *Late afternoon.* Seen by Mr C. G. Williams, bartender at the Dugout, the cocktail lounge beneath the Hotel Cecil, 634 South Main Street. Mr Williams reported that she and an unidentified blonde girl were having an argument with a sailor who was brushed off by the pair. A Los Angeles cab driver also came forward and told of picking up a 'big blonde' and a girl he was certain was the Black Dahlia.

Sunday, 12 January *Morning.* The proprietor of a hotel at 300 East Washington Boulevard reported that a couple had registered at his hotel as man and wife. He had seen in a newspaper a picture of Beth and an unidentified man, reproduced from a snapshot which had been found by the police in her baggage. 'I'll swear it was Elizabeth Short, and I'm almost sure it was that man in the photograph with her,' said the hotel-keeper's wife, and her husband nodded in agreement. 'They went to their room and we didn't see the girl again. The man was absent for a few days and then returned saying he expected his wife to join him. I think it was Wednesday (15 January). I said to him, "We thought you might be dead." Then he got very excited and left.'

Evening. Beth seen again alone in the Gay Way bar by the girl dancer who had seen her there previously on 9 January. She was also seen by bartender Robert La Gore in a café at 6818 Hollywood Boulevard. She was with two blonde girls, one of whom was a fairly regular patron.

Monday, 13 January The cab driver who had picked up the 'big blonde' and the girl he thought was the Black Dahlia, said that he met her again with this 'bossy blonde' at Hollywood Boulevard and Highland Avenue that Monday. 'They were in a 1937 Ford sedan. The blonde kept insisting they drove off, and finally they did. She seemed jealous because Beth talked to me.'

Tuesday, 14 January A Greyhound bus driver said that he saw the Black Dahlia board his bus at 1am at the Santa Barbara bus terminal. She alighted at the Los Angeles terminal at 4.15am. Jack Fleming, a grocery clerk, of 5833 South Hoover Street, told the police that at about 10am that Tuesday, he had seen a girl answering the Dahlia's description in the Daniel J. Regan Market. She had asked for change of a quarter, and made several calls from a 'phone booth. Later, Fleming had seen a man, who was making an obvious effort to conceal his face, studying the customers in the market. The man then hurried away. Fleming was not quite sure what he looked like, but, he said, it might have been a red-haired man.

Between 5 and 5.30pm the Black Dahlia was seen by two waitresses and a gas station attendant who knew her slightly in a car on Balboa Street, San Diego. They said that she was with a red-haired man, dressed in either a green suit or it could have been a marine uniform. Jadell Gray, a waitress at a Pacific Highway-Balboa Street drive-in restaurant, said that at 5pm that Tuesday evening she served a black-clad, black-haired woman accompanied by a red-haired six-footer. She said that she knew the woman customer as Beth, and that the couple drank beer and seemed very friendly, laughing and talking a lot. The man was about six feet tall, weighed about 12st 2lbs, had red hair and freckles, and was very vain. He kept preening himself before the mirror in the cigarette vending machine.

Another waitress, Mrs Adelene McSwain, recalled Beth's visit to the Pacific Highway-Balboa Street restaurant and was able to add a few details to the description of her red-headed companion. She said that he was 'very fair complexioned' and that his red hair was quite straight. He was slightly freckled and neatly dressed in a light suit with a wide stripe.

This red-haired six-footer began to assume importance. He kept on cropping up. Alex Constance, a Hollywood hairdresser who used to do Beth's hair, had seen her around with a husky red-haired marine. He said that she had confided to him that she was scared of the man and only went out with him because she was afraid to say no. He tallied with the red-haired man who had spirited Beth away from Mrs French's; the red-haired man Fleming thought he saw in the Los Angeles market; the red-haired man in the car at Balboa Street; Jadell Gray's red-haired preener and Adelene McSwain's recollected red-head. Finally, the detectives learned that, early in January 1947, Beth had been telling her friends that she had at last met 'the love of her life' – a man called 'Red'.

That did it. A red alert went out. The mysterious red-haired man had become Suspect No 1.

On 19 January, George Bennett of Los Angeles, riding a Greyhound bus from Bakersfield to Stockton, California, found himself sitting next to a tall, almost-good-looking, almost-red-haired fellow-traveller, name of Thorpe, Edward Glen Thorpe, thirty-two-year-old cook from Laramie, Wyoming. They got chatting and the talk came round, not unnaturally, to the current Number One Talking Point – the five days' old mystery murder of the Black Dahlia. Thorpe told Bennett that his wife had disappeared on 11 January, and that, before Elizabeth Short's body had been identified, the Los Angeles police had taken him along to view it, in case it turned out to be that of his missing wife. As the long distance journey wore on and conversation flagged, Thorpe dozed off. He began to talk in his sleep, and the thoroughly alarmed Bennett heard him muttering, 'I forgot to cut the scar off her leg.' The bus was passing through Fresno at the time and, so seriously did Bennett take the import of his enforced eavesdropping, that he got off and went straight to the Fresno police. Police Captain R. T. Wallace made instant contact with LAPD, and was told to nab Thorpe. This he did when the bus reached Merced. Thorpe appeared confused and gabbled out contradictory stories. It was observed that his jacket bore what could be construed as suspicious stains. He was arrested and headed back, in the fast police car which had overtaken the Greyhound, for the Fresno lock-up. But all hope of having caught the black gardener of Los Angeles faded when it was in due course revealed that Thorpe's conflicting tales were clumsy gallantries designed to shield a San Francisco damsel with whom he was enjoying an extra-marital dalliance, that his jittery manner was down to a pretty merciless hangover, and that the stains on his clothes were not blood. No, the 'Man from Laramie' was not the true Red.

Meanwhile, the search for that much-wanted gentleman had fanned out all over the country. The very next day after the shaken Mr Thorpe's adventure, the real Red was tracked down. He had been living all the time just five miles south of downtown Los Angeles, at 8010 Mountain View Avenue, South Gate. His name was Robert M. Manley. He was twenty-five, slender, neatly dressed, with carrot-hued hair. His first reaction was a vigorous denial that he had ever known Beth Short. An ex-Army Air Force band saxophonist, he had been

Robert 'Red' Manley and wife.
He was a suspect.

discharged in 1945, after spending some time under observation in an army psychiatric ward. Married for the past fifteen months to a twenty-two-year-old girl named Harriette, and father of a four-month-old son, he had got himself a job as a pipe clamp salesman. The marriage had not for some time being going too well, when, one December day in 1946, the clamp salesman had first clamped eyes on the Black Dahlia, who gave him the eye in the San Diego bus station. He told the police, 'It was just the thing I needed. It would be a good test to see if I was still in love with my wife.'

He admitted that he had collected Beth from Mrs French's on the evening of 8 January. They drove to a Pacific Beach motel. Their night together in a single room there was distinctly less than romantic. More frantic. Beth got sick with the food and drink and sat up all night in a chair, wrapped in blankets. He, disgusted, had turned his back on her and snored off in the bed. It was about eleven o'clock next morning when he awoke. Beth was sitting on the edge of the bed. They had a hurried breakfast and, at about 12.20pm, set out to drive on to Los Angeles, arriving there that afternoon. Beth checked her bags at the Greyhound bus terminal. He then took her to the Biltmore Hotel, where she said her sister from Berkeley would be waiting in the lobby, but she had not shown up by the time he had to leave her at 6.30pm. And that, he swore, was the last time he had seen Beth. She was then wearing a black collarless suit, fluffy white blouse, black suede shoes with high heels, nylon stockings, white gloves and a full length beige coat, and was carrying a large black plastic handbag with two handles. One other thing. 'I'd noticed she had scratches on both arms above the elbows and I asked her about them. She said she had a boy friend, an Italian with black hair, who lived in San Diego. She said she had been to his place on 6 January, and he was mean to her because he was intensely jealous.'

After going over his story millimetre by millimetre, and checking on his movements inch by inch, the police decided, rightly or wrongly, that Robert 'Red' Manley was not their man. True, he voluntarily submitted to a lie-detector test, but he proved to be so fatigued after hours of continuous questioning by relays of homicide investigators that he repeatedly fell asleep and the test was, according to police chemist Ray Pinker, inconclusive. His wife supported his statement that he had been visiting friends with her on the night of the murder.

Seven years later, in 1954, his wife had him committed to an insane asylum. – 'He hears noises, writes foolish notes and has a guilt complex,' she claimed. Although diagnosed as a paranoid schizophrenic, he was grilled by the police for the second time about the Dahlia's death, and was cleared once more after taking truth serum.

The hunt was on again. It felt very much like what it was . . . back to Square One. More than 400 suspects would be questioned and investigated before the detectives were done.

Beth's body was released – *circa* 21 January – by Coroner Ben Brown to Pierce Brothers Mortuary to be forwarded to the Grant Miller Mortuary, in Oakland, for funeral services. It arrived in Oakland on 23 January – for burial on Saturday, 25 January 1947.

Then – on 21 January – a funny thing happened. Jimmy Richardson, city editor of the *Los Angeles Examiner,* received a telephone call. He was to describe the voice on the other end of the line as 'soft and silky'. Smoothly, the voice proceeded to unwind a skein of minute details of the ante-mortem abominations perpetrated on the dead girl – details which only her true killer would know. 'I killed her,' the voice of syrup gloated. 'I'm going to turn myself in, but I want to watch the cops chase me some more.' Before ringing off, the voice told Richardson, 'You can expect some souvenirs of Beth Short in the mail.'

Three days later – 24 January – postal inspectors delivered a strange missive to the LA detectives; an unsealed envelope which had pasted on it, in printed letters snipped from newspapers and magazines, the painfully spelt-out message:

Los Angeles Examiner and Other Los Angeles papers. Here is Dahlia's Belongings. Letter to Follow.

The envelope which contained the genuine Black Dahlia belongings.

The envelope, measuring 8 × 3¹/₂in, received at the post office at 5 pm, contained a baggage claim check No RO6-97-79, dated Jan 9, from the Greyhound Bus Depot in Los Angeles. Elizabeth Short's Suffolk County, Massachusetts, birth certificate. A social security card made out to Elizabeth Short, No 022-18-4750. An identification card. A membership card of the Hollywood Wolves Association. Six snapshots. A newspaper clipping announcing the death in India of Major Matthew Gordon. The clipping quoted a letter from Matt Gordon to his family in which he stated that he might bring home a bride from Medford, Mass. The name of the bride or bride-to-be was scratched out. Friends of Beth's subsequently reported that she frequently showed the clipping to them, telling them that the name was scratched out because it was incorrect. An address book, bound in brown leather and with 1937 and the name Mark M. Hansen embossed in gold on the cover. Her comb and make-up. The envelope's contents gave off an odour of gasoline and police theorised that the sender might have intended to burn them and changed his mind. Both envelope and contents were rich in fingerprints, and the police thought they were in for their second lucky break, compensation for their disappointment over the red-haired man. The prints were telephotoed pronto to the FBI, but luck had run out; too many over-eager post office personnel had handled the package to make any meaningful identifications possible.

The address book proved a wet squib, too. It turned out to have been 'acquired' by the Dahlia from Mark Hansen. He said: 'She had lots of dates. There was a language teacher that I know of, and other persons, mostly hoodlums who I wouldn't even let in my house.' He said that the address book was his, and that a memorandum and a calendar were also missing from his desk. One page had been torn from the address book. Perhaps it had borne the sender's name and address. Following up the remaining seventy-odd names, and some of the business cards slipped in between the book's pages, the detectives discovered that Beth had in fact contacted a number of them. She had used Mark Hansen's appropriated list as a sort of 'mine' from which to quarry dates.

Saturday 25 January 1947. A day of swirling fog at Mountain View Cemetery, Oakland, California – the Black Dahlia's funeral.

The day after the delivery of the Dahlia envelope – 25 January – with fog swirling around Mountain View Cemetery, Oakland, Elizabeth Ann Short was laid in her hillside grave. Only her relatives were present. Eight floral pieces were placed upon the casket. The Reverend G. Raymond White, pastor of the First United Presbyterian Church, conducting the service, quoted from Deuteronomy, 'As thy days, so shall thy strength be.'

. . .The lonely end.

Another couple of days and, on 27 January, a Los Angeles newspaper received a printed snip-and-paste note. The promised letter. It read:

> Here it is. Turning in Wed. Jan 29, 10am. Had my fun at police. Black Dahlia Avenger.

Tuesday night, 28 January, the telephone rang at police headquarters. A man's voice. 'I killed her. I met Beth two weeks ago at Fourth and Hill. That's where I first saw her in '41.' He wanted to give himself up because he 'couldn't stand it any longer.' Was it *him*? The snippety-clip letter-man? Breaths were held. Was the case about to break wide open? The man's voice was droning on. Telling them to come and pick him up. He was downtown. Where else but at the corner of 4th and Hill Streets. Sure, they'd recognise him at once from the description he'd just given them over the 'phone. Yeh, yeh, he'd wait. He gave his name as Daniel S. Voorhees. He was thirty-three, an unemployed waiter. He had a wife and nine-year-old daughter in Phoenix, Arizona. The wiry, bushy-haired transient was booked into County Jail on suspicion of murder. He signed a one-line confession, 'I did kill Beth Short.' But when he was questioned there were so many discrepancies in his story that it became obvious that what they were listening to was the fantasy of a mentally sick man. Clearly this was not the snippety-clip man. Just a nut in his own right.

29 January. The promised day. The police waited. The turning-in time came – and went. Then, at 1pm an envelope bearing his typewritten name and address was handed to Captain Donahoe. Inside was one of those now familiar clipped print messages. It read, with simple, hope-crushing finality:

> 'Have changed my mind. You would not give me a square deal. Dahlia killing was justified.'

And that was, always supposing the note to be genuine, the closest the police ever got to the slayer of the Dahlia.

The unending stream of dubious tip-offs and misleading information from ordinary, and some extraordinary, members of the great American public kept on pouring in to bedevil police work and present a positive obstacle course to progress. Some of it was well-intentioned – like the Los Angeles waitress who telephoned in to tell how she had heard two sinister-looking men discussing the Dahlia murder in scary detail at her lunch counter. They had guns under their coats and one of them 'had an apprehensive look and ordered only a half-cup of coffee.' She gave the police a good description, so good that the 'killers' were promptly recognised as a couple of squad detectives who had nipped in for a brief off-duty coffee.

Some of it represented a desire for personal revenge, such as the blonde dancer who rang in, and, with an air of great secrecy, told them in a whispery voice, 'I'm meeting a man at First and Temple at nine o'clock, and I have reason to believe he's the Black Dahlia killer.' Detectives were waiting to arrest the pair and take them down to headquarters for questioning. The man proved to be a totally innocent, harmless business executive. He had met his blonde accuser during the war. They had been members of the same 'share-the-ride' group – a patriotic wartime scheme to save petrol, in which car owners gave regular lifts to people along their work route. Apparently they had, just once, shared a bed. She had 'dogged, threatened and slightly blackmailed' him ever since – and this was just her way of putting a bit more pressure on the already well punished sinner.

Much of it was motivated by exhibitionism and a desire for publicity. One man confessed because his wife was missing and he thought that she would contact him if she saw his picture in the newspapers. An old woman rang in to advise: 'Bury the girl with an egg in her right hand. The killer will then be found within a week. That's the way it works in Alabama.'

Clues may have been missing, but there was no shortage of crackpots and confessions.

On 24 January, a man walked into the station house at Inglewood, seven miles south-west of downtown Los Angeles, to announce blandly to the astonishment of the assembled officers: 'I'm afraid I might kill a woman.' Asked what he would do with the body, he knowingly replied, 'Cut it up and throw it into an empty lot.'

John N. Andry, a thirty-three-year-old chief pharmacist's mate in the US Navy, was hauled in after bragging loud and long several dozen times too often in a Long Beach bar of his great skill in carving up cadavers. Sitting coolly back in his chair at LAPD HQ, he insisted to the detectives that it was indeed he who had killed the Black Dahlia. Less calm and glib when subjected to high power interrogation, he was eventually forced to admit that he had not actually done the murder, adding a codicil of sulky defiance. 'Well, I'm *capable* of doing it.' Then, the final crumple up: 'I was just kidding.'

It was by no means a men only business, this confessing lark.

A six-foot-one, twelve-stone, twenty-one-year-old beefy brunette, Caral Marshall, hailing from Tulare, south central California, was overheard to say in a café-bar in Barstow, in the South Californian Mojave Desert, 'I know who killed Beth Short, but I'm afraid to tell.' Challenged, she had second thoughts. 'Sure I'll talk – if the reward is big enough.' At the police station she was questioned by a couple of detectives rushed up from Los Angeles. She alleged that two of her men friends had been involved in the murder. They had since walked out on her, so, to equal the score, she had decided to sing, but loud. The tale she told was palpably phony. All she knew was what she had read in the papers. But the lawmen's trip was not a total waste of time. The blonde's two recalcitrant *beaux* were hiked back to LA and booked as suspects in connection with an outstanding car theft.

On 28 January another two women tried this time to put themselves in the frame. Emily E. Williams alias Emily E. Carter, of San Diego, a tall, dark-haired, twenty-four-year-old waitress and former WAC, walked into the precinct yelling, 'Elizabeth Short stole my man, so I killed her and cut her up!' The San Diego police were not impressed. They soon had her down as a mental case. It did not take long for her to break under questioning and admit that she had made the whole thing up. That night a woman in Fullerton, 22 miles south-east of Los Angeles, telephoned in to her local police to tell them, 'I'm the killer of the Black Dahlia.' And just to fill in the interstices of 28 January, a note arrived at LA police HQ saying: 'I will give up in Dahlia killing if I get ten years. Don't try to find me.' He didn't. They didn't.

Confession hysteria had set in early. Black-bearded psychiatrist for the Los Angeles police, Dr J. Paul de River, had said it would. The case, he said, would 'spark a bevy of guilt-laden souls.' The confessions, he explained, did not arise just out of a lust for publicity. They could spring from masochism, exhibitionism, or a guilt complex engendered by some forgotten incident of childhood. He said, too, that the type of mind that conceived the Dahlia murder 'will one day have to boast about it,' and predicted, 'The confessors will keep coming.' He was right. There were more false confessions in the Dahlia case than in any other case in American criminal history. Fortunately, though, it was easier than usual to spot the bogus self-accusers. The savage way in which the victim had been treated provided a sort of key to the mystery. A key which only the true killer would recognize – because the full details of the injuries were unprintable and were known only to their perpetrator and the police. That meant that, by the asking of certain carefully planned questions, the detectives could rapidly establish whether or not the self-proclaimed murderer knew anything more than what had already been published, and, consequently, whether or not he or she was worthy of powder and shot. Although in all around forty men and women have to date confessed to committing the murder – some of them not even born when it took place – no confession so far has contained the vital 'key' information.

On 8 February 1947, Captain William Florence of the US Army Criminal Investigation Department announced the arrest of twenty-nine-year-old Corporal Joseph Dumais. The

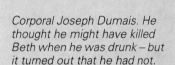

Corporal Joseph Dumais. He thought he might have killed Beth when he was drunk – but it turned out that he had not.

curly-haired, moustached, combat veteran, of Fort Dix, New Jersey, had just returned from 42 days' leave when he had a quarrel over money with a fellow-soldier whom he had told that he had known Beth Short and been out with her on 9 January. Not without malice, the soldier had hared straight off to report this to the military police. Bloodstains were found on Dumais' clothing and in his locker was a batch of newspaper cuttings about the murder. 'It is possible that I could have committed the murder,' said Dumais. 'When I get drunk I get rough with women.' And he certainly knew many details of the killing. When the detectives came to check his 'facts' against the *key* facts known to them, however, his whole house-of-cards story collapsed. They sent him to a psychiatrist.

Inevitably, there was some exploitation of the Dahlia, too. Local petty criminals and drunks soon cottoned on to ways of cashing-in. The criminals, muggers, small-time stick-up men and assorted others of like kind and calibre, quickly appreciated that to secure the fullest possible co-operation from their women victims, no half measures, as it were, they only had to whisper, 'Shut up, or you'll get what the Black Dahlia got.' The drunks would spin a plausible yarn suggesting that they knew something about the murder, and thus avoid for a precious day or two the dreaded discomfort of their regular cure in the city's 'drunk tank'. Far gone tosspots were even prepared to plead guilty to the slaughter on Norton for the price of a pot to toss.

Hope flared briefly in December 1947, when the Homicide men were informed that nineteen-year-old Mrs Helen Miller had complained that a man had cut his initials into her hip with a sharp knife. They remembered the 'B. D.' carved in Elizabeth Short's thigh. The man with the carving knife was Donald Graeff, twenty-eight and patently a raging psychopath. He had offered the homeless, penniless woman shelter, then held her prisoner in his hotel room for a week. Two days before she managed to escape, he had suddenly thrown her on to a bed and cut into her 'D. G.' in blood-oozing letters three inches high. His lame explanation was the sober declaration: 'When I get drunk I don't know what I'm doing.' The heat was turned up on him, but all questions involving the demise of the Black Dahlia found him adamantly ignorant. And that was the way he stayed throughout hours and hours of round-the-clock interrogation. His inquisitors failed, though not for want of trying, to uncover a single direct link between this unsavoury creature and Beth Short's death. They had no alternative but to accept his vehement denials.

Two years later, there was a flurry of police activity when a Florida bellhop came forward with a circumstantial account of how another bell-boy had killed Beth Short in a motel at 29th and Flower Streets. Picked up in Salinas, Western California, the second youth hotly denied the charge. Both men were closely questioned, but no evidence was forthcoming to back the original accusation, and they were turned free.

In September 1950, a very minor underworld figure, Max Handler alias Mack Chandler, gave himself up repeating the by now familiar *confessio necis*, 'I killed the Black Dahlia'. This time, though, the detectives thought there was a good chance they really had solved the case, because in the Dahlia's address book there had been inserted a business card bearing the name of a firm for which Handler had once worked. Moreover, he named two places to which he claimed to have accompanied the girl – and she was known actually to have been at both of them. A lie-detector test showed that he was just another poor deluded soul. That same month, thirty-four-year-old Mrs Christine Reynolds told police officers in Oakland, California, that she had committed the murder when Elizabeth Short left her for another woman. Because of this unpleasant novel twist, her confession took an hour or two longer than most to disprove.

Then, on 5 January 1956, nine years since Elizabeth Short was laid in her grave, forty-four-year-old New York dishwasher, aristocratically cognomened Ralph von Hiltz, came out of the kitchen, not, for once, to claim Dahlia blood upon his hands, but to assert accomplicity. He saw a friend kill Elizabeth Short. Afterwards he helped his friend reduce her to manageable proportions. What are friends for? Most of Mr Von Hiltz's facts were at critical variance with those in the official dossier. He seemed unable, or unwilling, to disclose his homicidal friend's identity, which remains a mystery. He was released as a tongue-wagging crank.

The Black Dahlia in her heyday – an eminently accessible flower for the picking.

The sorting and sorting-out of the cranks, crackpots and confessors fell mainly upon two LAPD stalwarts, Sergeants Harry Leslie Hansen and Finis Brown. Oddly enough, it was to be a man called 'Red', for that was Sergeant Harry Hansen's nickname – a name of very special significance for Beth Short, as indeed was also the name Hansen – who lived longest with the Dahlia after her death. For nearly a quarter of a century, until his retirement in 1971, he had charge of the cabinets, cram-full of swollen, red-inked files, their drawers still, symbolically, unlocked, which stood like so many metal tombstones to her memory. Red Hansen had his own strong views on the case which occupied so large a part of his professional life. He said:

I know for certain I never met the killer face to face. I know he didn't manage to slip through with the other suspects. We considered the possibility of his coming right in, making a confession, then cleverly side-stepping the key question. We watched for that. We'd taken measures to expose him in that event. We never underestimated this guy. You'd never believe the amount of checking we did on this case. We followed everything as far as it would go, then we'd turn right around and walk through it all again. We had some good leads, but they never panned out. Oh sure, I wonder about who the killer was, but I don't lose any sleep over it.

*Craig Rice. Novelist and crime
fiction writer. She had her
theories – especially about the
Dahlia case.*

In 1979, Hansen is on record saying, 'I think the killer's dead now.'

Since Red Hansen's departure the hundreds of Dahlia files have been handed on, like a jurisprudential legacy, to a succession of some half-dozen homicide detectives, each as he retires passing them solemnly down to his appointed legatee.

Up till comparatively recently the odd greying-headed would-be confessor was still swinging through the precinct doors to lay a claim to the prestigious killing. Never was such a prolonged spate of false confessions, people acting out their fantasies. Latest custodian of the Dahlia archive, Detective John St John says, 'Every time a documentary on the Black Dahlia is shown on TV here, we get letters and 'phone calls from cranks. It's some years now since anybody came in and confessed, but we still follow up any lead no matter how trivial it seems. Unless we solve it, the case will never be closed.' And he recalls the words of his predecessor, Sergeant Hansen. 'Unsolved murders have a way of clearing themselves up if you wait long enough and keep your files up to date.'

The police came up with three 'official' theories as to the motive for the crime: the girl was killed by either a pick-up sadist, a vengeful lesbian who had been repulsed, or by someone from whom she had attempted to extort money, and who then mutilated her to make it look like a sex crime.

Craig Rice, the well known American novelist and mystery writer, had a theory as to the sort of person the killer was likely to be. She believed that very considerable skill and anatomical knowledge was displayed in the bisecting of Beth – therefore, she deduces, either a doctor, trained nurse, undertaker, or undertaker's assistant as culprit. She favours one or other of the latter two, as a mortician's parlour would be a fine and private place in which to bisect. She pointed out that the purpose of the bisecting could well have been to convert the body into transportably convenient weights and measures – therefore, she deduces, either a woman, an undersized man or a cripple. It was not, she felt sure, a crime of sudden passion, perpetrated by a person of brief acquaintance. Rather was it the work of someone with a long-carried grudge, who pursued the unfortunate girl until she was almost insane with fear, before taking his or her well-savoured revenge.

Captain Donahoe had formed his own theory within two weeks of taking charge of the investigation. He thought that the killer was more likely to be a woman, for a number of reasons – primarily, the nature of the injuries and the peculiarly vicious spite with which they had been inflicted. ('The female of the species is more deadly . . .') Many of the wounds, he noted, were similar to those found in other mutilation murders in which jealous women had hacked the object of their spleen to death. Moreover, various bits of circumstantial evidence seemed to support his belief. There was the statement of the 4-Star Grill barman and the statement of the Los Angeles cab driver. They set one thinking about possible lesbian complications. And, tracking back, how about WAC Sergeant Mary Stradder, with whom Beth had lived after leaving Camp Cooke? OK, so that could mean something – or nothing. What was one to make of what Paul Simone, the painting contractor who had worked in the North Cherokee Avenue apartment house where Beth had lodged for a while with 'les girls', had told the detectives? He said that on 11 January 1947, he heard two women arguing bitterly at the rear of the building. He though they were going to fight, and walked towards them. When the one who was doing most of the swearing saw him, she said, 'Oh, nuts to you!' and stalked off. The other girl, who, said Simone, looked like Beth Short, asked him if there was a back way out. He told her no, walked with her to the front door, and watched her drive off in a cab. After that, as he was passing the door of the room which Beth had occupied, he heard a woman say, 'I'm tired of all this. It's getting too hot.' And the voice of another woman said, 'Didn't you know that Beth (or it might have been 'Bev', he didn't quite catch it) and Shirley were buddies?' That tied in, didn't it, with Mrs French's account of how, on the last night which the Dahlia spent at her Bayview Terrace home – Tuesday, 7 January – two men and woman had knocked at the door, and when Beth failed to answer, ran back to their car and drove away. Mrs French had learned of these nocturnal visitors from a neighbour. She herself was in bed and asleep at the time. 'I asked Betty about them. She admitted hearing them knock and said she peeped through the window. She was evasive when I asked other questions, so I gave up. She told me that a woman chased her and a friend of hers on Hollywood Boulevard, just before I met her early in December. Betty seemed constantly in fear of something. Whenever anyone came to the door she would act frightened.'

By now, other police officers were also beginning to wonder if Beth's avidity for men might not have been matched by an equivalent voracity for women. If that were so, it could well transpire that she was the casualty of one of those vicious bisexual triangles.

Was it a man? Was it a woman? Either way, Captain Donahoe had worked out a scenario which he was firmly convinced was a mighty close approximation to the truth. He reckoned that the girl had been held captive practically all that last week of her life, those missing 136 hours, in an isolated shack somewhere in the Los Angeles area. Her eyebrows and her naturally jet-black hair had been hennaed by the murderer in the hope of deflecting identification.

Elizabeth Short was really a trinity of people, a three-faces-of-Eve character – Betty the small-town daughter, Beth the hustler and down-and-out Hollywood drifter, and Dahlia the seductive, desirable *femme fatale* – all incarnated together at one and the same brief period of time in the short unhappy life of Elizabeth Short.

Hollywood and Vine.

In early January 1947, Beth told friends that she intended to reform, to find a regular job and a regular man – one who would not consider her just a piece of sexual merchandise. She wanted, she said, to settle down; perhaps have children. The Black Dahlia would be no more, she promised, adding that she had met 'the love of her life' – there goes that phrase again – a man she called only 'Red'.

It did not work out like that at all. Predictably. The way it did surely entitles her to elevation to poster place of Keith 'Hollywood Babylon' Anger's ultimate pin-up girl, for not only was she suitably gloriously depraved in life, but herself became, in death, another's monumental depravity. With parodist's apologies to Hood, one might characterise her: one more Hollywood hopeful, weary of breath, rashly importunate, tortured to death.

Like one of those exotic night-blooming flowers whose petals close tight against the daylight, the Black Dahlia has, in her withering and dying, folded in firm upon her secret self against those who have tried to bring to bear upon her the bright daylight of disclosure. She has passed out of life into post-mortem legend. She has become one with Pater's *La Gioconda* . . . 'She is older than the rocks among which she sits; like the vampire, she has been dead many times, and learned the secrets of the grave; and has been a diver in deep seas, and keeps their fallen day about her; and trafficked for strange webs . . .' In her end she has achieved a kind of black stardom; known, coast to coast, to millions of her fellow-Americans, and beyond the coasts to international fame. The celebrity which she so eagerly sought, but which shunned her in life, has dowered her in death, settled like a fur-black moth upon her marble face, wrapped and embraced her like a shroud. But it was immortality hard-won by the monstrous manner of her dying. Long after many of the stars she so envied, admired, and hankered to emulate, have ceased to twinkle, become coiled heaps of unremembered celluloid shadows, little Betty Short, from Medford, Mass, *scilicet* the Black Dahlia, will be remembered and celebrated the world over for the unique rôle which, at curtain fall, she was bidden to play – dark heroine of a truly classic case in the criminological repertory of the United States.

The short life . . .

The Black-Robed Killer Priest

Being the sad and monitory tale of a young cleric who so far forgot his sacerdotal vows as to cast another's bread of life on the waters of Lethe in a heptad of neatly parcelled fragments.

The Reverend Father Hans Schmidt's practice of the precept of sacrifice was Abrahamic rather than strictly twentieth-century theological, and his personal – very – sacrificial bread was cast, literally, upon the waters of the Hudson River.

It was a girl, herself only a small handful of years younger than the *bon père's* sacrificial lamb, who, on the morning of 6 September 1913, made what was lip-smackingly described by the more ochreous broadsheets as 'The Ghastly Catch'. Eighteen-year-old Mary Bann and her eleven-year-old brother, who lived in a tar-paper house by the riverside at Woodcliff, New Jersey, spotted an odd-shaped bundle bobbing in the water. Mary prodded it with a pole, manoeuvred it ashore on to a landing dock, and then, with the flighty mercurialism of adolescence, abandoned her interest in it. Later, two boys, brimful of the curiosity of youth, came upon the surprise package, fumbled open the brown paper and twine. The surprise was not a pleasant one. Inside was the fleshy mass of a woman's torso – severed at the waist, head and arms sawn off.

The New York coroner, Israel Feinberg, was able to state that the remains were those of a woman between twenty and thirty years of age, who, in his opinion, had been dead less than a week. The torso had been wrapped in a pillowcase, to which there fortunately remained attached the manufacturer's tag.

The following morning – Sunday, 7 September – a second parcel floated ashore three miles downriver, at Weehawken, north-eastern New Jersey. In it, also wrapped in a pillowcase, which this time bore the embroidered initial 'A', was the lower part of the torso. Parcel No 2 provided two further clues: included along with the heavy tar-paper wrapping was a newspaper dated 31 August 1913, and a piece of greenish-grey schist, peculiar to the original bedrock across the river in Manhattan, had been used to weight the package.

Finally, several days later, a third *trouvaille*, a neatly parcelled leg, was brought forth from the water at Keansburg, New Jersey.

Lower Manhatten *by Louis Lozowick.*

Father Hans Schmidt in lay garb.

Meanwhile, the police had not been idle. To Police Detective Inspector Joseph A. Faurot, of the New York City Detective Bureau, had been allocated the rather more difficult job of putting a name to the torso. Even as he sat in his office debating with his assistants a strategy to cope with what the press had already labelled 'The Mystery of the Dismembered Woman', another of her 'members', to wit one leg, the contents of Parcel No 3, was being fetched in from Keansburg by a police officer.

Scarcely overwhelmed with alternatives, Detective Faurot decided to follow the clue of the garish pillow-bere. Four fragments were snipped off the oddly-patterned, although patently extra-fine quality, ticking pillowcase, which had been manufactured, they knew, in New Jersey, and, each carrying his sample, the Inspector and his three sharpest detectives – James O'Neal, Frank Cassassa, and Richard McKenna – set off for those areas of the city in which were located the lofts and sample-rooms of the manufacturers' agents who dealt in bedding and upholstery. The hunt dragged unproductively on, day succeeding weary, foot-tramping day. Then, just as the detectives were coming up to what was practically their last listed call, their luck dramatically changed. Yes, said this ultimate manufacturer's agent, yes, he certainly recognised the sample of ticking. The expensive pillows from which it came had been made up by way of an experiment. It had been a

costly failure. The pillows had not sold well. Too gaudy, he explained. They had been a drag on the market, and he had eventually sold them off at bargain prices to a number of small neighbourhood shops. Incredibly, he still had a record of the destination of every pillow that had left his warehouse.

Armed with copies of the delivery slips, Inspector Faurot reasoned that, since the pillow-bere shroud had been floating down the Hudson, the shops most likely to produce a lead might well be situated in that district of upper Manhattan in the vicinity of the river. He drew the dividend upon his hunch at No 2762 Eighth Avenue, up near 137th Street, the store of George Sachs, dealer in household furnishings. Mr Sachs had sold two of the pillows. He remembered the purchasers – a young couple recently married. The young woman had been quite attractive, but it was the man whom he especially remembered. Peculiar customer. Slender. Pale of face. Brilliant brown eyes. Mr Sachs discovered the date of the purchase – a sales slip dated 25 August, for a chair, bed springs and enamelled bed, plus two pillows and pillow-slips.

The delivery firm used by Sachs had duly transported these articles to a four-room rented apartment, the third floor back, at No 68 Bradhurst Avenue. The police turned up what struck them as a useful piece of corroborative evidence when they located a shop near Sachs' which had sold the tar-paper wrapping, and another which had supplied two sheets of medicated manila paper. From the superintendent at No 68 Bradhurst Avenue, the police learned that the flat had been rented, on that same 25 August, to a Mr H. Schmidt. He had said that he wanted it for a young relative of his who was getting married.

For the next few days, a day and night watch was kept on the apartment, but no one was seen to enter or leave it. Then, on Saturday morning, 13 September, Faurot and his men decided to go into the third-floor back. They knew at once that they had found in that deserted love-nest the scene of the dismemberment. Bloodstained floors, a gory bathtub, a blood-encrusted knife, all unarguably bespoke the bloodiest butchery. There, too, a sort of stamp or seal of confirmation, was one of Sachs' two gaudy pillows. The only furniture in the place was Sachs' chair and bed and a trunk. Behind the blind flap of a woman's handbag, found by one of the detectives in that trunk, were some letters, bearing Hungarian stamps and postmarks, addressed to Miss Anna Aumüller, c/o The Rectory, St Boniface's Church, Second Avenue, New York, a marriage licence issued in New York and dated 26 February 1913, and a marriage certificate stating that Anna Aumüller had been married six months before to one Hans Schmidt by the Reverend Hans Schmidt.

That afternoon, Faurot paid a call at St Boniface's Church, at 47th Street and Second Avenue. He met there the rector, the Reverend Father John S. Braun, the priest's sister, who acted

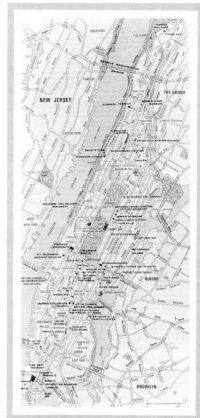

The Island of Manhattten including the Audubon Terrace area.

Anna Aumüller – a sacrifice.

as his housekeeper, and a maid. Faurot asked about Anna Aumüller. He was told that she had been about twenty years of age and had worked at the rectory as a maid since the time of her arrival from Oedenberg, Hungary, in the week before Christmas 1910, until the summer of 1911. She had then left of her own accord. She had, however, returned on Thanksgiving Day – 28 November – 1912, and asked for her old job back. She had remained until 30 August 1913, when she had told Father Braun that she was in fact married, and that she was going to live with her husband in Ohio.

According to another account, Anna had been discharged by Father Braun on 31 August 1913, because he 'was not satisfied with her way of life', thus referring obliquely to a suspected pregnancy which had not been confirmed by the autopsy. In any event, what is indisputable is that Father Braun informed Inspector Faurot that neither he nor his sister had the faintest inkling as to where Anna Aumüller was now.

What Faurot needed next was positive identification of the bipartite torso. Surely the maid at St Boniface's who had after all shared a room with Anna could recall something that would help. She wrinkled her brow. Well . . . yes . . . Anna had had quite exceptionally smooth, creamy coloured skin. Very beautiful. Faurot nodded. That satin-textured, creamy-white skin had been remarked by the pathologists. But was there not something else? More brow wrinkling. Then: 'Yes. Down under one shoulder there was one small scar, a little pink patch you'd hardly notice. Anna told me once she'd had it since she was a little girl.' That was it.

And that was when Father Braun told Faurot of the young man who had come from Trenton, New Jersey, to live in the rectory. He had arrived at about the same time as Anna. Looking back, he did seem to have been more than usually attentive to the girl, but Father Braun could not bring himself to think that it was anything other than a perfectly innocent relationship. The young man in question had left in November 1912. What was the name of this young man? Hans Schmidt – Father Hans Schmidt. He was a Roman Catholic priest. He had been Father Braun's assistant. Where was he now? In Harlem – at St Joseph's Church, West 125th Street and Morningside Avenue. It was now 11.30pm, and the detectives sped over to St Joseph's.

The door was opened to them by a Father Quinn. He, disappearing back into the dim-lit recess of the hall, went off to summon Father Schmidt. A thin, pale-faced, brilliant-eyed young priest entered the room into which the police had been ushered.

'Are you the Reverend Father Hans Schmidt?'

'I am he.'

'I am Inspector Faurot of the Detective Bureau. These men are my assistants.'

Father Schmidt was shown a photograph of Anna Aumüller.

He dropped his head upon the table. His shoulders shook. He began to weep.

'Did you kill her?' No messing about. Sharp as a whip. Just like that.

'Yes. I loved her.'

They took him over to the Bradhurst Avenue apartment. It was now the early hours of Sunday morning. Back on the killing ground, Schmidt made a series of horrifying admissions. He described how the girl had been killed and dismembered. He had, he said, received a message: 'Anna will be a sacrifice of blood and atonement.' Acting on this instruction from on high, he had cut her throat while she slept, then taken her body to pieces in the bath. He admitted to drinking her blood and having intercourse with her after he had killed her. He had then wrapped the parts of her up in several bundles and, in the course of a number of trips aboard the 125th Street crosstown car to the Fort Lee Ferry, which he rode to mid-stream, dropping his grisly parcels off the end of the boat, disposed of her.

After hearing all this, they hurried the thirty-two-year-old priest away to a cell in the Tombs – but not before he had tried to cut his throat with a razor-blade, and then asked shame-facedly to be allowed to change from his clerical garb into a suit of layman's clothing. Seen at the Tombs by the Roman Catholic chaplain, the Reverend Father L. J. Evers, he made a strange confession. 'I was directed to kill Anna Aumüller by Saint Elizabeth. Saint Elizabeth is my patron, and she directed me to make the sacrifice of the girl I loved; the sacrifice to be consummated in blood as was the sacrifice of Abraham.'

Some evidence was adduced at Schmidt's trial, in December 1913, which seemed to indicate that he was grossly abnormal to the possible extent of insanity. His sister testified as to his visions at the age of ten and subsequent disposition for cutting off the heads of geese, with an unnatural interest in the blood. His father also spoke of his son's excessive interest in blood and gloating visits to slaughterhouses. On the other hand, the prosecution presented evidence that Schmidt had attempted to insure Anna Aumüller's life. An insurance company doc-tor said that he had examined a girl represented to him as Schmidt's wife. And the Postal Life Insurance Company had refused the application for a 5,000 dollar policy. They gave no reason. There were other strange and disquieting revelations to come. Rental receipts found among Schmidt's papers at the rectory, led the police to another flat at 516 West 134th Street. And there they found a printing plant for the produc-tion of counterfeit ten and twenty dollar bills. Schmidt had purchased the equipment and rented the premises under the name of George Miller, and his associate in this venture was a Dr Earnest (sic) Arthur Muret, practising, without benefit of licence, as a dentist. Muret had written a letter to Schmidt in which he referred to Anna's death as being due to an illegal operation, not murder, and claimed that the body had been cut

The Tombs, New York. From presbytery to prison house: Father Schmidt's last pilgrimage.

up to conceal the real cause of death. A cell-mate of Schmidt's in the Tombs, Philip Musica, told one of Schmidt's attorneys, Alphonse Koelble, that Schmidt had admitted to him and others that Anna had died during an abortion, and that it was to protect his friends from prosecution that he had admitted killing the girl. Schmidt said that the apartment at Bradhurst Avenue had been hurriedly rented after Anna had been ordered out of St Boniface's Rectory. He had bought her some furniture, but the bed collapsed on Anna, hurting her back and possibly bringing on complications in her pregnancy. She was in pain, and it was she who suggested the abortion. Muret agreed to do it. With a woman named Bertha Zeck acting as his assistant, Muret duly carried out the abortion, removing the foetus and disposing of it down the lavatory. But Anna had a haemorrhage which Muret was unable to stem, became unconscious, and finally died. The hazard of calling an undertaker was too great, as he would assuredly inform the coroner. It was agreed that they would try to dispose of the body themselves. Schmidt obtained the necessary tools – a saw and a knife – and Muret performed the dismemberment. The parts were bundled up, and Schmidt, Muret and Zeck carried them to the ferry and cast them into the river.

This latest story of Schmidt's was not believed, but Father Schmidt, a teleologist to the end, went to his death rigidly averring that he was going to the chair for lying and not for murder.

The Electric Chair. The grim terminal of Father Schmidt's ultima culpa.

The Three Black Crows

Concerning the practice in an East Orange bathroom of a sinister kind of aquatic horticulture, wherein, attended by three mad sisters, an urban Ophelia floated like a strange water-flower.

There hangs in the Tate Gallery a famous painting by John Everett Millais, which depicts Hamlet's mad love, Ophelia, drowning in a glassy brook, with wild flower petals trapped in the tresses of her hair. If Dr Herbert Simmons were familiar with that painting – and there is no reason to suppose that he was a man devoid of aesthetic sensibilities – he would, perchance, have recalled it when he first looked down on the body of Oceana Snead.

The beautiful girl, prophetically named, had reverted to her element, to cold, cold water. Her drained-white, naked corpse was bent in a bathtub, with her head submerged underneath the tap. Long, auburn hair, beaded with bubbles, silver as mercury, streamed on the surface like seaweed. A flannel was loosely cupped in her left hand. She was extremely thin, wasted, even.

The doctor examined the lovely, blank face – perfect, classical features, and large, clouded brown eyes. *Cover her face; mine eyes dazzle: she died young* – he might have thought, now, in the words of Webster. The pity of it moved him, and he turned away to inspect the stark, comfortless surroundings, into which Death had entered before him. It was not much of a bathroom, with no form of heating, although it was late November. No furniture, no towel, only a heap of clothes on the floor, with a note carefully pinned to them. Written in ink in a bold, flowing hand, it read:

> Last year my little daughter died; other near and dear ones have gone before. I want to join them in Heaven. I have been prostrated with illness for a long time. When you read this I will have committed suicide. Do not grieve for me. Rejoice with me that Death brings me a blessed relief from pain and suffering greater than I can bear.
> O.W.M. SNEAD

A model suicide note. Clear, comprehensive, and unambiguous. But Dr Simmons sensed, in every atom of the scene

Oceana Snead, victim of the Crows.

Miss Virginia Wardlaw.

set before him, a discordance, an artificiality, a lack of connectedness.

It had been a strange call-out on that afternoon of Monday, 29 November 1909. He had little information; Sergeant Timothy Caniff, stationed at East Orange police station, New Jersey, an un-smart residential suburb of New York, had asked him to visit 89 North Fourteenth Street, where a woman had reported an 'accident'.

The doctor had hurried on foot through cheerless streets to a gloomy, wooden frame-house, which, with its attic, shutters and porch, breathed out a menace of its own. The door opened sharply, and an apparition loomed in the murky cave of the hallway: a towering woman, draped and caped entirely in black, with thick veils shrouding her face. The veils stirred, and were sucked in and out as she spoke. 'Please come in,' she said, in an unexpectedly soft, cultured, Southern voice. 'I am Virginia Wardlaw.' For the moment, she evidently considered that was all the explanation that was required, and, in lofty silence, she led the doctor up an echoing, uncarpeted flight of stairs, and along a first floor landing, past the doors of empty rooms. The house appeared to be bereft of furniture and was no warmer than the morgue which was waiting to receive Oceana Snead.

Fiercely, now, Dr Simmons addressed himself to the watching black pillar of a woman – 'When did you find the body?'

'Only a short time before I called the police station,' she replied calmly.

'But she has been dead fully twenty-four hours!' The doctor's voice was incredulous.

'Well, perhaps she has.' Virginia Wardlaw was unshaken. 'The truth of the matter is, my niece asked me yesterday afternoon to start a fire in the kitchen range to heat water for her bath. She intended to take a nap first. I started a fire and then, having business to attend to, went away, leaving her to sleep undisturbed.'

Haughty and slippery, she parried further questions. She and her niece, dead Oceana, lived alone in the house. It was only temporary accommodation. She herself had had no reason to visit the bathroom. (One presumes that the WC was situated elsewhere!) She did not check her ailing niece's condition, because she had asked not to be disturbed.

The woman in black was not doing very well; she was not doing well at all, and the doctor could hardly wait to edge past her and make for the nearest telephone to report the apparent suicide with suspicious circumstances attached.

This time, it was Sergeant William O'Neill who came rapping at the door of No 89. Ignoring the supercilious response of Virginia Wardlaw, he raked the place over from attic to cellar. Only one small upstairs room was 'furnished', with a truckle bed and a cloth-covered barrel which served as a dressing table. That bare house of death was dotted with sparse relics of the dead girl, like rare flowers in a great desert. A solitary, silk maternity gown hung in a closet. There was one painting – of a ballerina. The aunt appeared to have slept on the floor. Orange peel littered the floorboards in a ghastly fungus.

Downstairs was only marginally better. The dining room table was a packing-case. One cupboard was stuffed with cheap, unbleached muslin, left over from the yards of the stuff which had been used to blanket out the windows. The kitchen, seen in wan gaslight, was empty, except for a few scraps such as a dog would leave. There was neither pen nor ink in the house.

It was the cellar that held the most important clue of all. The rusty old boiler was as dead as a dodo. It had not yielded hot water in living memory.

Sergeant O'Neill needed no more. He bore Virginia Wardlaw off to the police station for questioning. Why was her niece so thin? Because she had lost the will to eat. What was the flannel doing in her hand? It was not clasped: it had just drifted there. How did she write the note? She had written it previously – and it was not the first.

The next day, an autopsy showed that twenty-four-year-old Oceana had died by drowning in the four-foot bathtub. Even more disturbing was the mute testimony of her pale, crinkled body. She weighed less than six stone. Did she have the strength to climb into the bath? Had she been carried there? If it were murder, the flannel demonstrated muddled thinking: the murderer could not have it both ways – the note signalled suicide, but the flannel signalled accident. The aunt betrayed no grief and she would not reveal her background.

The case was beginning to stir nightmare memories of the infamous, English, Staunton murder of 1877, when just such a young woman as this was starved to the threshold of death by those who were her nearest, and should have been her dearest. Harriet Staunton had been held captive in a remote Kentish cottage before being removed to her death in Penge. Detectives soon discovered that Oceana Snead had suffered in Brooklyn and had been brought to East Orange to be dispatched.

A trail of addresses led to No 1693, East 48th Street, Brooklyn, an old, dark house, christened by neighbours the House of Mystery. Virginia Wardlaw had lived there, sure enough, but there were *three* of them, all dressed in black. Three Black Crows – that is what they called them. At dead of night, they caught glimpses of the three grim figures, veiled and cloaked, hovering round bonfires in their back-yard, like the three witches in *Macbeth*.

There were rumours – of a beautiful, young girl, and an ancient, wrinkled crone, hidden away behind the shuttered windows – and others, wild and fanciful. The devilry began on Sunday, 14 November 1909. Two figures emerged into the night – one gaunt 'Black Crow' and a limp, fragile young girl. A cab whisked them off to New Orange, where No 89 North

Fletcher Snead, Oceana's husband and first cousin. He disappeared mysteriously, eventually turning up as a cook in Canada.

*89 North Fourteenth Street,
East Orange. The Crow's Nest.*

Fourteenth Street was to become a *second* House of Mystery. The cab driver remembered that the girl was so weak that he had helped her into the house.

A fortnight had gone by in quietly deceptive darkness. Then, suddenly, on the night of Sunday, 28 November, the house lit up like a lighthouse, with lamps winking and twinkling in the first floor windows, and shadows of *several* people jerking about, as if they were puppets behind the muslin curtains. Then, just as suddenly, total darkness . . . total silence. Until the call, next afternoon, to the police station, which set off a massive feat of unravelling. The case was now teetering on the edge of total illumination, total revelation.

Sergeant O'Neill tramped through the bare rooms of the first House of Mystery in Brooklyn with a horrible sense of déjà vu. Broken shards of furniture. Tatters of clothing. Decaying food. Cobwebs. And, crammed into the kitchen range, a clump of matted, yellow hair wrapped round two animal bones. To this day, no one knows what *that* was all about.

The Crows' nest was empty. One crow was under wraps and the two other flown crows would have to be traced. A Dr William Pettit was found. Yes, he had seen the Three Black Crows, and the ancient crone, and they must all have slept on the floor, because only his patient, Oceana Snead, had a bed to lie in. Several months previously, she had given birth to a sickly baby boy, who never seemed to thrive, and was now in

St Christopher's Hospital, Brooklyn.

The young mother was undernourished, but the three guardian women in black ignored his recommendations. She seemed afraid of them. Once he spotted a bottle of chloroform on the mantelshelf. To gain access on his last visit, he had to climb in through a window. He thought they had left the house to escape his attentions. They refused to let him take the stitches out of an operation wound – and, in fact, the stitches were still in Oceana's corpse.

In her cell, Virginia Wardlaw scoffed down grapefruit and cereal inside her veils and called for strong coffee and stronger cider. They were certain now to charge her with murder. Gradually, a web of jiggery-pokery was beginning to mesh together. There were complicated insurance fiddles. Oceana Snead was insured for 24,000 dollars. And she had been 'helped' to make will after will.

Who were these frightful women? The astonishing truth emerged from the caches of documents and newspapers which the Three Black Crows deposited like droppings as they migrated from nest to seedy nest. These were no ordinary eccentrics, but real old American aristocrats brought down by their own weird behaviour. Indeed, the Wardlaws were one of the great families of the American South. Back in Scotland, Bishop Henry Wardlaw had founded St Andrew's University.

The three women in black were sisters, all former teachers. Virginia Wardlaw, aged fifty-seven, had been a headmistress, but had left her school under a cloud, the previous year. The second sister, Mrs Mary Snead, aged sixty-one, was a widow. Oceana had married her son, Fletcher Snead – Oceana's first cousin. He had disappeared. Mary Snead was the one who rented the death house at East Orange. She was run to earth,

The Three Furies – Mary, Caroline and Virginia

Mrs Caroline Martin, Oceana's mother. The inset picture is of Mrs Mary Snead.

holed-up at 466 West 22nd Street, Manhattan, together with the aged crone, Mrs Martha Eliza Wardlaw, aged eighty-four, who was the sisters' mother, and Oceana's grandmother. Only Martha stood between the dead girl's property and the three sisters – the ultimate beneficiaries. There was no food in the house.

The third sister, Mrs Caroline Martin, aged sixty-four, was Oceana's *own mother*. She had unwisely booked herself into the Bayard Hotel, Manhattan, calling herself Mrs Maybrick. A bizarre touch. It was an earlier Mrs Maybrick who was convicted at Liverpool in 1889 of poisoning her husband with arsenic! Inside a tin box in her hotel room, reporters discovered three practice 'suicide notes' – all in the same hand as the one positioned beside Oceana's corpse.

Fletcher Snead, Oceana's lost husband, for whom she had pined, her first cousin, and scion of a proud family, was located in a small Canadian town, St Catherine's, Ontario, working as second cook at the New Murray Hotel. He seemed a broken man, and he refused to return to New York under any circumstances.

Public prosecutor for Essex County, Wilbur A. Mott

reckoned that he had enough evidence now to go ahead. The Wardlaw sisters were put up at Newark Court, New Jersey, indicted for the murder of Oceana Snead. They all pleaded not guilty. Family connections stood them in good stead; they were well represented. Planted side by side at the bar, robed and veiled in black, they looked like the three Furies incarnate. They were duly committed to the higher court. But it was not to be.

Virginia Wardlaw, crippled with shame and pride, swore that she would never stand trial, and deliberately starved herself to death. She died in Essex County Jail, Newark, on 9 August 1910, five months before the trial date, finally set for 9 January 1911.

Caroline, without doubt the ringleader and worst of the bunch, pleaded insanity at a special hearing to determine her state of mind. The proceedings were farcical, as her unquenchable interruptions demonstrated only too clearly that she was in the grip of some complicated paranoid illness, but the judge stoutly declared her to be sane. He did, however, later accept her plea of guilty to the reduced charge of manslaughter – her learned comment was, 'How can it be manslaughter when she was just a lovely little girl?' – and sentenced her to seven years' imprisonment.

At New Jersey State Prison, the veils were, at long last, stripped away from her flinching face. Within a year, no one doubted that she was mad, and she was transferred to the State Hospital for the Insane. She died there on 21 June 1913. It is irresistible to hazard that the three sisters were implicated in a form of *folie à trois*, with the infection spreading out from the dominant, and truly deranged, point of the triangle, Caroline Martin. Absurd family pride also played its part.

That left Mary Snead – and a rather complicated legal position. Since, as a matter of law, there was no accessory to manslaughter, therefore it followed that Mary could not be brought to trial for anything that Caroline had done. She was set free – a solitary Black Crow, doomed to roost – and brood – alone.

Two of a number of 'practice' suicide notes found in the possession of Oceana's mother.

The suicide note found near the body of Oceana Snead.

Place the Face:
A Ripping Old Game

It is a game which, down a hundred-year-long corridor, the baffled generations have continued to play – Hunt the Ripper. Ever since, in 1888, a faceless horror stalked the mean streets of one square mile of London's East End, slaughtering most horribly five pathetic women, the game's been afoot. The hazards as to the unvisaged slayer's identity have ranged wide – and wild. Here are six favourite guesses. But does the face fit?

Montague John Druitt (1857-1888)
Candidacy supplied by Tom Cullen in *Autumn of Terror* (1965), and Daniel Farson in *Jack the Ripper* (1972). Confirmed by Martin Howells and Keith Skinner in *The Ripper Legacy* (1987).
Supported by specific nomination in the private papers of Sir Melville Macnaghten, Assistant Chief Constable, Scotland Yard, from 1889.
Failed barrister and dismissed schoolmaster. Drowned himself. Body taken from the Thames December 1888. No real evidence against him, other than temporal coincidence of suicide and cessation of accredited Ripper killings.

HRH Prince Albert Victor Christian Edward, Duke of Clarence (1864-1892)
Proposed by Thomas Eldon A. Stowell in Nigel Morland's magazine, *The Criminologist* (November 1970).
Enthusiastically seconded by Frank Spiering in *Prince Jack* (1978).
Indirectly supported, and with infinite complications which, exonerating Prince Eddy personally, involve royal physician, Sir William Gull, the artist, Walter Sickert, and one John Netley, royal coachman, by Stephen Knight in *Jack the Ripper: The Final Solution* (1976). No real evidence. A tissue of genuine, and manipulated, coincidence.

James Kenneth Stephen (1859-1892)
Accused by Michael Harrison in *Clarence* (1972). Tutor to HRH Prince Albert Victor. Son of Mr Justice Stephen. Cousin of Virginia Woolf. Alleged to have been Prince Eddy's homosexual lover; driven to murderous distraction by the jilting of the Prince's betrothal, sacrificed symbolic 'Women' at the altar of his ruined passion. Fanciful stuff. No hard evidence whatsoever.

George Chapman otherwise Severin Antoniovich Klosowski (1865-1903)
The choice of Chief Detective Inspector Frederick George Abberline, who was actually involved in the real-life Ripper hunt. Chapman, a Pole, poisoned three of his female consorts, and was hanged. The sole evidence against him seems to be Abberline's curious and inexplicable observation to his colleague, Inspector George Godley, who had just arrested Chapman, 'You've got Jack the Ripper at last.' Hargrave L. Adam in *Trial of George Chapman* (1930) tries to make a case for Chapman being the Ripper, but it is not particularly convincing.

Dr Thomas Neill Cream (1850-1892)
Guilt pointed to by persistent, evidentially unsupported, legend that on the Newgate scaffold his strangled confession, 'I am Jack —' was cut short by Mr Hangman Billington's noose. Grierson Dickson in *Murder by Numbers* (1958), states that it was Billington himself who reported hearing Cream call that out. Cream's guilt canvassed by Donald Bell in the *Criminologist* (Summer 1974). Most dubious.

Dr Roslyn D'Onston Stephenson (1841-?)
Adopted candidate of Melvin Harris in *Jack the Ripper: The Bloody Truth* (1987). Previously put forward by Aleister Crowley and Bernard O'Donnell. Baptismal name, Robert Donston Stephenson. Mage, medical man, esoteric author, journalist and man-about-Whitechapel. It is suggested that the killings were black magic ritual murder. After 1904, when he would have been sixty-three, D'Onston Stephenson just vanishes from the scene as totally and finally as Jack the Ripper, leaving behind, like him, a gigantic question mark.

Before placing the face, you should take a look at the evidence put forward by the authors of the various books mentioned. You should also take into the reckoning the views expressed by high-ranking contemporary police officers.

Sir Melville Macnaghten mentioned two suspects in addition to Druitt – a Polish Jew named Kosminski and a crazed Russian doctor, Michael Ostrog.

Chief Inspector Donald Sutherland Swanson also identified the prime Ripper suspect as Kosminski.

Martin Fido in his *The Crimes, Detection and Death of Jack the Ripper* (1987), pursues the Polish Jew theory and comes up with the discovery of an Aaron Kozminski, admitted to Colney Hatch Asylum on 6 February 1891. But he dismisses him. He elects instead, Nathan Kaminsky, whose Colney Hatch incarceration and death, in October 1889, was, he thinks, recorded under the incorrect name of David Cohen.

The Rabbit-Pie Murders

A doctor named Sprague was accused at the Exeter Autumn Assizes of 1865 of poisoning his wife and entire household with atropine. The evidence? A quantity of that poison found by an analyst in the remains of the rabbit-pie, and the eyes of the decedents had all exhibited the significant symptom of much dilation.

Fortunately, after long retirement the jury brought in a not guilty verdict. It was not until a considerable time later that scientists discovered the strange fact that rabbits can eat any quantity of the deadly-nightshade (Belladonna) plant – the source of the virulent vegetable alkaloid poison, atropine – without suffering any harm, although their flesh becomes fatally poisonous.

The First Murderer Arrested by Telegram

John Tawell, the not quite quick enough Quaker.

Crippen was the first murderer to be arrested by means of wireless telegraph, but, sixty-five years before that, a murderer was arrested through a telegram.

The year was 1845. His name was John Tawell. A professed Quaker, he was a man with a chequered career behind him. Now about fifty, he had been arrested for a bank forgery at the age of twenty. Transported to Australia, good conduct had procured him a ticket of leave after seven years. He had established a prosperous chemist and druggist's business. He had on his return to England married and settled in some style at Berkhampstead, in Hertfordshire. His wife died, and he seduced Sarah Hadler, who had entered his service only weeks before. He set her up as his mistress, first in London, and then, with their two children, at Slough, where she was known as Mrs Hart, a widow.

Tawell married again. Another Sarah: Sarah Cutforth. His finances seem to have plunged and he apparently decided that Sarah Hart was an appurtenance he could no longer afford. He accordingly removed her from his debit column with a bottle of porter laced with Scheele's prussic acid. A neighbour, Mrs Mary Ann Ashley, heard stifled screams coming from the widow Hart's cottage, and saw a man dressed like a Quaker walk down the garden path. She asked him what was the matter. He made no reply and walked quickly away. Mrs Ashley found Sarah Hart dying. Tawell was spotted getting on to the train at Slough station, and an electric telegraph message was sent to Paddington, where a railway policeman was waiting. He followed Tawell to his lodgings. Next day he was questioned and arrested. He was hanged on 28 March 1845.

The Greatest of the Locked-Room Murder Mysteries

Isidor Fink was found lying dead in the rear room of his locked, bolted and barred two-room laundry at 4 East 132nd Street, Fifth Avenue, New York City . . . and there was just no way of explaining the bullet holes in his body. Life was imitating that classic Agatha Christie-style – out of Queen, out of Carr, out of Chesterton, out of Poe – detective story puzzler – the locked-room mystery.

It happened in real life at 10.30 on the night of Saturday, 9 March 1929, and the Fink-file still lies officially open and dust gathering on its high shelf at police headquarters.

Isidor Fink arrived in America, as a twenty-year-old refugee from Poland, around the year 1918. A Fairy Tale of New York character, he might have come straight out of the pages of Isaac Bashevis Singer. He is, fictively, in those of Ben Hecht – 'The Mystery of the Fabulous Laundryman.' Starting from nothing, he beavered away for long years of sixteen-hour days to save up for his own business. Independence. And in the end he made it. Not that it added up to much. Just a Lilliputian one-divided-into-two-room laundry, and a single-divided-into-double apartment at 52 East 133rd Street, shared with a shoemaker named Max Schwartz.

The thirty-year-old Fink was a lonely figure. Poor. Unmarried. No relatives. No women friends. His punishing work schedule did not leave him much time for socialising. At least he had no known enemies either. Although you would never have guessed it from the Fort Knox-like defences he set up at his laundry. You could believe that all the dybbuks of ancient Poland were out to take up their abode with and in him. Was it, as Schwartz said, that he feared robbers and hold-ups? Or was it, perhaps, the exile's deeper psychological need of husbanding the hard-won evidences of howsoever meagre security?

His kingdom, his hired patch of America, consisted of what had been a sizeable single room, forty feet long, twenty feet wide, now partitioned to make two rooms, on the ground floor of a typical East Side tenement building. 'One of those edifices that seem built out of sweat and refuse.' There were two windows. One looked out – or would have looked out had it not been totally obscured by a coat of thick grey paint – on to the front street. The other, similarly greyed-out, looked on to an alley that ran down the side of the house. Both windows were fitted, like mort-safes for the living, with stout iron bars, set six inches apart. There was a front door opening directly

Ben Hecht. He wrote a short story based on the Fink Case – The Mystery of the Fabulous Laundryman.

into the front 'room' of the premises. It was furnished with the heaviest lock that the devotedly saved-up money – fruit of how many scores of washing-baskets – could buy. Above the front door was a small transom window. Less than twelve inches high, it, too, was grey-painted. According to one report it was securely nailed up. Another account states that the hinge was broken. And there was a rear door. This adjoined another largish ground-floor room, occupied by another tenant, Mrs Locklan Smith, a coloured woman. This door was not only securely locked and bolted, but it was definitely nailed up.

Within this mini-fortress or watertight chamber, Fink had at first had his cabined and confined being. He had slept on a cot at the rear and rigged up a sort of makeshift bathroom behind a screen. He washed and ironed herein, taking his meals at nearby cafés. Such was the mode and manner in which he had contentedly invested the hours of his days before moving in with Max the cobbler.

It was at about half-past ten on the night of 9 March that Mrs Locklan Smith, disturbed by alarming alien sounds issuing from her secluse abutter's hermetically sealed quarters, made haste to communicate with her friendly neighbourhood policeman. And, with commendable promptitude, Patrolman Albert Kattenborn brought his calming presence to the, by now chaotic, scene.

Moving with the balming influence of respected authority through the wide-eyed, chattering locals knotting themselves in garrulous groups about the firm-closed laundry door, the intrepid Kattenborn began his cool, calm, collected investigation of 'the incident'. And as he moved from bolted door to barred window, and back from barred window to bolted door, it was borne in upon Patrolman Kattenborn that someone had been doing his dirty washing in private in Mr Fink's secure, soap-sudded kingdom.

Casting a momentarily bewildered eye about him, Patrolman Kattenborn spotted a likely lad of thirteen. One Lloyd Fox. Master Fox was hoisted aloft to the transom window, handed a truncheon and, to his delight, told to smash the glass. He did so with a will and was instructed that, after taking care to remove all jagged edges, he should, with equal care, clamber through, drop to the floor and open the front door.

Inside, some thirty feet back from the doorway, lay the corpse of Isidor Fink, two bullet holes in the left side of his chest, a third bullet lodged in the left wrist.

Robbery it was not. There was money in the cash register and money in Fink's pocket had not been touched. A hot iron on the lighted gas stove betokened the fact that Fink had been ironing.

Suicide? It *had* to be. No one could have got into or out of that inexpugnable place.

Suicide? It could *not* have been. There was no gun to be found anywhere in that impregnable room.

Murder? *Impossible.* A murderer simply could not have got in or out. The windows were all unbroken and all nailed up from the *inside*.

During the weeks of total puzzlement that followed, police literally tore the premises to pieces. Walls, floors, ceiling were probed for secret entrances, sliding panels, trap-doors.

Nothing.

All manner of theories were tested. Perhaps Fink had attached the gun to some sort of elastic device that pulled it out of sight after its discharge. Perhaps not. Every theory, no matter how crazy, was given a hearing.

Nothing was revealed.

To this day the New York police remain baffled by the big Fink riddle. As one detective officer succinctly expressed it after a year's work on the case ended for him in utter bafflement: 'That damn two-for-a-cent mystery gives me the creeps.'

It certainly is a puzzler, but I suspect that it is a plain case of murder, and, with the help of the celebrated Edinburgh Professor of Forensic Medicine, the late Sir Sydney Smith, I think I can supply the solution.

What in all likelihood happened was that Isidor Fink answered a knock at his front door, was shot twice in the chest – the police doctor had opined that the shots were fired from a distance of about two feet – and the third bullet hit him in the wrist when he instinctively brought up his hand to protect himself.

Fink then re-locked the front door and walked the best part of thirty feet before dropping dead to the floor.

Impossible?

A dead end – hard-won, but hardly luxury.

Hear ye. Professor Smith cites a case in which an elderly professional man in Edinburgh walked out of his hotel, went into a public garden and shot himself. The bullet travelled up from under his chin into the brain. Blood and fragments of brain and bone were found spattered about the roof, just above the seat in the shelter where, around 6am, he shot himself. At 7.30am the man returned to the hotel, spoke to the maid, placed his umbrella in the hall-stand, hung up his coat and walked upstairs to the bathroom. There he collapsed. He was taken to the hospital, where he did not die until three hours later.

Such cases of tenacious survival are rare – but far from unknown. There is good reason to believe that Isidor Fink may have been one of them.

How Murderers Kill Time

Even the keenest, kinkiest multicide can't be 'at it' all the time. So how does he fill in the dull hours between kills? What were the homicides' hobbies?

For relaxation George Joseph Smith played the harmonium. Charlie Peace was an accomplished violinist, inventor and tombstone designer. Wallace (not a murderer) scraped on the violin and tinkered with his chemistry set: chess and the reading of Stoic philosophy were more serious. Dr Palmer set up his own racing stable. Henry Wainwright was keen on amateur theatricals and was well known as a reciter in the Whitechapel district. Dr Pritchard's hobby was the delivery of self-aggrandising lectures about his travels and adventures. James Greenacre was interested in politics and is said to have been connected with the Cato Street Conspiracy. Maundy Gregory, undoubted killer of Edith Marion Rosse, was a bibliophile. Major Armstrong kept a decent library, played tennis, took dancing lessons, and had a passion for aggressive gardening. Dennis Nilsen was a good cook, and played classical records, especially Bach, his favourite. Samuel Herbert Dougal gave bicycling lessons. Christie collected pubic hairs. (Although some deny this.) And poisoner Graham Young's hobby was – the study of poisons!

Beams and Motes

Clues and court room exhibits come in all shapes and sizes.

A huge wooden beam from the hut in which he lived on his chicken farm, at Crowborough, Sussex, and where, in 1924, Norman Thorne murdered his sweetheart, Elsie Cameron, was carted into court at Lewes to show that there were no rope marks on it, although Thorne claimed that she had committed suicide by hanging herself from it. He it was who was hanged – judicially, at Wandsworth.

A button and badge, by way of contrasting magnitude, sealed the fate of David Greenwood. The raped and strangled corpse of sixteen-year-old Nellie Trew was found on Eltham Common, in suburban south-east London, on 10 February 1918. Beside it lay a bone overcoat button and a cheaply produced replica of a regimental badge in the shape of a tiger (Leicester Regiment). Both were traced to the possession of the twenty-one-year-old discharged soldier. Greenwood was sentenced to death, but this was subsequently commuted to life imprisonment.

A pair of gloves helped the police to seize hold of ex-Army officer, Frederick Rothwell Holt. On Christmas eve 1919, the bullet-holed body of his mistress, Kitty Breaks, was found on the sandhills of St Anne's, near Blackpool. Close by was a pair of gloves. They belonged to Holt. The prosecution's case was that he had killed the girl he described as the lodestone of his existence for the £5,000 for which she had insured her life, and which he had persuaded her to to bequeath to him in her will. Despite an ingeniously energetic defence by Sir Edward Marshall Hall, he hanged. After being sentenced to death he remarked, 'Well, and that's that! I hope they won't be late with my tea.'

A nose reformer was a curious exhibit at the trial of Lance-Corporal Jack Goldenberg, accused of the murder by shooting of William Edward Hall, the young manager of the one-roomed bank hut on the fringe of Bordon Military Camp, Hampshire. It was stated that Goldenberg had used this instrument in an endeavour to reduce the size of his nose. It did nothing to reduce the gravamen of the charge, or the menace of the noose. The eighteen-year-old was hanged at Winchester in 1924.

Eye Ball Ballistic Revelation

The great Austrian criminologist, Hans Gross, author of the classic Criminal Investigation, was first set thinking of forensic ballistics by a curious family relic. His grandfather, serving in the Austrian army, had been shot in the head by one of Napoleon's soldiers in 1799. The ball lodged behind his eye and remained there all his life. When, in 1845, he died, it was removed and kept as a memento. Years later, Gross saw it, noticed that traces of powder still adhered to it, and wondered . . . could such things ever help in the investigation of criminal deaths by shooting?

The Dog-Watches of Murder

Mr Holmes, They were the Footprints of a Gigantic Hound!

A tail-wagging, heart-warming profit-and-loss account of the uncanny commerce between man and his canine amicus curiae *in the dogdays of sundry matters homicidal.*

When murder has been done, sometimes a lonely figure is glimpsed, padding in and out of deserted rooms, an innocent victim, and, as likely as not, a witness of the deed. This disregarded mourner is the dog in the case, which, through sheer closeness to his master's side, or his mistress' skirts, has become implicated, and even part of the evidence. His own life may be forfeit, especially if he is greatly loved, when the malice of the murderer spills over to include him in the killing.

Such was the fate of the little lap-dog which belonged to Miss Elizabeth Jefferies of No 6 Trenchard Street, Bristol. A wealthy woman, it was her pleasure to abuse and starve the succession of timid servant-girls who came to her fresh from country cottages. In 1849, her latest maid, young Sarah Harriet Thomas, from the village of Pensford, through some difference in her character, although she was of respectable background, turned against her tormentor and battered her head in. The butchered body of the dog was found, thrust down the water-closet, a horrible act, presignificatory of the Constance Kent affair, which reflects the savagery of the passions aroused in the unhappy household.

Jacko, a small brown and white spaniel, was the devoted pet of a very much nicer woman, Miss Camille Cecille Holland, and she should have named him Lucky. That frightful, lusty rogue, Samuel Herbert Dougal, who profitably shot Miss Holland and secreted her body in a drainage-ditch at the Moat Farm, appears to have lacked all inclination to include Jacko in the elimination procedure, even though his story that his 'wife' had left, but would return, might have been more convincing if she had not, notionally, abandoned the love-object so important to her.

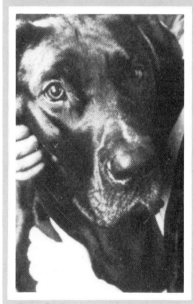

Poor Rinka.

Samuel Herbert Dougal, Miss Holland's killer, in the arms of the law, outside Audley End station, Essex.

During Dougal's four years of living it up, and bedding them down, before the body was discovered, *someone* must have fed Jacko, because we know that, as the farm was turned over in the search for Miss Holland, he was seen wandering around the excavation trenches, very stiff in the legs, nearly blind, and totally deaf. He was not the type of dog that could easily live by scavenging, and one must envisage the rough hand of Dougal setting down a daily supper for him. The constant sight of his dead lady's pet did not exacerbate his sensibilities beyond endurance.

Did Jacko, like Greyfriars Bobby, who kept long vigil for fourteen years beside his master's grave, stand guard at first over his mistress where she lay in her shroud of blackthorn bushes? Did Dougal shoo him away with fruity curses? Had he given up, or forgotten, by the time that help arrived? He did not assist the police, stand pointing or whining at the spot . . .

After pining and puzzling for some sixteen months, the spaniel formed the resolve to mount an expedition from the Moat Farm to look for his mistress, and, in so doing, entered the evidence. His objective was the bow-fronted house in Saffron Walden where Dougal, Miss Holland and Jacko had lodged for a couple of months before the move to the Moat Farm. He remembered it as a happy place, where a canary sang, and breakfast came up every morning, on a tray. Surely she would be there, as of old?

Miss Henrietta Wisken, the landlady, welcomed him warmly as a naughty stray who stayed to dinner for three weeks, after which she felt it her duty to write a letter to Miss Holland at the Moat Farm asking her what she was to do with her canine visitor. Dougal chose not to ignore the letter – which, in his scheme of things he had automatically opened – and replied that she should turn Jacko out one dark night, and he would find his own way home. This was not, of itself, a cruel suggestion, incidentally, but a countryman's remedy. Outraged,

Murder hunt in full cry – excavations at the Moat Farm.

Mrs Wisken did not comply, and, realizing that he must take action, Dougal appeared at her side door and declined to go round to the front.

'Come along, Jacko,' he addressed the spaniel. 'You have no business to run away from your mistress like this!' Humbly, little Jacko shambled back to the Moat Farm with him, leaving Mrs Wisken much exercised by Dougal's parrying of her enquiries about the welfare of Miss Holland – as she later told the Court in her capacity as chief witness for the Crown. She did not forget Jacko, who had come to her, and she rescued him from the wreckage and took him home to care for him. When eventually, he died, she had his body preserved and mounted in a glass case, for all to see.

By her dying, Norman Scott's Great Dane bitch, Rinka, assumed the crucial centre of the evidence in the trial of Jeremy Thorpe, the Liberal leader, in which, with others, he was charged with conspiracy to murder Scott, and acquitted. When, allegedly acting as Thorpe's remote agent, Andrew Gino Newton shot Rinka, did he then, having put out of the way the guarding dog 'as big as a donkey', intend to turn the gun on Norman Scott and either shoot him or deliver a warning shot past his head? Did the gun really jam? Or did Newton merely intend to frighten Scott? Was the slaying of the dog sufficient in itself, an extempore improvisation? Or did Newton, a squeamish man, according to his mother, lose his nerve and his intent to kill as the beautiful dog lay dead in her blood, and Scott, refusing to flee, tried to revive her with the kiss of life?

We can be sure that Rinka was trained to a nicety by Scott, although he had, in fact, acquired her only as an adult dog, the gift of friends, and would, indeed, have been a threat to an aggressor, if so commanded. Scott said that he took her with him on the car trip for Newton to meet a person in Porlock because he was uneasy. Many dog-lovers wrote letters of condolence to Norman Scott about the death of Rinka. 'I wasn't very good with people,' he said once, 'but with animals I know I'm all right.'

There was much public sympathy, too, for the plight of Bleep, a rough-haired, black and white mongrel bitch, the property of Dennis Nilsen, mass-murderer of Cricklewood and Muswell Hill, and the wincing, flinching spectator of his dispatches. Even people generally indifferent to the charm of dogs were touched to hear that when Carl David Stotter woke up on a sofa, half-strangled, half-drowned by Nilsen, Bleep was licking his face.

It was no life for a dog, even though Nilsen claimed, 'The dog was not disturbed. It never went near anyone dead. I taught him (sic) not to. It behaved quite normally.' Nilsen bought Bleep as a six-month-old puppy from a pet shop round the corner, and was fond of her in his way, without protecting her from vicissitude as a really dedicated pet owner would

Miss Camille Holland, Jacko's owner and Dougal's victim.

Bleep, Dennis Nilsen's gentle mongrel showing her bad eye.

Myra Hindley crouching over the grave of John Kilbride – the photograph which led to the death of Puppet.

have done. She gave birth to a litter of puppies – in a shed which he built specially for that purpose in the garden: he drowned some, and gave the rest away. She had a fight with a cat, which left her partially blind in one eye from an infected scratch. He told the man from Dyno Rod that he never fed her fresh meat. He may not have kept her inoculated against infectious diseases, because when she was removed by police to Battersea Dogs Home, where she *was* inoculated, it was too late, and, miserable, she succumbed to the deadly Parvo virus. Although the vets put her on a drip, they could not save her for the good home already found for her. She was eight years old and she had witnessed fifteen murders.

Illogically and unfairly, there was no surge of decent public feeling for Myra Hindley's pet, Puppet, on whom revulsion was Freudianly displaced, so that she was, as it were, contaminated by her mistress's guilt. It incensed people that Myra Hindley loved her like a baby. It disturbed them that Puppet was a part of the indecent poses photographed by Brady.

Puppet was just a little dog, ordered by Brady during the performance of unspeakable acts to 'Get in the f— basket'. Like Rinka, she, also, became deeply involved in the case, and died for it. There seems to have been a general opinion that she was better off dead, anyway.

The police were anxious to prove that the photograph of Myra Hindley in a crouching position on the site of the hidden grave of John Kilbride was taken after the boy had vanished, not before, as she claimed. There was a clue, in the shape of Puppet as a puppy, recognizable by her tri-coloured markings, tucked snugly into Myra Hindley's jacket to shield her from the moorland winds. Now a grown dog, Puppet was hailed off to a veterinary surgeon so that he could, by X-raying her teeth, indicate her age, and thus, by simple subtraction, the approximate date of the photograph could be established. Unfortunately, Puppet had a kidney condition, and died under the anaesthetic which is necessary to keep a dog immobile while X-rays of this kind are taken. Myra Hindley believed that the police had deliberately arranged Puppet's death, to punish her. 'You f— murderer!' she screamed at Chief Super-intendent Benfield when he told her what had happened – an unenviable task.

John Reginald Halliday Christie, reviled necrophile, kept a dog and a cat, and he cared for them. He was in the habit of going out to buy fish and chips for the mongrel bitch, Judy, and five-year-old, black and white cat. Ludovic Kennedy inter-viewed a Mr Giradot, whose window looked on to Christie's back-yard, and he said that both pets were eager to please their master; when he called them, they would have a race to get first to the prized position on his shoulder. There is a story – a quite persuasive one – that Christie's dog dug up a skull from Muriel Eady's skeleton, buried by him in the back-yard, at the time when the bodies of Beryl and Geraldine Evans were found in the wash-house: Christie took it under his raincoat and dropped it on a bombsite at St Mark's Road. Just before he decamped from 10 Rillington Place, he had Judy destroyed by a vet, which demonstrates that he had some feeling for her. Was he upset? He left the cat, which went berserk when the police came to dig and delve. With difficulty, the RSPCA caught it, but it was too wild to be re-homed, and it, too, was put down. Both Judy and the cat must have witnessed monstrous scenes in those small, cramped rooms that smelt of gas and decay.

Christie's cat, winner of the Shoulder Race.

Even John George Haigh spared, and very adequately looked after, the Irish Setter, Pat, which had belonged to his victims, Dr and Mrs Archibald Henderson, until he was no longer able to keep him at the Onslow Court Hotel, and gave him away. A terrible liar, of course, Haigh romanticized the dog's disposal, but, although Pat soon became unwanted, and was destroyed, he did *not* end his days in an acid bath.

The mysterious business of Edwin Bartlett's worm introduced into the Adelaide Bartlett case – not immediately, but *post hoc*, by way of conjecture – the noble, benevolent presence of the St Bernard. Already a powerful fancy by the year of Edwin's demise in 1886, the breed was first brought into Great Britain in some numbers in the 1860s, although the earliest recorded import, in 1815, was 'Lion', painted by Landseer at the young age of sixteen.

Rather engagingly, Edwin Bartlett kept and showed his own small kennel of St Bernards: not a poor man's hobby. On 9 December 1885, the second day of his terminal 'illness', he attended a show – his last. It was suggested by Yseult Bridges that the lumbricoid worm displayed for Dr Leach's attention was, in fact, a dog's roundworm (*Toxocara canis*) garnered by Edwin's wife, Adelaide, from the St Bernards' kennels. Both worms are similar in appearance, indeed, as Adelaide could well have known, and Dr Leach, if so fooled, should not be scorned. The worm, of whatever provenance, influenced the tragi-comedy by so far setting back the invalid's progress as to rule out the proposed trip to Torquay away from Adelaide's influence – and the *coup de grâce* by chloroform.

At this time, the Bartletts lived in Claverton Street, Pimlico, not a suitable milieu for a kennel of large dogs, and the St Bernards were still kept in the South London suburbs, some distance away. One is given the impression that Adelaide never left her husband's side from 9 December until his death, nor ceased from holding his toe, but it is not impossible that she was able to visit the kennels on some pretext, especially during the period of remission before the Torquay release. Alternatively, she could have snaffled a dog-worm before the 'illness' – she was brewing up a whole hotch-potch of symptoms for Edwin, and it might have been a reserve – and preserved it. There was no necessity for the worm to be produced to the doctor *in vivo*. Perish the thought that the Reverend George Dyson brought the nasty object to her hand as faithfully as he retrieved for her the bottle of chloroform!

In the absence of any suspicion at the time, the worm was not kept and subjected to proper examination. The human body does not carry the dog roundworm, only its larvae. If it *had* been found to be a dog-worm, think what evidence that would have been against Adelaide, who was so famously acquitted. . .

The fine figure of the St Bernard makes a later appearance in the Armstrong case of 1922, this time as a victim, happily by rumour only, its great size affording no protection. Pocket-sized Major Herbert Armstrong, come to think of it, was just the sort of man to select a giant breed for his own self-aggrandisement.

Robin Odell, in *Exhumation of a Murder*, while in no way endorsing the story, reports that a local resident said that Armstrong used to beat his St Bernard after a bad day at the office. The authors, in 1987, have been unable to trace a resident who can place a St Bernard at Mayfield, although lesser data are surprisingly well remembered.

It is curious that, as Odell goes on to relate, another St Bernard is linked with the Armstrong case: a neighbour of Armstrong's, from his early days at 52 Durning Road, Edge Hill, in Liverpool, claimed that Armstrong, with his mother and aunt, lived next door to a doctor who bred St Bernards. One morning, a bitch, named Lassie, was found dead. The doctor's daughter said, 'You know that Lassie was Herbert's last victim. My father always knew that Herbert poisoned her, only he had no positive evidence.'

There *must* have been a St Bernard somewhere in the affair! Is it feasible, though, that Armstrong would twice select a St Bernard for ill-treatment? Or, supposing that both stories are true, did St Bernards first come to his notice when simply convenient for experiment, and did he then idly muse that they were a decent kind of dog for a gentleman to have about his grounds, an ambition fulfilled when he proudly acquired Mayfield, set in its dandelion lawns in Cusop Dingle?

Exotic, large dogs appealed strongly to the Victorian imagination, especially if anthropomorphic characteristics were reputed to be attached to them. Bloodhounds, with their romantic history in this country, dating from the Norman Conquest, were regarded with awe. However, the performance of two champion hounds, Barnaby and Burgho, in tracking Jack the Ripper, was popularly considered to be a farce, with both dogs getting lost in fog on Tooting Bec Common, until Donald Rumbelow revealed the truth – not farce, but bathos.

Apparently, Barnaby and Burgho never got a sniff of Jack's handiwork; Sir Charles Warren, Metropolitan Police Commissioner, could not decide whether or not to use them, having tested them himself in rural surroundings in Regent's Park. It was not such a ludicrous idea as some have suggested; they might have been successful, even on a badly foiled line in city streets. A modern expert writes: 'The line may be hours cold

William Fish, child murderer and singing barber of Blackburn.

and crossed many times (sheep and cattle may trouble him) but nothing will stop him.'

It is a matter of record that a bloodhound, or, rather, a bloodhound-retriever cross, together with a Clumber spaniel, achieved, in 1876, a spectacular triumph in the little-known case of William Fish, the singing barber of Blackburn.

Morgan, the hybrid bloodhound, had already proved himself and secured a conviction by tracking down a gang of thieves through wild country and across a ford, but success had made him over-sharp and keen to attack any person of shifty, shabby mien. His master, Thomas Parkinson, of 18 Church Street, Preston, sent him for remedial training to Peter Taylor, of 72 Nelson Street, Preston, who was anxious to demonstrate his expertise with dogs when the killer of Emily Mary Holland was sought.

Morgan and Clumber spaniel hot on the scent of Emily Holland's remains.

Emily, aged seven, whose home was in Moss Street, Blackburn, had disappeared on 28 March 1876, after attending the Roman Catholic School of St Alban, at Larkhill. Two days later, the incomplete remains of the little girl were found in a field near the Blackburn cemetery. The head, arms and clothing were missing. The murderer had obligingly left a text-book clue: sticking to the torso and the blood-saturated newspaper in which it was parcelled, were wads and wisps of cut human hair of assorted lengths and colours. . .

There were not a great many barbers in the neighbourhood, and William Fish (an ill-starred name in the history of crime, shared with Albert Fish, the sado-masochistic cannibal, electrocuted at Sing Sing in 1936) who had put up his pole at No 3 Moss Street soon became a beleaguered suspect. A married man, with two children, he blandly carried on singing and snipping and lathering: business boomed. *'Tomorrow will be Friday, and we've caught no fish today,'* he warbled, and the children of the street sang back, *'Barber, barber, who killed the girl?'*

Morgan finds his quarry.

Morgan with his magic powers was needed. On 16 April, Chief Constable Potts decided to let him see what he could find on Fish's premises. Taylor brought the Clumber spaniel along as well, as back-up, and as soon as their leashes were slipped, they lunged around the shop, whining and quivering. Then Morgan ran into the back room, and put his paws up on the sink-stone. Fish turned green at the gills.

Taylor opened the door at the bottom of the stairs, and the dogs galloped upstairs, Morgan leading and giving tongue. First he sniffed around some clothing in the back room, and then he followed a line into the front room and straight to the fireplace, where he stood pointing, his hackles bristling and his head half up the chimney. 'There's something here!' Taylor cried, pulling Morgan away by his collar and groping in the sooty recess before bringing down the burnt skull and bones of a child, and pieces of grey calico and a chemise – Emily Holland's pathetic clothes.

William Fish, whose only previous offence had been theft

from his master's till, made a full confession – 'I tried to abuse her, and she was nearly dead. I then cut her throat with a razor.' After that, so the story goes, he slunk downstairs and shaved some customers with the same Todd's razor. It can't be true – can it? That evening, carefree as Mrs Dyer, he went to the Amphitheatre of Varieties.

The barber who sang no more was hanged at Kirkdale Gaol, Liverpool, on 14 August 1876. His parting homily was a gem of excusatory thinking: 'You can see my bad end through breaking off Sunday School. Avoid those bad, cheap journals on which I wasted so much time.' Morgan was a hero, celebrated in a special presentation card.

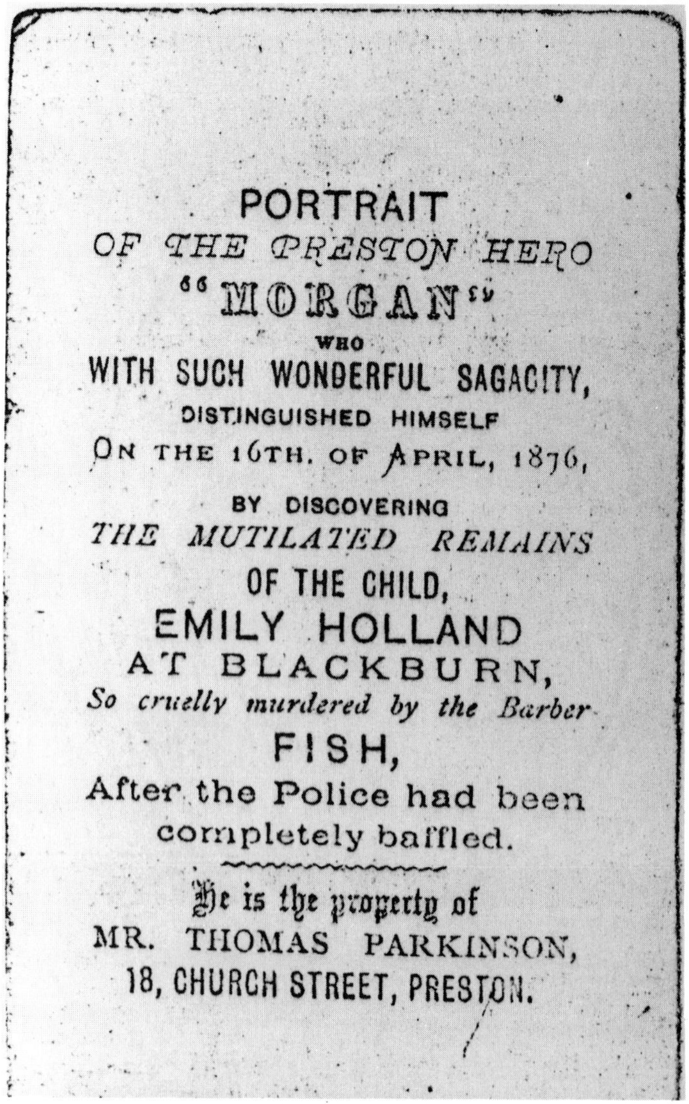

PORTRAIT
OF THE PRESTON HERO
"MORGAN"
WHO
WITH SUCH WONDERFUL SAGACITY,
DISTINGUISHED HIMSELF
ON THE 16TH. OF APRIL, 1876,
BY DISCOVERING
THE MUTILATED REMAINS
OF THE CHILD,
EMILY HOLLAND
AT BLACKBURN,
So cruelly murdered by the Barber
FISH,
After the Police had been
completely baffled.

He is the property of
MR. THOMAS PARKINSON,
18, CHURCH STREET, PRESTON.

A Will – But No Way

Jean Pierre Vaquier, hanged for the murder of Alfred Poynter Jones, landlord of the Blue Anchor Hotel, Byfleet, Surrey, in 1924, sought in his last will and testament to provide in a rather curious way a permanent memorial to himself.

An outstandingly vain little man, he was also outstandingly knowledgeable about wireless, having worked at a wireless depot during his service in the French army. After his demobilisation, he maintained a lively interest in the subject and took a job as wireless operator at the Hotel Victoria, Biarritz. It was while working the wireless set in the guests' drawing room, that he met Mrs Mabel Theresa Jones, recuperating in Biarritz after a nervous breakdown. Mabs and the passionate Frenchman had an intense affair. Besotted, he followed her to Byfleet, and poisoned Mr Jones.

Executed at Wandsworth, he left behind a will in which he asked that a certain wireless company in France, with whom he had previously been in negotiation regarding a special listening-in set of his invention which he had patented, should broadcast each year on the anniversary of his death – 12 August – the fact that his trial and conviction had been 'one of the most tragical errors of British justice.' His request was not, of course, acceded to.

Love Will Allaways Find a Way

In the contrary, unpredictable, out-of-evil-cometh-good way of things, it can sometimes happen that even a circumstance as evil as murder may, in a roundabout way, lead to romance.

There was certainly nothing romantic about the cold-blooded way in which thirty-six-year-old Thomas Henry Allaway, chauffeur to Mr Arthur Warwick Sutton, of Barton Close, Southbourne, lured thirty-one-year-old Irene Wilkins, of Streatham, to Bournemouth by a bogus telegram offering her work, and battered her to death.

However. . . . after Allaway's trial and conviction, one of the prosecution witnesses, a pretty young girl whom Allaway had also attempted to decoy, married a policeman who was present at the trial – the first time that the couple had met – and it was a case of love at first sight.

Thomas Henry Allaway listening to sentence of death being pronounced upon him by Mr Justice Avory on 7 July 1922.

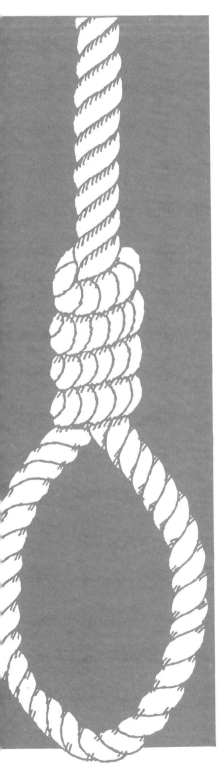

How They Met the Hangman

The condemned cell. The last morning. Your first sight, the white faces of the warders: most of those due to hang had to be woken from a deep sleep. A hearty breakfast – surprising how many could get it down. The tot of whisky or brandy that few refused. Sitting waiting for the door to open and the hangman to sidle in. The cigarette drops from your fingers. Off with your spectacles: they lie still warm on the table. Straps. Then follow the hangman. In the execution shed, if you looked up, you could see the rope . . .

John Reginald Halliday Christie

The Notting Hill necrophile. Killed at least six women.
Executed: Pentonville. 15 July 1953.
Gone the braggadocio of the prisoner on remand in Brixton, nicknamed Chris the Chess Champion. Now a lonely, broken man, with nothing and no one to live for. Professor Camps, conducting the post-mortem, noted that he had refused neither the breakfast, nor the whisky, although he was a teetotaller.

Dr Hawley Harvey Crippen

Poisoned his wife, for love of Ethel Le Neve.
Executed: Pentonville. 23 November 1910.
He had turned to writing poetry: *When the heart is breaking, and the way is long.* At midnight before the appointed day, presented to Prisoner Governor, Major Mytton-Davies, his rosary and crucifix ring (now in the authors' possession). Last request – to have Ethel's letters and photograph buried with him – granted. Secreted half the steel part of his spectacles in seam of trousers, hoping to puncture an artery and bleed slowly to death in bed – thwarted.

Ruth Ellis

Shot her lover outside Hampstead public house.

Executed: Holloway. 13 July 1955. No terrible scene. Fortified by brandy and a crucifix, famous blonded hair become streaky, dry-eyed and calm, went to her death without hysteria. Not true that Albert Pierrepoint resigned because of stress of hanging her.

Frederick Edward Francis Bywaters

Stabbed mistress' husband.

Executed: Pentonville. 9 January 1923.

Stoical and resolute, his only wish was that Edith Thompson should not suffer pain. The night before his dispatch, he talked to the Governor of the beauty of the Aurora Borealis.

Edith Jessie Thompson

Bywaters' mistress: also convicted of murder.

Executed: Holloway. 9 January 1923.

According to our executioners, a woman about to be hanged was generally braver than a man, but Edith Thompson was an exception, for her anguish was extreme, and she had to be carried to the scaffold. She may have been drugged.

George Joseph Smith

Drowned three wives in the bath.

Executed: Maidstone. 13 August 1915.

Tearfully turned to religion. Sandy hair said to have turned white. Terrified. Unrepentant. 'You'll have me hung the way you are going on!' he shouted at the judge during his summing-up, and so, indeed, Ellis the executioner sent him on his way, nearer to God. For all his balneal obsession, he never came clean. Last words: 'I am innocent.'

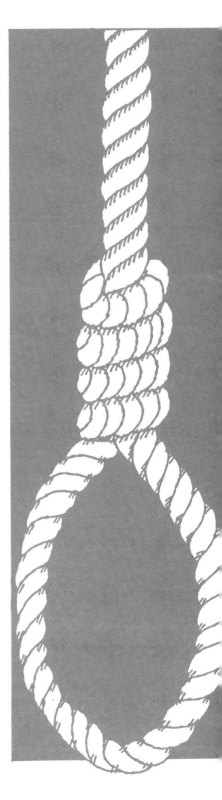

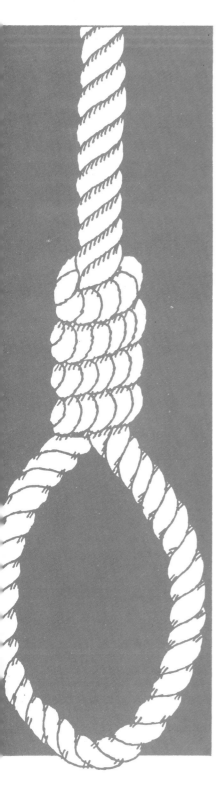

Neville George Clevely Heath

Riding-whip-wielding sadist. Killed two women.
Executed: Pentonville. 26 October 1946.
'It's just another op,' he said, in anticipation, having been a some-what tarnished RAF pilot. 'Only difference is that I know I'm not coming back from this one.' Albert Pierrepoint used his own, special wrist strap on him – pliant, pale calf-leather – and marked its use with red ink in his private diary; it was a rare sign of personal involvement in the execution. Last reported words – to offer of alcohol – 'You might make that a double.'

Charles Peace

Master criminal, ruthless burglar and murderer.
Executed: Armley Prison, Leeds. 25 February 1879.
'Bloody poor bacon, this,' he grumbled about his last breakfast on earth. When he lingered in the lavatory recess, and a nervous warder knocked, he complained, 'You're in a hell of a hurry. Who's going to be hanged this morning, you or me?' Poised on the scaffold, he delivered a homily. Then he asked for a drink: request ignored. 'The rope fits very tight,' he remarked. Departing words: 'Goodbye and God Bless. . . .' Best aphorism: 'What is the scaffold? A short cut to Heaven.'

Mary Ann Cotton

Multiple poisoner of at least fourteen.
Executed: Durham. 24 March 1873.
Her last infant had been taken from her. She woke at 4am. The wardresses helped her to dress. She prayed, with three Wesleyan ministers. Then she walked through ranks of reporters, shivering, sobbing and praying. Her hanging body shuddered and jerked for three minutes.

John George Haigh

Acid-bath killer of at least six.
Executed: Wandsworth. 10 August 1949.
Smiling and imperious to the end, prating of metaphysics, penning epistles to Dearest Mum and Dad from Sonnie, he specified the costume for his effigy in the Chamber of Horrors. Perished briskly, without a murmur.

Dr Neill Cream

Gave strychnine pills to prostitutes: killed four.
Executed: Newgate. 15 November 1892.
'They shall never hang me,' he boasted, after he had been sentenced – but they did. Spent a sleepless last night, pacing the cell, tossing on his bed, moaning, twitching. Refused breakfast. As the bolt on the scaffold was drawn, he is supposed to have said, 'I am Jack —' (*sic*) – *not* 'I am Jack *the* —'.

Henry Wainwright

Murdered his mistress and buried her in chloride of lime.
Executed: Newgate. 21 December 1875.
Dressed with scrupulous care, and bore himself with conspicuous fortitude. 'Come to see a man die, have you, you curs!' he addressed the crowd of sixty or so privileged visitors, and died like a man.

Frederick Browne

Shot PC Gutteridge in furtherance of car theft. Executed: Pentonville. 31 May 1928.
Intent on *felo de se*, he tried both to hang himself, and to cut his throat, with a broken button and then a razor blade. Prevented, he devastated his cell, raging with an inhuman strength. His last stroke was a hunger-strike, and he was forcibly fed. When the hour came, he made no such trouble. On the eve of his execution, he wrote a letter to the newspapers, giving as his address for reply, the Prison Mortuary.

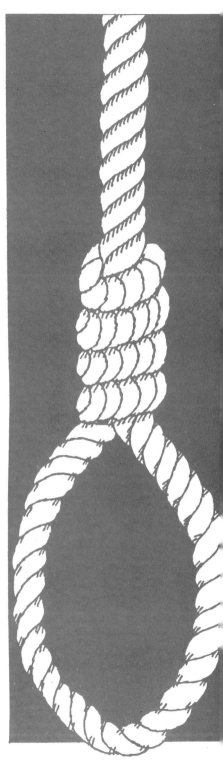

Paper Clues

*Percy Mapleton, alias Lefroy.
The* Daily Telegraph *sketch.*

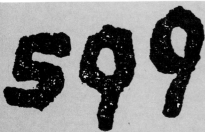

The identity mark of murder.

Long before the days of television and Police Five and Crime Watch, *newspaper detectives were doing a good job. It was a rough portrait-sketch in the* Daily Telegraph, *made also into a poster, that led to the arrest of Percy Mapleton alias Lefroy, who murdered Mr Frederick Issac Gold in a Brighton-bound express in June 1881. Lefroy vanished completely after the crime, and about this time a man calling himself Clarke took a single room at six shillings a week with Mrs Bickers, in Smith Street, Stepney. The neighbours of the new arrival saw the sketch of him and the offer of £200 reward, but it was not so easy to see the new arrival himself. He seemed very reluctant to come out of his room, declaring that for his health's sake he was forced to remain indoors all day, the blinds of his window – which looked out on to the street – pulled down, because the light was too strong for his eyes. The story is that a woman did contrive to get a good stare at him, and that what she saw sent her hastening to the police station. There are other tales told, but* whatever, the police certainly turned up at Smith Street . . . and it was the beginning of the end for Percy Mapleton.

It has been claimed that the first light was thrown on the Yarmouth Sands murder of 1900 by the Weekly Dispatch. A woman was found dead on the beach with a bootlace twisted tightly round her neck. For weeks the police were unable to find out anything about her, or trace her previous movements – for the simple reason that she had assumed the false name of 'Mrs Hood' when she came to the seaside. The sole clue was a washing number marked on the victim's clothing. It was 599. This was reproduced in the Weekly Dispatch, together with the offer of a reward of £5 for any information. A woman who worked in a laundry recognised it as the mark of a Mrs Bennett, of Bexleyheath, Kent. Police found her murderer-husband, Herbert John Bennett, in his secret retreat at Woolwich. Tried and convicted at the Old Bailey, he was hanged at Norwich, on the first day of spring, 1901.

When Murder Put Up the Chain

Few people realise that the widespread practice of putting a chain on the front door dates from the time of the Ratcliffe Highway murders of 1811 and 1812, when John Williams' wholesale slaughter of two families in the East End of London produced a panic even greater than that later aroused by Jack the Ripper. Never since the time of Bonaparte, had the British mind been afflicted with a more fearsome bogey than the imagined form of the Ratcliffe Highway Murderer, who came like a thief in the night to rob folk of their lives, and vanished into nothingness, like an evil phantom. After dark, no one dreamt of opening their door without being fully satisfied as to the caller's identity. This led to the almost universal adoption of the chain – and a brisk fillip for the ironmongery trade.

Kiwi Murder

The Near-Martyrdom of Arthur Allan Thomas

A tantalising down-under confoundment, in which some blood-spilling person or persons unknown, killed the parents, and some life-saving person or persons unknown, reticent and sub-visible as the shy and cautious kiwi, gave erratic succour to the victims' orphaned baby.

Who fed baby Rochelle? Answer that question, and you have the solution to the abiding mystery of Bitter Hill. Even the police, who thought, wrongly as it turned out, that they knew who killed Harvey and Jeanette Crewe, never came anywhere near explaining whose hand fed and changed their baby daughter at some time during the five whole days before their blood-stained farmhouse was discovered, empty, except for the abandoned survivor alone in her cot.

Bitter Hill is one meaning of the Maori name, Pukekawa, which was, in 1970, a small farming community of only six hundred souls, situated twenty-five miles south of Auckland, New Zealand. The area has a violent history; Pukekawa Hill itself rustles with memories of past conflicts, a kind of Maori Culloden, and modern domestic murder has thrice visited its isolated farmhouses – in 1920 (the Eyre case), in 1932 (the Lakey case) and now, in 1970, the Crewe case.

In June of that year, however, Pukekawa was a peaceful, pastoral scene of roundy hills where sheep could safely graze,

The scene of the murders, the Crewe farmhouse, Pukekawa, New Zealand.

although it was, remember, in that upside down country, bleak mid-winter. The landscape, too, was deceptive: the underlying rock was slashed by deep gashes and tunnelled by 'tomos' – limestone caverns, while through it all curled the wide, winding, muddy Waikato River on its way to the wild Tasman coast.

The Crewe farmhouse – not as it sounds, but, incongruously to British readers, a small, newish, single-storied chalet-type dwelling built of plain brick – was shielded both from passing Highway 22 and from the prevailing gales by rows of conifers, macrocarpa cypresses, their dense foliage bearing the scent of verbena. Outside the back door, a hibiscus bush was planted, but, even so, this was a place of toil, not of beauty.

Dourly, the Crewes, both thirty years old, kept themselves to themselves – they would accept hospitality, but not return it – and Harvey laboured from dawn to dusk on the 365-acre farm, to prove himself. Jeanette, not he, had brought the money to the marriage, and he was acutely aware of the inequality. Half the farm had been inherited by Jeanette, and Harvey had raised a mortgage to buy out her sister Heather's other half-share. It may be a mere coincidence that on 16 June, the day before the Crewes vanished, Jeanette called at her solicitor's and learnt the full details of a substantial new inheritance under her mother's estate – that is, half her parents' farm, in addition.

The couple were respected, but not popular. Nor were they precisely unpopular. But *someone* had it in for them. Three separate incidents, which were not interpreted, at least by Jeanette, as random happenings, had marred the four years of their marriage: in 1967, they were burgled, and only Jeanette's valuables were taken; in 1968, when, one evening, Harvey returned from visiting his wife and new-born baby in hospital, he found the spare bedroom ablaze; and in 1969, a haybarn went up in smoke. Jeanette, an ex-teacher, had become nervous, and did not like to stay in the house on her own.

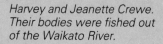

Harvey and Jeanette Crewe. Their bodies were fished out of the Waikato River.

Rather pathetically, she used to sit out in the fields in their car, nursing baby Rochelle, near to the comforting presence of her burly husband, until he had finished his work for the day. *How right she was to fear the unloved rooms of her home!*

Quite apart from the threat from the outside world, something else seems to have been seriously amiss within the walls of the marriage. Devoid of ornament or personal identity, such as one would expect from a person of Jeanette's college background, the farmhouse was more like a beaten-up furnished rental, or a half-way hut on a mountainside, than a love-nest, a haven from the grinding work and the elements. It was as if, in marrying a rough-cut shepherd – all sixteen and a half stone of him, fond of rugger, and with a well-proved nasty temper – Jeanette had abnegated the niceties of life which had once become available to her. Who knows but that the scent of lemon from the macrocarpa trees sometimes drifted through her curtainless windows, and poignantly reminded her of literature and lawns? More will be said later of those blank windows . . .

One should not, perhaps, make too much of the unprepared interior of a working farmhouse, especially one which has been ravaged, but scene-of-the-crime photographs do not lie – well, hardly ever – and the matrimonial bedroom and the spartan 'nursery' are particularly cheerless. When you changed your clothes in this household, you simply dropped the dirty set in a corner. On the other hand, the bed was made, the laminated surfaces in the kitchen shine, the carpet seems to be clean (except for the blood) and the dining table is laid in a civilized manner, while gumboots were routinely changed for slippers on coming in from the mud.

Jeanette Crewe came from a farming background, so that life on a farm was no gross culture-shock to her – although it was certainly lonely. Her father, Len Demler, liked to mount a bronc and ride the range over his larger spread down the road from the Crewes, clad in check shirt and New Zealand version of a Stetson. He it was who made the discovery of the crimes. It says much for the Crewes' relationship with the community that even Jeanette's own father suspected no ill when they were incommunicado for five days, but, finally, on 22 June 1970, at about one o'clock in the afternoon, when a stock-agent reported no joy on the Crewe telephone, and that meant lost business, which was important, Len Demler decided to mosey over to investigate.

The low, cold house was waiting for him. It clamoured with clues which spoke of a deed which had transformed the familiar into the alien. Milk, bread, newspapers and mail for the first two of the five missing days – until the roundsman decided the Crewes had gone away without telling him – lay uncollected. A couple of lights were blazing. Entry was easy – through the back door, turning the key, which was on the outside. Bloodstains, some diluted, maculated the lounge floor

Len Demler riding the range.

and furniture, the kitchen lino, and the wall outside the front door. A cleaner-up, who lacked stickability, had been at work. Saucepans held diluted blood. Ashes in the fireplace were probably the remnants of a burnt hearth-rug and a cushion. The TV was disconnected. Jeanette's knitting, stranded on the couch, cried out with a voice of its own; one needle had fallen to the floor, bent and twisted out of shape. The louvre windows were unseasonably open.

The dining table made a tantalizing contribution to the *mise en scène*. Either lunch *or* supper had been consumed, and not

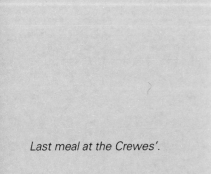

Last meal at the Crewes'.

cleared away. Two dirty dinner plates, their knives and forks correctly placed, were still on their table mats, and one sad, flat flounder fish, never to be eaten, lay in the centre of the table, on a different type of plain dish. Opened mail, delivered on Wednesday, 17th June, was scattered about.

We, and Len Demler, come now to the heart of the mystery – Rochelle Crewe, eighteen months old, trapped and neglected in her cot, but alive. The house was unheated, but although cold, she had escaped frank hypothermia. Let Demler speak: 'Rochelle looked very thin. She had been crying a lot and her eyes were sunk in but she wasn't crying at the time. She had a pyjama top on [and a woollen singlet] and napkins and she had no blankets on her at all. The napkins [under her plastic pants] were dirty.' In fact, the cot did contain the usual bed-clothes, including a blanket, and also pyjama trousers and one loose, soiled napkin.

At this stage, Len Demler, not so young as he used to be, and recently widowed, apparently panicked, and entered upon a course of action for which he was much criticized, because, in his attempt to preserve reality by marshalling practicalities (in the wrong order) he gave the impression of callousness. Instead of snatching up the infant and bearing her off to a place of safety, before raising the alarm, *he left her there*, drove home, and, as a priority, telephoned the aforementioned stock-agent to cancel his visit, before calling on the assistance of a neighbour, Owen Priest. 'The bugger's killed her and done himself in. I tell you

Harvey's killed her,' he kept saying to Priest as the two men searched the premises, afraid of what they might find. Then, at last, the grandfather took the child from her cot to the care of a motherly friend, Mrs Willis.

Now, not before time, the police were called in, and they, too, entered upon a course of action and behaviour which was severely criticized. Detective Inspector Bruce Hutton's first apparent breakthrough led him precisely nowhere. Bruce Roddick, a young man who had been working on the Chitty farm, over the road from the Crewes', reported that at about 9am on the second lost day, Friday, 19 June, he saw a green Hillman car parked outside the Crewes' front gate, and, standing just inside the fence, a tall woman with short, light brown hair, wearing dark-coloured slacks. That woman was never traced.

Even more puzzlingly, on the following afternoon, at 1.30 Mrs Queenie McConachie, driving past with her husband, saw a toddler on her own in the Crewes' garden, wearing clothes of the same description as those worn by Rochelle on the previous Wednesday. Did this mean that a person, or persons, had been secretly caring for Rochelle? A person who was local. Who was hiding a secret. Who cared what people thought. A humane person, who also fed the three working dogs, kennelled at a distance from the house, and fed hay to the cattle in the winter fields. Who, like, or in the same person as, the goblin in the house, *gave up* looking after Rochelle at some time during the five-day gap – say half-way through – because her condition on discovery was poor.

Or were Bruce Roddick and Queenie McConachie honestly mistaken? Both of them? Was Rochelle *never* fed or changed? Was the so-called accomplice a fantasy? David Yallop, in his influential and pioneering study of the case, entitled *Beyond Reasonable Doubt,* goes into this aspect thoroughly, and is convinced that the caring person did exist. Jeanette would not have left a soiled napkin in the cot, nor some (where the police found them) on top of the refrigerator, nor (a stronger point) would she have entirely run out of clean napkins, since there were none at all in the house. Mrs Willis, to whom the child was taken, remembered that she was wearing two napkins, arranged in a way which David Yallop considers to be complicated and to reveal the hand of a woman. It certainly shows that the napkins were meant to last for some time. The balance of the medical opinion (there was conflict, of course) was that Rochelle *had* been fed. She was not moribund when she was rescued, and did not even require hospital treatment, although hungry, thirsty, apprehensive and piteously dirty.

Few doubted that Rochelle was now an orphan, and on 16 August 1970, two fishermen found Jeanette's body floating in the flooded Waikato River, at Devil's Elbow, about half an hour's drive from the farm. She had been shot straight through the head from right to left with one .22 bullet, possibly while

Rochelle Crewe, aged eighteen months and sole survivor of the slaughter.

The Other Mystery of Hanbury Street

To every murder-fancier, and a great many other people too, the name Hanbury Street means only one thing – Jack the Ripper. For it was at No 29 of that East London street that poor Annie Chapman met her sticky end on 8 September 1888. But, twenty-three years later, at Christmas 1911, murder most mysterious paid a second visit to Hanbury Street.

There was there at that time a prosperous and respectable eating-house run by Samuel Millstein and his wife. Below the premises there was a cellar. The back part of the cellar was used as a kitchen, but it was the front portion, abutting upon the street, which gave grievance and affront to the Millsteins' neighbours. He had let it to tenants who promptly turned it into a gambling-den, and it was the night after night-long noise of perpetual yelling and quarrelling issuing forth from that subterranean gaming-place that sent a deputation of frantic,

lying on the floor, because her face had received a heavy blow, probably before death, as from a rifle butt. She was fully dressed in indoor clothes, and there had been no sexual interference. *Someone* had wrapped the body in bedclothes and tied up the whole bundle with wire – the type used multifariously on farms.

Harvey's body surfaced exactly one month later, four miles upstream, similarly wrapped, and with one .22 bullet in the head; it might have been weighted with an axle, but the police team failed to recover both corpse and axle as a joined entity. The wire broke.

It is no secret that the police first suspected Len Demler of the double murder. He notoriously did not aid his own cause by failing to help in the search for the missing bodies, preferring to ride the range and to throw a birthday party. Worse, traces of Jeanette's blood were found in his car, but apparently she had used his car from time to time.

David Yallop's book is weighted towards the exculpation of Arthur Thomas, the man convicted and ultimately pardoned, but almost casually interjected within the dense argumentation directed towards that end, there occurs this important sentence:

When one realises that not a single piece of evidence has ever been produced to refute the theory that one of the Crewes killed the other and then turned the gun on themselves, who can deny the possibility of murder/suicide being the explanation of the deaths of Harvey and Jeanette Crewe?

That is why Yallop considers the indications of the Crewes' indifferent marriage to be relevant. By this thinking, if Harvey violently attacked his wife, and were some kind of psychopath, he himself could have been responsible for the incidents on the farm which had so greatly frightened her.

As in all interesting cases, its components turn and whirl whichever way you look at it. Let us take the curtainless windows, to see if they support the murder/suicide theory, starting from the known fact supplied by David Yallop that the fire in 1968, *two years previously,* had destroyed some curtains, which had not been replaced. Jeanette did have material for new ones on order from two separate stores in Auckland, but on 15 June, two days before the crimes, Yallop continues, Harvey Crewe rang up one of the stores and cancelled the order.

Why did he do this? There are a number of possible explanations:

1 They were intending to move, because Jeanette was afraid to stay at the farm? There is no evidence that they told anyone of such an intention.
2 He was mean, and worried about the expense, even though Jeanette might not have been thus worried.
3 He had quarrelled with the store proprietor? (In

character.)

4 It was an act of spite against Jeanette?

5 He thought the curtains might go up in flames again? A sinister idea!

6 They had decided on a different pattern?

7 They, or he alone, had decided that curtains were an unnecessary excrescence on their life-style?

The possibilities are typically open-ended and inconclusive. One is bound to say, however, that the concept of a third person or persons coming upon the postulated murder/suicide, elaborately concealing the bodies, and secretly succouring the child, but then abandoning her (when it became too risky?) is extremely far-fetched. That notional person of conscience then allowed an innocent man to serve nine years of a life-sentence without a saving word. Or did that person come upon a double murder inflicted by an unknown assailant, and wrongly interpret the scene as matrimonial murder/suicide?

It must be far more likely that some other, unhinged, local person, never in the frame, killed both Crewes, and concealed the murders to the best of his ability. Either he, or an intimate of his, cared for Rochelle. Covering up two murders committed by a living man is a stronger motive for letting an innocent man take the rap than covering up the shame of a matrimonial tragedy, whose participants are both dead.

Baffled and floundering, the police closed in upon Arthur Allan Thomas, a thirty-two-year-old farmer, who lived with his wife, Vivien, nine miles away from the Crewes. His misfortune was that, by his own admission, he had had 'a real schoolboy crush' on Jeanette Crewe, and had later courted her unsuccessfully, before both were otherwise married. Forensic connections were extremely tenuous – his fingerprints were not present in the farmhouse, for example – and there seems little doubt that the police planted a cartridge case from his rifle in the Crewes' garden, in an area which had been previously pattern searched and sieved. David Yallop must have been wonderfully gratified, in a triumph which few writers experience, when his book powerfully went towards the report made by Mr R. A. Adams-Smith, an Auckland QC, who devoted an entire year to studying aspects of the case at the Government's instigation, and concluded that 'It seems that injustice may have been done.'

On 17 December 1979, Arthur Thomas, twice tried and convicted, was pardoned and released. He was granted compensation of £400,000 at the recommendation of a Royal Commission set up by New Zealand's Prime Minister, Robert Muldoon, following the Queen's Pardon. On 28 November 1980, in a report to Parliament, the Commission described Arthur Thomas' imprisonment on the basis of evidence by police officers as an 'unspeakable outrage'. The cartridge case, they said, was put in the garden 'by the hand of one whose duty

red-eyed, sleep-deprived local inhabitants round demanding that an end be put to the nocturnal uproar. Millstein, not wishing to lose his customers, gave his gambling tenantry peremptory notice to pack up and quit.

After a busy Christmas and Boxing Day in their café, the Millsteins took 27 December off. They had a day out. Neighbours saw them return home around midnight that Wednesdy. In the small hours of 28 December, smoke and flames were seen billowing from the Millsteins' bedroom. The alarm was raised. The police had no difficulty getting into the shop, for the door was unfastened. They rushed to the Millsteins' room. That door was locked. The key was in the lock – outside. They turned it, flung the door wide . . . there, on the floor, surrounded by flames that were rapidly licking up the walls, were the bodies of Samuel Millstein and his wife. The identity of the perpetrators of that double event has remained as mysterious as that of their illustrious predecessor in Hanbury Street.

Arthur Allan Thomas and wife, Vivien.

was to investigate fairly and honestly, but who . . . fabricated this evidence to procure a conviction of murder'.

The freed man had two choices – he could disappear abroad, anonymous, or he could go home – which is what he did, using his compensation to buy a new 125-hectare dairy farm. Rochelle Crewe is said to have grown up in the USA: inside her brain is locked, irretrievably, the face of the person, not her mother, who looked after her in the house hidden behind the macrocarpa trees.

Murder Car Numbers

Thomas Henry Allaway The Bournemouth Murderer	1922	Mercedes	LK7405
Major Herbert Rowse Armstrong The Hay Poisoner	1922	Triumph Combination	CJ3973
Browne & Kennedy The PC Gutteridge Murderers	1927	Morris Cowley	TW6120
Evelyn Foster The Otterburn Victim	1931	Hudson Super-Six	TN8135
Miles Giffard The Cornish Parricide	1953	Triumph	ERL 1
Michael Gregsten The A6 Murder Victim	1961	Morris Minor	847BHN
John George Haigh The Acid Bath Killer	1949	Alvis	BOV463
George Edward Heath The Cleft Chin Murder Victim	1944	Ford V8	RD8995
Arthur Albert Jones The Brenda Nash Murderer	1961	Vauxhall 14	FAN342
Raymond Leslie Morris The A34 Child Murderer	1969	Austin Cambridge & Ford Corsair	158BOC 492LOP
Alfred Arthur Rouse The Blazing Car Murderer	1931	Morris Minor	MU1468
Dr Buck Ruxton The Lancaster Wife Murderer	1936	Hillman Minx	ATC272

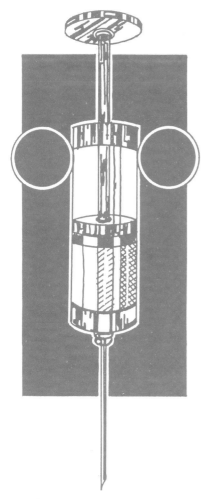

Dr Pepper.

The Death Doctors

The Beastly Science, that is what — opposed to the *art* of pure medicine — they called the anatomising, the cutting up, of the dead, whether for the academic purpose of the study of human anatomy, or for the more severely practical reason of uncovering homicidal foul play. Its more seemly title was, originally, Medical Jurisprudence, superseded later by Forensic Medicine.

A discipline hailing, like so many other dubious practices, from the Continent, it was not until the end of the eighteenth century that an interest was displayed in it in Britain. And then it was in Scotland that the cradle of jurisprudential medicine was to be found. In 1807 the Crown created the first Chair of Medical Jurisprudence at the University of Edinburgh. Thirty-two years were to elapse before a similar Regius Professorship was established at Glasgow University.

South of the Border, it was not until 1831 that Dr Alfred Swaine Taylor, accepting at the tender age of twenty-five a newly-created Chair at Guy's Hospital, in London, became the first English Professor of Medical Jurisprudence. He brought to his novel position the benefit of a great deal of special knowledge and experience acquired in the course of prolonged tours of the medical schools of Europe. In 1844 he published what became a standard text-book, *A Manual of Medical Jurisprudence*, and the new branch of medicine seemed to be gaining recognition and respectability. And then, in 1859, came a crashing blow.

A Dr Thomas Smethurst was charged with the murder of his bigamous wife. Professor Swaine Taylor, in his capacity as leading toxicologist, was called in. At the magistrates' hearing he confidently declared that he had discovered arsenic in the tissues of the dead woman's body, but by the time of the trial he found himself obliged to tell the Court that he had since concluded that the arsenic had come from an imperfection in the apparatus which he had used in his tests. As a result, Smethurst, who was undoubtedly guilty of dispatching the lady with ignominy and antimony, escaped his just dues. It was a terrible setback for medical jurisprudence. Press, public and orthodox medicine lost all faith in it, and for the next fifty years never viewed its pronouncements with anything other than healthy suspicion.

The redemption of British forensic medicine, the smoothing of the ruffles caused by the disastrous Smethurst affair, fell to the lot of three doctors – Pepper, Luff and Willcox – on the staff of St Mary's Hospital, in Praed Street, Paddington, London, and their protégé, young Dr Spilsbury. The year was 1910. The occasion, the Crippen case.

Dr Augustus Joseph Pepper, senior of the quartet, had come to St Mary's in 1879 as surgical tutor and pathologist. A great character, well read and never at a loss for an apt quotation from English literature, he was affectionately nicknamed 'Professor' Pepper, after a well known comedian of the time. A surgeon of very considerable skill, he operated at St Mary's from 1882 until 1910. His prowess in pathology, too, was such that he had been appointed pathologist to the Home Office. Among Pepper's previous triumphs was the Druce case, with its weird riddle of the draper or the duke, only to be answered by an exhumation; the Moat Farm murder, with his classic identification of a body which had lain in a drain for three years, and his astonishing determination from the evidence of such ancient wounds that the death had been a murder and not a suicide; and his unravelling of the grisly secrets of the trunk in the Devereux case.

Slightly junior to Pepper was Arthur P. Luff. Born in 1855, he had first come to St Mary's as Lecturer in Forensic Medicine in 1887, and had been a staff physician since 1890. Before that he had been a colleague of the great Sir Thomas Stevenson – successor to Swaine Taylor at Guy's, Toxicological Adviser and Analyst to the Home Office for thirty years, and foremost forensic expert of his day. Luff, too, was a Home Office analyst.

William Willcox had arrived at St Mary's as a student in 1895. Twenty years younger than Pepper, he had proved exceptionally gifted. His special interests were chemistry, pathology, toxicology and forensic medicine. In 1907 he also had been appointed an analyst to the Home Office.

Bernard Henry Spilsbury had, at the age of thirty-one, ascended at Pepper's retirement, and on his recommendation, to his old master's position of Senior Pathologist to St Mary's.

The medico-legal performance of Pepper and Luff and Willcox and Spilsbury in the Crippen case completed the work of restoration begun by Pepper back in the 1880s. The mantle of Luff fell upon Willcox. The mantle of Pepper fell upon Spilsbury, who for the next three decades would dominate a new era in the refurbished practice of forensic medicine.

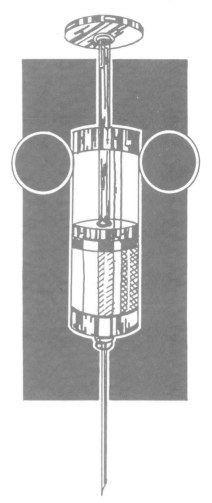

Dr William Willcox.

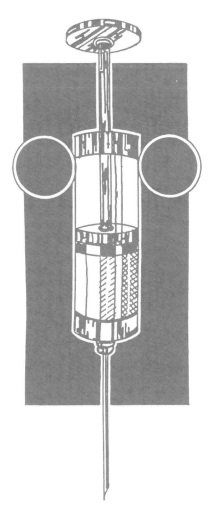

Dr Bernard Spilsbury.

Case Card on Sir Bernard Spilsbury

Sir Bernard Henry Spilsbury was a charismatic figure. For nearly forty years he shared top billing with all the great murderers and mutilators of the post-Victorian Great Age of Murder. To the man on the Clapham omnibus he was a sort of Sherlock Holmes – no pipe, but fifty cigarettes a day – of the mysterious world of mortuaries and lantern-lit midnight exhumations. 'He stood for pathology as Hobbs stood for cricket or Dempsey for boxing or Capablanca for chess,' said Edgar Lustgarten.

Tall, handsome, sprucely suited by Savile Row, bowler-hatted by Lock of St James's, always a blood-red carnation in his button-hole, he nonetheless contrived, with his ruddy complexion and bucolic air, to look more like a gentleman farmer than an habitué of morgue and dissecting room. But his shirt-sleeves gave the Holmesian clue. He had them made detachable, so that his cuffs would not crease from continual rollings-up.

Born in Leamington Spa, Warwickshire, in January 1877 – eleven years before the Jack the Ripper murders – he was the son of an analytical and manufacturing chemist. In 1899 he entered the St Mary's Hospital Medical School, Paddington, London. He qualified in 1905 and was immediately appointed Resident Assistant Pathologist, thus joining the holy trinity – Doctors A. J. Pepper, A. P. Luff and William Willcox – in direct apostolic succession to the founding father line of English medical jurisprudence.

His breakthrough to enduring celebrity came in 1910, when he identified the filleted flesh mass dug up in Dr Crippen's cellar as, despite absence of head, limbs, bones and genitals, Mrs Crippen, and that good lady's goodnight drink as hyoscine. From that time forward, Spilsbury (knighted in 1923) plied skilful scalpel, mean microscope and trusty test tube with dour, obsessive thoroughness to such effect that, in the words of Dr Richard Gordon, 'he could achieve single-handed all the legal consequences of homicide – arrest, prosecution, conviction and final post-mortem – requiring only the brief assistance of the hangman.' Such was the clarity of his expert witness and the weight of his utterance, that his word became positively biblical, his authority seldom challenged, save once, a chirrupy young barrister of recent call asking him: 'When did you last examine a *live* patient, Sir Bernard?' His single-minded purposiveness could shade into the macabre. Wishing to know the precise effect of a bullet penetrating skin, he practised shooting into an amputated leg donated by an obliging surgeon (memories of Holmes beating the subjects in the dissecting room to ascertain the

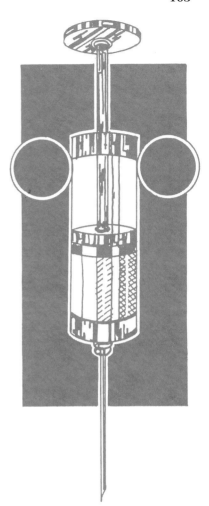

extent of post-mortem bruising). To discover the modus operandi of Joseph Brides-in-the-Bath Smith, he practically drowned a volunteer St Mary's nurse.

The latter part of Spilsbury's life was overshadowed by domestic tragedy. He and his wife were apart. A close woman friend died. His devoted sister died. His doctor son was killed in an air raid in 1940. Another son died of tuberculosis in 1945. In the mid-1940s Sir Bernard suffered three strokes. Severe arthritis made dissection difficult and painful. On 17 December 1947, he carried out at Hampstead the last of some 25,000 post-mortems, dined at his club, and gassed himself in his laboratory in University College, Gower Street – just a few streets away from where, in Store Street, his first 'big' murderer, Crippen, had once in the long-ago lived. Dr R. H. D. Short post-mortemed the post-mortem man. His finding: Death due to coronary thrombosis and carbon monoxide poisoning.

A lecture in progress at St Mary's Hospital Medical School 1904. Spilsbury is seated at the near end of the front row. Also in the picture is Willcox, seated in the front row on the near side of the gangway.

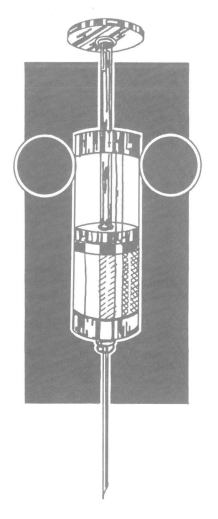

Case Card on Professor Keith Simpson

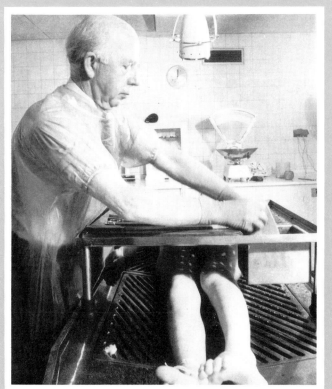

Dr Cedric Keith Simpson, upon whom the mantle of Sir Bernard Spilsbury fell, was, physically at any rate, somewhat swamped by it. A small, almost dainty man, with a great domed, bald head, fringed around with sandy-grey hair, dapper but sartorially undistinguished, what he did share with the Master was the quality of supreme thoroughness. He did not like Spilsbury, though. He believed that the great man was jealous of him.

The son of a Brighton family doctor of the old school and Scots descent, he was born there on 20 July 1907. Educated at Brighton Grammar School, he was admitted to Guy's Hospital Medical School, in London, in 1924. An outstanding student, the winner of five major prizes, including two gold medals, he qualified in 1930. He was to stay on as a teacher at Guy's for the whole of his professional life, becoming ultimately the head of its Department of Forensic Medicine. He began as Senior Demonstrator in Pathology, 1932-1937. Then, 1937-1946, London University Lecturer in Forensic Medicine, and, 1946-1962, Reader in Forensic Medicine. In 1962, he was appointed first Professor of Forensic Medicine in the University of London. Retiring in 1972, he was made Professor Emeritus.

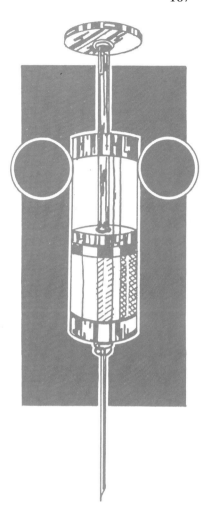

It was, according to himself, a soft heart that directed his steps towards the charnel-house and bone-yard. He could not stand the spectacle of living pain. He loathed to see people crying, distressed, dying in agony. He felt, like that worthy and humane philosopher, George Joseph Brides-in-the-Bath Smith, that 'When they're dead, they're dead', or, as the poet put it rather more elegantly, 'Beyond the need of weeping, Beyond the reach of hands . . .' He did not see the poor twisted and battered fragments of humanity that were his daily staple as men, women and children, but as three-dimensional jigsaw puzzles. He did not ask who is this? Who did this? His merely was to resolve how did this come about – murder, suicide, accident, natural causes?

When those little plump, pink, well-scrubbed hands of his were not busily unpicking the seams of one of his departed-hence fellow-creatures, they would very likely be coaxing the melodies of Mendelssohn or Brahms from the piano which he kept in his Weymouth Street mansion flat. He would sit there, wrapt, cascading notes of lovely music swirling all about him, his mind drifting away to the stone-slabbed problem in some dank morgue and, like as not, a murdered woman's severed head he had brought home with him sitting in the bath.

The little doctor figured in many of the important murder trials of his time – Sangret, Heath, Haigh, Hanratty, the Lucan murder – but that which was for him what the Crippen case was for Spilsbury, was the Dobkin case of 1942, when, from a handful of old bones turned up under a blitzed Baptist chapel in South London, he produced the complete evidence that sent a wife-killer to the gallows. Almost as spectacular was his spotting of two gallstones which led to his resurrection of Mrs Durand-Deacon from her acid-bath grave, and the consignment of John George Haigh to his via the scaffold. He was a pioneer of forensic dentistry, identifying for the first time, in 1948, a killer's teeth marks left on the victim's body (Goringe case), and an original percipient of the Battered Baby Syndrome, securing, in 1965, the first murder conviction for that abomination. He wanted to see the return of hanging.

Thrice married – in 1932 to a Guy's nurse, in 1956 to his secretary, and in 1982 to the widow of a coroner friend – and with a son, two daughters and ten grandchildren, Simpson professed to be a happy man. 'I enjoy life. I'm only sorry it is so short,' he once said. 'I never have any trouble getting out of bed ready to begin another day.' On 21 July 1985, the day after his seventy-eighth birthday, he was finally unable to get out of bed. He died, tragically, reduced by a brain tumour to a state of shambling confusion.

The Charnel House. The interior of the Old Paris Morgue.

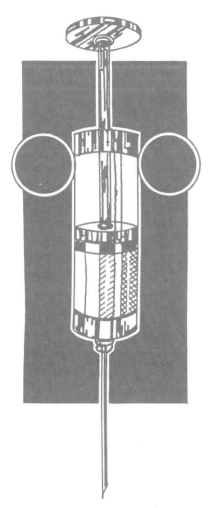

Case Card on
Professor Sir Sydney Smith

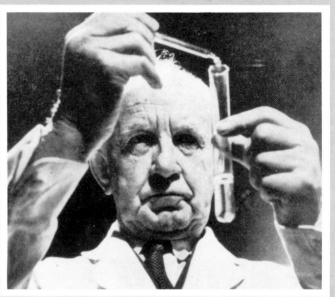

The Caledonian counterpart of Sir Bernard Spilsbury, the forensic Wizard of the North, embattled in his great granite laboratory north of the Border, was Sir Sydney Smith, who had come a long way round – via New Zealand and Cairo – to occupy the oldest Chair in Forensic Medicine in the British Isles. As a man the very reverse of Spilsbury, he was a warm, sociable, kindly human being, acutely aware of the pathos of crime and killing, tolerant of human nature, sensitive to other people's problems, paternalistic to young struggling doctors, such as Keith Simpson, for whom he became an *alter pater*. As a forensic pathologist, he displayed flair, ability and an enthusiasm for police problems well on a par with, if not surpassing in some respects, those of the slightly older Sir Bernard.

Veritably a Smith of Smiths, the son of an émigré Cockney, a road construction contractor, and a Yorkshirewoman, widowed and with six children from her previous marriage, Sydney Alfred Smith was born on August 4th, 1883, in the small New Zealand village of Roxburgh, in the heart of the Otago goldfield; a remote territory of gold-mining, sheep-farming and fruit-growing, where stage-coaches still ran, and the boy did not see a train until he was nearly fourteen.

It was, frankly, because it seemed to offer the best way to escape from the village to the adventures of the beckoning wide world, that Smith picked on medicine as a career. After leaving school he was lucky enough to land a job as apprentice at the local chemist's. He was also lucky when he invested the capital of his slender wages in speculation at the time of a gold-dredging boom, and made quite a lot of money, which he banked towards his future. His next move was to a position as assistant to a chemist in Dunedin, where he studied in his spare time, passed the exams and became a qualified pharmacist. That meant a better salary to save up. By 1908 he had enough to send himself to Edinburgh University, where, aided by various scholarships, he duly qualified as a doctor in 1912, and got married a week later. He had been awarded a research scholarship. He chose ophthalmology, but learning that a vacancy existed for an assistant under Professor Harvey Littlejohn in the department of forensic medicine, and that this carried a salary of £50 per annum, he went for that instead. Thus, almost accidentally, did he take up forensic medicine.

In 1914 he returned to New Zealand. The First World War broke out and he served in the New Zealand Army Corps, as well as continuing to carry out the civilian work of a Medical Officer of Health. At last, in 1917, he secured the post of Principal Medico-legal Expert to the Ministry of Justice in Egypt, and Professor of Forensic Medicine at the University of Egypt, and spent the next eleven years in Cairo, amassing enormous forensic experience.

In 1927 Professor Littlejohn died, and the following year Smith returned to Scotland to take up his Chair. He continued to occupy it with distinction as Regius Professor for the next quarter of a century. During that time he brought his formidable expertise to many celebrated cases, including that of Annie Hearn, in which he made himself available as a defence witness; Jeannie Donald, the Aberdeen child killer; and, with Glasgow colleagues, the Ruxton case. He crossed swords memorably with Spilsbury in the Sidney Fox case, and soldiered uneasily beside him in the battle to save Peter Queen in the Chrissie Gall strangling case.

Retiring from his Chair, and from the office of Dean of the Faculty of Medicine of Edinburgh University, which he had held since 1931, Smith was, in 1953, made Emeritus Professor. He died, weighed down with honours, on 8 May 1969, leaving a widow, a son and a daughter.

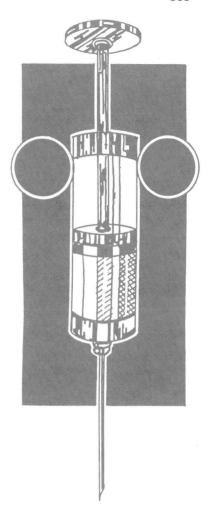

The dissecting room.

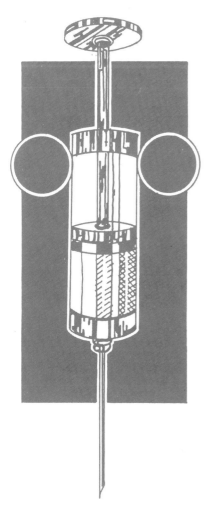

Case Card on Professor John Glaister

Westward some fifty miles across the narrow neck of lowland Scotland, Sir Sydney Smith's Glaswegian rival, Professor John Glaister, perched upon the commanding eminence of Gilmorehill, a fine eyrie overlooking as splendid a spread of criminous terrain at the hillfoot as heart of forensic pathologist could desire, coped valiantly with his geographically accorded portion of Scotia's unburiable dead.

Glaister, born, in May 1892, bred and schooled – the venerable High School – in Glasgow, enjoyed there a wonderful, middle-class, period childhood. A fine, comfortable Townhead home; a big garden with greenhouses; Norwegian pony in the stables where the brougham and the landau were kept; unforgettable Christmases, with special marzipan and almond cakes ordered direct from Germany, amazingly shaped ices and spun-sugar baskets with crystallized fruits; the scent of log fires, the cosy reek of oil lamps, flames in polished brass fenders, lace and velvet curtains, bobble-edged on thick, shining poles, securely drawn against the *other*, cold, grey, pinched, starving, cobbled Glasgow. Early in life he decided that unlike his father, also John, Regius Professor of Forensic Medicine in the University of Glasgow, he would go on the stage. Or if, by any mischance, an actor's life was not to be for him, then he would go to the bar as an advocate. His father persuaded him into medicine.

He qualified in March 1916, and within a few weeks was commissioned into the Royal Army Medical Corps. He served in Egypt. He married, in 1918, Isobel Rachel, the daughter of Sir John Lindsay, Town Clerk of Glasgow. She bore him two daughters. From 1919 to 1925 he worked as assistant in forensic medicine at Glasgow University, and in 1926 was called to the bar at the Inner Temple. Now doctor and barrister, he was appointed Lecturer in Forensic Medicine at Glasgow University.

In 1927 Sir Sydney Smith returned from Cairo to Edinburgh, and Glaister went out from Glasgow to Cairo, to act as Medico-legal Consultant to the Government of Egypt and as Professor of Forensic Medicine at Cairo University. He stayed out there until 1931, when he was appointed to his father's old Chair at Glasgow University. And there he remained for the next thirty-two years.

Unquestionably, the most spectacular of the thousands of cases in which Glaister was involved – not even forgetting his peripheral concern in the celebrated Merrett matricide case – was that of Dr Buck Ruxton, who, in 1935, murdered and cut up the bodies of his wife, Isabella, and their children's nursemaid, Mary Rogerson, and disposed their *disjecta membra* about a ravine at Gardenholme Linn, near Moffat. Working in conjunction with Edinburgh University's Regius Professor of Anatomy, James Couper Brash, and a team of other specialists, Glaister was the principal architect of a fantastic reconstruction and systematic identification of the bodies, employing the then novel technique of superimposing upon the positive portrait photograph of the deceased in life, the negative of a photograph of the skull, to demonstrate coincident features of identity, which is still regarded as a classic triumph of forensic medicine. Ruxton was hanged. For Glaister, an outstanding memory of the trial was, characteristically, theatrical. He had managed to get a seat in court for an old boyhood friend and fellow swimming club member, matinée idol actor, Jack Buchanan.

Resigning his Chair in 1962, Glaister was created Professor Emeritus. A kenspeckle character, pioneer of the precipitin test for the identification of human blood, author of several standard text books, acknowledged by Erle Stanley Gardner to be 'the man who furnishes Perry Mason with so many authentic facts', long remembered for his song and a smile piano performances with Sir Harry Lauder when both were house-guests of the millionaire Glasgow grocery baronet, Sir Thomas Lipton, John Glaister, a surviving character from a rapidly vanishing world, died in his eightieth year on 4 October 1971.

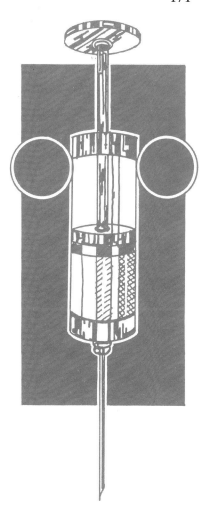

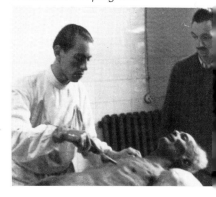

A dissection in progress.

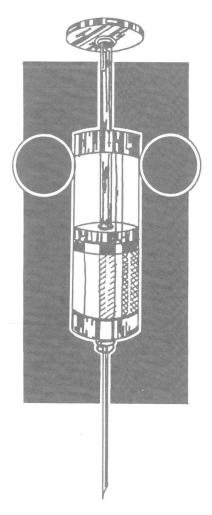

The horrors of identification.

Case Card on Professor Francis Camps

Francis Edward Camps, the son of an extremely wealthy physician and surgeon who tended the rich burgesses of turn-of-the-century Teddington, there first saw the light of day, a Wednesday's child, on 28 June 1905. After Marlborough, young Camps enrolled at Guy's, where he qualified in 1928. There followed a period in general practice at Chelmsford, Essex, before he decided, after a brief flirtation with obstetrics, to specialise in pathology. By 1945 he had got a first-footing into the London Hospital Medical College as a lecturer. By 1954 he had consolidated his position there by becoming Reader in Forensic Medicine. Finally, in 1963, he achieved the professorship. A truly wonderful type-specimen model of empire-building.

Throughout the nineteen-fifties and sixties, he appeared in a number of celebrated cases, including those of Donald Hume, Sergeant Emmett-Dunne, Dr Bodkin Adams, Master Sergeant Marymont and, most famous of all, the Christie case. To the public at large, as to himself, Camps was the pipe-smoking, English medical Maigret, but his medico-legal colleagues mustered rather less enthusiasm for him. He was the stormy petrel of pathology, provoking dislike, resentment and downright anger among his confrères.

It is a rebuttable presumption that doctors do not make good witnesses. Camps thought to identify the source of the defect as a fundamental lack of knowledge of court procedure, but unfortunately he proved incapable of himself bridging the gap between accurate diagnosis and effective therapy. Lord Justice Lawton, before whom he often appeared professionally, was not impressed by his performance, and Sir David Napley, Camps' close friend as well as his legal adviser, was disconcerted to find how he would say one thing in conference and something quite different in court.

Possessing, when he wished to exert it, great charm, he was also a difficult, unpredictable man, capable of sustaining a grudge. He ruined his own retirement dinner in 1970. Rising to reply to the toast to his health and happiness in his retirement, Camps launched into an unexpected, vicious and boorish attack on his non-attending fellow-pathologist, Keith Simpson, of whom he was known to be jealous, and what should have been a memorable and pleasant evening broke up prematurely in an atmosphere of embarrassment and rumbling disapproval. The final irony resultant upon Camps' intransigent nature was his unnecessary death – entirely due to his own wrong-headedness. Terrified to consult a doctor – he had no faith in them – about stomach pains which he was convinced were the symptoms of incurable cancer, on 8 July 1972, he collapsed and died – of a treatable ulcer. His greatest fear – other than that of cancer – had always been that his arch-enemy, Keith Simpson, would do the post-mortem on him. That did not come to pass either.

He married three times, and had a son and a daughter. His second wife, a consultant pathologist in Essex, was a lonely, tragic figure. After her death, he married again, in 1972, shortly before his own, Dr Ann E. Robinson, a forensic scientist.

With for many years a flat in Welbeck Street – latterly he moved to the Barbican – and a pleasant country house at Purleigh, in Essex, Camps lived well. His recreation was fishing. His clubs were the Savage and the Savile. He enjoyed good wine and good food, and went to the best restaurants, never more pleased than if he saw people there nudging one another and recognising him. His behavioural pattern – dawn rising after only four hours' sleep, a twenty-five-hour-day taken at the run, relentless monologue, whirlwind pm room methodology, passing through a mortuary like fire through a cornfield – points clearly to hypomania. It was buttressed though by alcohol and amphetamines.

Perhaps he was cantankerous, arrogant, querulous and despotic, but, warts and all, he was a visionary, a man of imagination and enthusiasm – albeit oft-times misplaced. The fact that the currency of his life was death, left unaffected a sense of fun that set him singing lusty sea-shanties with Lord Chief Justice Goddard at the Savage. Then . . . back to the mortuary to add one more to his highly questionable grand total of 88,000 post-mortems.

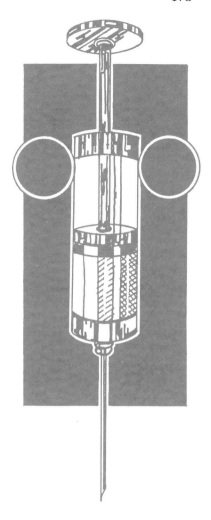

The Old Paris Morgue, a popular excursion place.

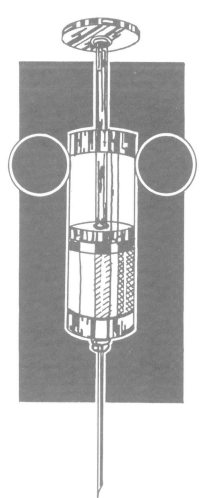

Case Card on Professor Donald Teare

To the Metropolitan Police, the principal trio of on-tap pathologists regularly called in on cases of irregular demise during the mid-decades of this century – Drs Simpson, Camps and Teare – were affectionately known as the Three Musketeers.

Dr Robert Donald Teare, although over the years involved in many leading cases – Jones and Hulten, Camb, Raven, Timothy Evans, Hume, Straffen, Chesney, and Podola – never courted or received the publicity which surrounded the other two, flashier swordsmen. But his reputation was of the highest where it counted; among the professionals.

According to Sir David Napley, who knew all three musketeers well, both in his public practice of law and in private friendship, Teare was the best pathologist; not only because of his ability, judgement, and lucid explanation of his investigations in the witness-box, but because also of his constant, overwhelming desire never to be unfair. A rather plain, thickset man, whose looks belied the attractiveness of his character, he was universally popular with his colleagues. Kind, gregarious, always ready to oblige, his brand of quiet unassuming charm is well illustrated by an incident at the Old Bailey. He and Simpson were both giving evidence, from different sides of the fence, in an abortion case. In cross-examination defending counsel put it to Teare: 'Can you think of any single person more experienced in this field than Dr Keith Simpson?' Teare, side-stepping, with a disarming smile: 'You embarrass me.' A 'situation' was avoided. Hardly surprising that Simpson should describe him as 'a much more endearing colleague than Camps: a solid, likeable man, with a good sense of humour,' echoing Napley's 'a most delightful person to know as a friend'. Indeed, Simpson could not recall a single occasion in forty years of their having any substantial difference of opinion. He described Teare as being competent both in the field and in the witness-box. Napley thought he had a streak of laziness in him. His approach to his cases seemed casual. In fact, he was 'the quintessence of thoroughness'. He had also an intellectual generosity which made him always prepared to consider any possibility and lent a sweet reasonableness to his attitude which made his firmly expressed conclusions all the more devastating.

He did not always confine his activities to the post-mortem room. In the so-called Cleft Chin Murder case of 1944, in which an American GI and his Welsh girlfriend shot a West London hire-car driver, Teare borrowed a skeleton, put it in the car seat where the dead man had been sitting, and, using a steel rod, traced the path of the bullet backwards from a dent in the near-side door panelling, through the skeleton's bones to the position in the back seat from which the gun was fired – proving its discharge, not in panic, but with murderous intent.

Born on 1 July 1911, Teare was educated at King William's College, Isle of Man, and went on to study medicine at Gonville and Caius College, Cambridge, and St George's Hospital, London. After qualifying, he specialised in pathology at St George's, where he ultimately became Consultant Pathologist. He, Simpson and Camps, all at the beginning of their careers in wartime London, used to meet regularly to wine and dine together at L'Etoile French restaurant, in Charlotte Street, and, in the late 1940s, over a meal to which they invited Sir Sydney Smith, at a little Soho restaurant, the Bon Accord, founded an Association in Forensic Medicine, which came to number in its membership every crime pathologist in the United Kingdom. Sadly, with growing success there came growing tensions between the Three Musketeers. Simpson and Teare realised that Camps was interpreting 'All for one' in a very personal sense, and increasingly grudging them cases, especially the headline-grabbing ones. There were frequent clashes between Simpson and Camps, who were not temperamentally dissimilar. Teare, being more self-effacing than the other two forensic turkey-cocks, was not much troubled by internecine confrontations. In 1960, Camps betook himself off and founded his own Academy of Forensic Sciences.

Teare became Lecturer in Forensic Medicine at St Bartholomew's Hospital Medical College. In 1963 he was appointed Reader in Forensic Medicine at Charing Cross Hospital Medical School, and, in 1967, Professor there. Married, with three sons and a daughter, he lived in Putney, London, and had also a house at Castletown, on the Isle of Man. He enjoyed gardening and golf. He retired, Professor Emeritus, in 1975, and died on 17 January 1979. He was only sixty-seven.

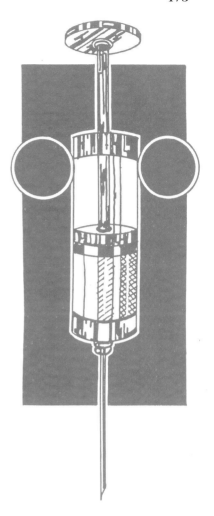

A scene from the New York Old Morgue on the shore of the East River.

Bang! Dead on Target

While the shadow of the noose lay across the muzzle, Britain had little in the way of gun crime, but over the years there were quite a few cases of 'private enterprise'. Here is a selection of fifteen 'rounds' of killers and calibres. . .

1903	Samuel Herbert Dougal	Murdered his mistress at the Moat Farm, Essex	Revolver .32
1910	John Alexander Dickman	The Newcastle Train Murder of John Nisbet	Two weapons used Automatic pistol .250 Pistol .350
1919	Ronald Light: Green Bicycle Case	The murder of Bella Wright	Webley Service Revolver .455
1920	Frederick Rothwell Holt	Shot his mistress	Webley Revolver
1923	Madame Fahmy	Shot her husband, Prince Ali Kamel Fahmy Bey at the Savoy	Browning automatic pistol .25
1924	Corporal Jack Goldenberg	Shot bank manager, William Hall, in course of robbery	Webley Revolver .455
1926	Alfonso Smith: Stella Maris Case	Shot his wife's lover	Webley Revolver
1927	Browne and Kennedy	Shot PC Gutteridge	Webley Revolver .455
1927 1954	John Donald Merrett	Shot his mother Committed suicide	Spanish 'King' automatic .25 Colt automatic
1932	Elvira Barney	Shot her lover	Smith and Wesson .32
1947	Antiquis Case	Shot by jewel thieves	Revolver .320
1952	Craig and Bentley	Shot PC Sidney Miles	Eley Service Revolver .455
1955	Ruth Ellis	Shot her lover	Smith and Wesson Revolver
1959	Guenther Podola	Shot Detective Sergeant Raymond Purdy	'Random' automatic pistol 9mm
1962	James Hanratty: The A6 Case	Shot Michael Gregsten	Revolver .38

Murder: A Poetic Truth

Oscar Wilde and the Hanged Man

The poetic chronicle of how a great writer, himself in dire straits, cast an artist's eye on a horseman and Death as they passed him by, and transmuted the base metal of common disaster into the gold of noble tragedy.

If revenants there be, surely the echoing halls, the brooding landings, the dank and stone-deaf cells of Reading Gaol are territories of ghosts; the haunting ground of two sad wraiths at least – the Poet and the Soldier.

They came, these twin unhappy shades, each by his separate *via dolorosa*, close on a hundred years ago now, to this iron-bound station or terminus.

The poet was Oscar Wilde. The prison gates clanged behind him here on 21 November 1895. All out of the blaze of fame and yellow nineties' sunlight, into the murk and gloom of the hard-stoned yard, a heartbreak's odyssey by horse-drawn Black Maria – to Reading by way of Bow Street, the Old Bailey,

Reading Gaol.

Holloway, Newgate, Pentonville, Wandsworth and that plat-form at Clapham Junction, where, like one much greater than he, he was spat upon, *in vinculis*. A six months' journey, or way of the cross, to the personal crucifixion of C.3.3. – Block C. Landing 3. Cell 3.

The soldier, Trooper Charles Thomas Wooldridge, of Her Majesty's Royal Horse Guards, arrived on a capital charge, at Reading in April 1896.

> *Like two doomed ships that pass in storm*
> *We had crossed each other's way:*
> *But we made no sign, we said no word,*
> *We had no word to say;*
> *For we did not meet in the holy night,*
> *But in the shameful day.*

Oscar Wilde at about the time of his imprisonment.

The first weeks of March 1896, found Trooper Charles Thomas Wooldridge of the Royal Horse Guards extremely dejected. His regiment had only recently been ordered back from Windsor to Regent's Park Barracks, in London, and the prime cause of the trooper's dissatisfaction was his wife – or, rather, the lack of her.

It was in the course of his two years of service at Windsor that Wooldridge had met and fallen in love with a twenty-two-year-old local assistant postmistress, Laura Ellen Glendell. The couple had married, secretly, on 9 October 1894, at St Martin's Church, in Kentish Town, North London – secretly because in those days a soldier was required to seek and obtain his commanding officer's consent before he was permitted to marry. In Wooldridge's case, this necessary permission had not been given. Perhaps it had not even been sought. In any event, the result was that, in the army's eyes, Charlie and Nellie, as he called his wife, were not officially married; which meant that when his regiment moved to London there was no provision for a wife to accompany him. Nellie had, therefore, had to stay behind in Windsor; remaining in the house in Arthur Road, a pleasant, leafy thoroughfare running from Windsor railway station to the village of Clewer, which she and her husband had shared with Miss Annie Cox, a relative variously described as a cousin or niece of Wooldridge's. Laura Wooldridge continued to be known by her maiden name. She carried on, too, with her job, working in the post office at Eton.

Rumour has it that the marriage had for some time not been a happy one. There was an alleged history of ill-treatment by the husband. The situation is said to have become one of such acute bad usage that Nellie complained, presumably without revealing her marital status, to Wooldridge's CO, who warned him forthwith that he should not visit Miss Glendell again. All this, so far at any rate as Wooldridge was concerned, was in the past, and now, bereft of his wife's company, feeling strange and out-of-water in his new metropolitan surroundings, needing the comfort of reassurance, Wooldridge got himself aboard a Windsor-bound train and turned up unexpectedly on the doorstep at Arthur Road. It is not – bearing in mind those recent past events which Wooldridge had so conveniently put out of his – perhaps surprising that his wife received this sudden appearance with extreme frigidity, expressly pointing out to him, in fact, that he had 'a pretty good cheek' in coming there at all.

Nothing if not optimistically persistent, Wooldridge, within days, called again. His reception was similarly Icelandic. But, stoked up by a two-way flood of hot words, grew more heated. The steam thereof built to an explosive pressure. Suddenly, beside himself, all noble resolutions evaporated in the climbing temperature, Wooldridge lashed out, landing a stinging blow full on Nellie's face, sending her crashing to the floor.

Alice Cox, upstairs, hearing the scuffle and weeping of the

rapidly blown up turmoil, came hurrying down to find out what was the matter. Wooldridge was standing distraughtly contrite over his prostrate wife, swaying slightly, fingers twitching like panicky pink-white mice, muttering 'Oh, what have I done now? What have I done now?' Then, seeing Alice, his voice rose hysterically, and shouting a rhetorical 'Oh, why does she try my temper so?' to the inattentive universe at large, he fled wildly out of the house: only to return, sheepish, shame-faced and crestfallen, a while later, bearing in tentative hand a letter addressed to Nellie. It was very pathetic, abundant in repentance, lush with protestations of affection and brimful of terms of endearment – an emotional drunkard's promissory pledge-taking lament. And about as reliable. A full-foaming glass of penitence, topped with a fine froth of good intentions. In it he assured her that she was safe from all thought, word and act of molestation by him. In it he promised never to darken her door again until she invited him. Was there, he inquired, anyone else that she cared for? He begged her humbly to be faithful. He reminded her that he had only two more years to serve in the army, and hinted that perhaps she might love him again and join him when he had finished his time. He took upon himself all the blame for their recent and sudden estrangement. 'It's very hard lines,' he wrote, 'but it's all my own silly fault.' Deeper than that, self-abasement could hardly go. His wife received this submissive missive without comment. Meekly, the lion-turned-lamb bowed himself out of the little house which he had with such violence defiled. He asked Alice Cox to walk with him to the train, and all the way to the station poured forth a ceaseless cascade of contrition and an endless expression of bewilderment at the upsetting way in which Nellie had been behaving lately.

As a consequence of that little marital visitation, 'Miss Glendell' was so facially disfigured that she had perforce to dissemble to the solicitous postmaster, explaining that she had 'fallen downstairs'.

The trooper's next ill-starred appearance at Arthur Road – without, it must be pointed out, benefit of invitation – was on Friday, 27 March. This time he behaved impeccably; spoke and conducted himself in a warily affectionate manner, kept his fists unknotted. But the iceberg did not melt. He did, nevertheless, before going quietly, succeed in extracting from Nellie a promise that she would come up to London and meet him outside the barracks on the following Sunday afternoon, 29 March. As she was giving him this promise, she at the same time handed him a document to sign. Although she had written it herself, she had obviously been advised in the matter by a lawyer. It was an undertaking that he would not molest her in any way in the future.

On Sunday afternoon Wooldridge *did* wear his scarlet – figuratively, but actually his *blue* – coat. As Oscar Wilde protested, when taken to task by an overly literal-minded undergraduate who wrote to point out that the trooper was in the 'Blues', it would have been impossible to open his poem:

> *He did not wear his azure coat,*
> *For blood and wine are blue . . .*

Togged out all spick and span, pill-box cap and swagger-cane, he eagerly awaited his Nellie's arrival. He asked the main-gate sentry to keep a look out for her and signal to him the moment she appeared. The watches ticked by. The sentries changed. Nellie did not appear. Came dusk. Then darkness. Still no sign. Trooper Wooldridge took a deliberate decision. He counted up his money, pennies and shillings and sixpences of loose change. Found that he had enough to get him to Windsor. From a fellow-soldier he borrowed a cut-throat razor. Fatal indication of preformed intent – *mens rea*. This would, as in the fullness of time things turned out, militate disastrously against him in the matters of manslaughter and judicial recommendation to mercy. He stuffed Nellie's 'legal' document, signed and stamped, in his pocket. Then, telling a puzzled sentry, 'I have to go to Windsor tonight. I must go. I'm going to do some damage', walked out of barracks without leave.

On the interminable-seeming train journey down, Wooldridge brooded on what Alice Cox had told him, or perhaps hinted at – as good as told him; that Nellie was sweet on a corporal in the 2nd Regiment Life Guards, stationed at Windsor. The blood rushed in his ears. His head ached. Heat welled up from the very centre of him.

Arrived at last at Arthur Road, everything there looking somehow strange, hostile and menacingly different from usual, he obtained entrance, as the police phrase goes, by saying that he had brought some papers relating to a separation which he needed his wife to sign. Alice Cox left him in the parlour and retired tactfully upstairs. Presently Nellie came down. The parlour door closed. Mere minutes later, a terrible scream cut like a scimitar through the warm, safely fusty atmosphere of the house, striking a piercing chill into the heart of Alice Cox. It was followed by the sound of someone running, bursting out of the front door.

Shaking with fright, Alice Cox dashed to the window – and froze in horror at what she saw. Nellie was lying puddled in blood in the middle of the road, her crazed-looking husband kneeling over her. What had happened was that when Charlie and Nellie had started discussing their situation, another row had flared up, and, in a blind fury, Wooldridge had slashed his wife across the face with the razor. She had rushed screaming out of the house, but before she had reached the iron gate separating the forecourt from the road, he had caught up with her. As they struggled, locked in lethal embrace, he slit her throat twice, completing his dreadful knife-work in the middle of the road.

Drawn by the appalling commotion, people were already

Oscar Wilde's Cell, C.3.3, in Reading Gaol.

THE ILLUSTRATED
POLICE BUDGET
THE LEADING ILLUSTRATED POLICE JOURNAL IN ENGLAND

No. 148.   SATURDAY, APRIL 4, 1896.   ONE PENNY

Trooper Wooldridge murders his wife.

running towards, and gathering in mesmerised shock about, the obscene tableau at the road centre. One of them was the beat policeman, Constable Henry Miles. Wooldridge, rising from his transfixion, casting wide about him his unseeing gaze, like one awakening from a dream, surrendered himself immediately into the rurally mittened hands of the law. 'Take me,' he said. 'I have killed my wife.'

How disappointing to discover that Wilde's noble trooper was a mere common or garden wife-battering psychopath. Obviously, Wilde knew none of this, and probably saw him as the undeserving victim of some poisonous harpy.

The trial was held at Reading Assizes, before Mr Justice Hawkins, on 18 June 1896. Counsel for the defence, Mr Walsh, submitted that, in the light of his wife's unfaithfulness, Wooldridge had acted under great provocation, believing, rightly or wrongly, that, in his own words, his wife had been 'carrying on a fine game.' That she *had* formed an attachment elsewhere, and that her husband knew of it, emerged early in the trial. What was not, and never has been, established, was the extent of that attachment, and whether it was guilty or perfectly harmless. Counsel, citing a persuasive dictum of Mr Justice Blackburne's, suggested that the jury might, in such circumstances, properly reduce Wooldridge's guilt to that of manslaughter. But 'Anging 'Awkins would have none of it, and summed up strongly against the prisoner. The jury, absent barely ten minutes, brought in a verdict of guilty, with a rider recommending Wooldridge to mercy. Mercy was not forthcoming. Petitions, numerously signed, to the Home Secretary, Sir Matthew Ridley, and begging gracious clemency of the Queen, were rejected.

Wooldridge displayed throughout considerable courage and fortitude. Asked by the Clerk of Arraigns if he had anything to say why sentence of death should not be passed upon him, he stood smartly with folded arms and replied firmly, 'Nothing, sir.'

Mr Justice Wills.

The Judge then told him: 'The law does not permit me to pass upon you any other sentence than that of death . . .'

> The man in red who reads the Law
>   Gave him three weeks of life,
> Three little weeks in which to heal
>   His soul of his soul's strife,
> And cleanse from every blot of blood
>   The hand that held the knife.

As the last solemn words of the death sentence, '. . . And may the Lord have mercy on your soul,' died away, the prisoner, having listened calmly to the pronouncement of his doom, smiled at two or three people at the back of the court, before, still holding himself very erect, he passed out of sight.

Trooper Wooldridge was brought back to Reading Gaol and placed in the condemned cell, where the warders watched

> His anguish night and day;
> Who watched him when he rose to weep,
>   And when he crouched to pray;
> Who watched him lest himself should rob
>   Their scaffold of its prey.

For Wilde and the other convicts, in an atmosphere of mounting tension and dread, prison routine clanked as ceaselessly and implacably on as the treadmill.

> We tore the tarry rope to shreds
>   With blunt and bleeding nails;
> We rubbed the doors, and scrubbed the floors,
>   And cleaned the shining rails:
> And, rank by rank, we soaked the plank,
>   And clattered with the pails.

The last photograph. Wilde in Rome.

> *We sewed the sacks, we broke the stones,*
> *   We turned the dusty drill:*
> *We banged the tins, and bawled the hymns,*
> *   And sweated on the mill:*
> *But in the heart of every man*
> *   Terror was lying still.*

It was the first time for nineteen years that an execution was to take place at Reading, so it was, naturally, an event that loomed large and menacing upon the prison's circumscribed horizon. In fact, the scaffold there had been used only once since its installation for a double execution, that of Henry Tidbury and George Francis, hanged on 12 March 1877, for the murder of two policemen while trying to avoid arrest for poaching.

In key with the brutal tenor of the times, the authorities made no attempt to hide from the other prisoners their bustling preparations for the grim Gallows' Lupercalia. The scaffold was erected in a little shed – wooden, oblong, narrow, with a glass roof – like, said Wilde, 'a photographer's studio on the sands at Margate. For eighteen months I thought it *was* the studio for photographing prisoners. There is no adjective to describe it. I call it "hideous" because it became so to me after I knew its use.' The shed was situated distressingly close to the exercise yard.

Trooper Wooldridge's three clear Sundays in the condemned cell drained inexorably away. He seldom referred to his crime, but he is said to have listened to the ministrations of the chaplain in a humble spirit, to have shown true penitence, and to have expressed his sorrow at having taken his wife's life, saying that he hoped to meet her in heaven.

On the afternoon before the execution, Monday, 6 July, the hangman, apparelled in appropriate black clothes, black necktie and black skull-cap, relieved only by the sporting of the blue ribbon of the teetotaller, Billington, hairdresser of Bolton, arrived at the prison. Having viewed his client from a hidden vantage point and assessed his height and weight, he arranged for a 6ft 6in drop, and tested the gallows. Mr Hangman Billington's attention was drawn to the fact that the drop of his choosing was considerably in excess of the scale officially laid down, but he insisted that in the circumstances his drop was the correct one.

In the course of that same afternoon, Wilde, tramping with other prisoners in from work to the cells, passed an open grave

> *With yawning mouth the yellow hole*
> *   Gaped for a living thing;*
> *The very mud cried out for blood*
> *   To the thirsty asphalte ring:*
> *And we knew that ere one dawn grew fair*
> *   Some prisoner had to swing.*

> *Right in we went, with soul intent*
> *On Death and Dread and Doom:*
> *The hangman, with his little bag,*
> *Went shuffling through the gloom:*
> *And each man trembled as he crept*
> *Into his numbered tomb.*

Then fell night upon the prison, its swaddling dark pinions blotting out every last vestige of the light of day, peopling the corridors and long steel landings with forms of Fear.

> *And up and down the iron town*
> *Stole feet we could not hear,*
> *And through the bars that hide the stars*
> *White faces seemed to peer.*

And warders' eyes that night at Judas holes beheld 'men knelt to pray, who never prayed before.'

> *At six o'clock we cleaned our cells,*
> *At seven all was still,*
> *But the sough and swing of a mighty wing*
> *The prison seemed to fill,*
> *For the Lord of Death with icy breath*
> *Had entered in to kill.*

At a quarter to eight the great bell of St Lawrence's Church nearby began solemnly to toll. Breath held, the prison waited for the stroke of eight. At this moment Wooldridge, who we are told had submitted to the preliminary pinioning 'with marvellous firmness', was being conducted from the condemned cell to the gallows shed, both of which were situated only a few steps away from the entrance to the three ordinary cell blocks. The procession was made up of the Governor, the chaplain, the doctor and Under-Sheriff, in addition to the executioner, two warders and the condemned man. Arrived in the shed, Wooldridge is said to have taken his stand on the trap-door under the beam almost as if he were on parade. Billington fastened his feet, adjusted the white cap, and drew the bolt . . . Wooldridge died bravely, without a struggle, word or cry.

Wilde never saw the condemned man after his conviction, but he told one of the prison warders with whom he had become friendly that 'those moments when the bell rang out, and my imagination conjured up the execution scene, were the most awful of a time rich in horror.'

> *And as one sees most fearful things*
> *In the crystal of a dream,*
> *We saw the greasy hempen rope*
> *Hooked to the blackened beam,*
> *And heard the prayer the hangman's snare*
> *Strangled into a scream.*

There is no chapel on the day
On which they hang a man:
The Chaplain's heart is far too sick,
Or his face is far too wan,
Or there is that written in his eyes
Which none should look upon.
Illustration by Arthur Wragg

The Hotel d'Alsace, Rue des Beaux-Arts, Paris, where the shadow he had long been expecting lay in soft wait for him.

At a quarter past eight, the employees of the the local biscuit factory, Huntley & Palmer's, passed the portals of the prison on their way to breakfast. Not a single one paused to discuss the tragedy enacted within. Few even glanced at the black flag hoisted and fluttering like a throttled rook from the pole above the entrance to the gaol.

In accordance with the law's decree, Wooldridge's body was left to swing and turn on the gently oscillating, squeaking rope's end in the execution shed for a statutory hour. It was then taken down, hauled from the pit for rapid inquest, and pronounced coldly dead by the prison doctor, who, in Wilde's memorable phrase, 'said that Death was but a scientific fact.' Then, in a burning winding-sheet of lime, they hid the crook-necked corpse away.

> *The Warders strutted up and down,*
> *And kept their herd of brutes,*
> *Their uniforms were spick and span,*
> *And they wore their Sunday suits,*
> *But we knew the work they had been at,*
> *By the quicklime on their boots.*

The gates that had closed behind the Poet and the Soldier, had opened for Trooper Wooldridge.

> *And he of the swollen purple throat,*
> *And the stark and staring eyes,*
> *Waits for the holy hands that took*
> *The Thief to Paradise;*
> *And a broken and a contrite heart*
> *The Lord will not despise.*

The Soldier had slipped away.

For the Poet, the prison gates would never really open at all. Throughout the short remainder of his life, he would be, like all of us, only more so, Dumas' condemned man under indefinite reprieve. When, after his release from prison, Wilde visited a palmist in Paris, she looked at the palm of his pudgy right hand and said: 'I am puzzled. By your line of life you died two years ago.'

It was ten months after the hanging of C.T.W. that, on 18 May 1897, Oscar Wilde left Cell 3. Landing 3. Block C. to be released out of Pentonville early the following morning. On the evening of Wednesday, 19 May, he caught a train from West Croydon to Newhaven, and the night boat to Dieppe. Settled, under the name of Sebastian Melmoth, in the little Normandy village of Berneval-sur-Mer, Wilde began to write *The Ballad of Reading Gaol*. It was, he later claimed, 'an idea that came to me while I was in the dock, waiting for my sentence to be pronounced.' If that is really so, another romantic notion perishes in the rose-red dust of Petra. What is certainly true, is that Wilde had been reading Housman's *A Shropshire Lad*, and derived inspiration for both metre and subject from it.

What is also true, is that even short distance from it seems to have lent enchantment to Wilde's view of Reading Gaol. According to his friend, Robert Ross, it became for him, in retrospect, a sort of enchanted castle. Its kindly governor, Major Nelson, successor to the ill-wished, ill-favoured, ill-natured governor, Major Isaacson, whom Wilde likened to Sulla, 'a mulberry-coloured Dictator', and described as having 'the eyes of a ferret, the body of an ape, and the soul of a rat', was the presiding good fairy. On the discredit side, along with the despotic Isaacson, was the chaplain, the Reverend T. Martin Friend, an ineffectual and not especially noble specimen of the human species, and Brutality's greasy-white-bearded lackey, the prison doctor, Oliver C. Maurice, who 'resembled a bullying director of a sham city company', and whose Hippocratic Oath had better been designated Hypocritic. But now, within mere hours of release, 'the prison's machicolated turrets were turned into minarets, the warders were benevolent Mamelukes', and Oscar's three companions at Dieppe – More Adey, Robbie Ross and Reggie Turner – paladins reclaiming him after his captivity.

Did the execution of a fellow-prisoner provide, in that claustrophobic milieu, the vital traumatic catalyst that made to coalesce vague notions weaving and wavering in Wilde's mind as, in May 1895, he stood in 'the black dock's dreadful pen'? Was the writing of *The Ballad* a kind of acting-out at one remove of Dr Johnson's shrewd, 'Depend upon it, Sir, when a man knows he is to be hanged in a fortnight, it concentrates his mind wonderfully.' And was the fruit of this new concentration the cathartic vision that the tragedy was *his* every bit as much as Wooldridge's?

Wilde had sounded previously the cry of Marsyas in an earlier poem, *Panthea*:

> . . . *for we are part*
> *Of every rock and bird and beast and hill,*
> *One with the things that prey on us, and one with what*
> *   we kill.*

And echoes it in *The Ballad*:

> *Yet each man kills the thing he loves,*
> *   By each let this be heard,*
> *Some do it with a bitter look,*
> *   Some with a flattering word,*
> *The coward does it with a kiss,*
> *   The brave man with a sword!*

There was, of course, a liberal element of the dramatist's self-dramatisation, but Wooldridge, the image of reality, guilt made flesh, and Wilde himself, his own parable's mirror image of guilt, became merged identities in the fevered alembic of his displaced artist's imagination. He *was* Wooldridge. Wooldridge *was* him. Each had killed the thing he loved.

Wilde's last room at the Hotel d'Alsace.

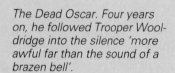

The Dead Oscar. Four years on, he followed Trooper Wooldridge into the silence 'more awful far than the sound of a brazen bell'.

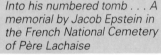

Into his numbered tomb . . . A memorial by Jacob Epstein in the French National Cemetery of Père Lachaise

The first draft of the poem was completed by mid-July. Wilde was not at all sure that he liked it. 'Catastrophes in life bring about catastrophes in art,' he observed tartly. Nevertheless, *The Ballad* was completed at Posilipo, in October 1897. It was to be his swan-song, the only work of literature that he wrote in the last three years of his life. It was also his one great and really sincere poem. And it was an immense success.

Too late . . . too late . . . Now, for Sebastian Melmoth, the wanderer, the albatross days were closing in. . . . yellow brilliance to umber and penumbra, as came still evening on. The lost Lord of Language, with 'a level of suavity that, like the lawns of Oxford had centuries of culture behind it,' stammered his well-practised litany of roseate regrets between the fireflies, the begged cigarettes and bestowed wine of charity. His Calvary and his conversion, long put-off when the blood was still thick and fast-flowing, awaited him in the dingy first-floor apartment with the lethal lees-of-wine, magenta wall-paper. His last *pension*. His condemned cell. It was not the hangman, but the shadow which he had for some time now been expecting, that he found lying in soft wait for him in the doorway of the Hôtel d'Alsace, in the Rue des Beaux-Arts, in Paris. This was the appointment in Samarra made in Reading not, it seemed, so very long ago.

On 30 November 1900, life struck the fetters from the lamed limbs of Oscar Wilde; death finally opened the prison gates for the Poet. On his tomb in Père Lachaise they carved the epitaph that in his poem he wrote for the Soldier and himself . . .

> *And alien tears will fill for him*
> *Pity's long-broken urn,*
> *For his mourners will be outcast men,*
> *And outcasts always mourn.*

Murder in Fact and Fiction

Do you like to take your murder neat – or do you prefer it filtered through fiction? There is no denying that life supplies the best plots. Here is a select library list of real-life murders and the novels which they inspired.

Adelaide Bartlett	Ford, Elbur. *Poison in Pimlico* (1950) Symons, Julian. *Sweet Adelaide* (1980)
Black Dahlia Case	Ellroy, James. *The Black Dahlia* (1987)
Mary Blandy	Morgan, Joan. *The Hanging Wood* (1950) Stubbs, Jean *My Grand Enemy* (1967)
Lizzie Borden	Wilkins, Mary. *The Long Arm* (1895) Dougal, Lily. *The Summit House Mystery* (1905) Lowndes, Mrs Belloc. *Lizzie Borden* (No date) Bierstadt, Edward. *Satan Was a Man* (1935) Hunter, Evan. *Lizzie* (1984)
Deacon Brodie	Bramble, Forbes. *The Strange Case of Deacon Brodie* (1975)
Elizabeth Brownrigg Elizabeth Canning	Tey, Josephine. *The Franchise Affair* (1948)
The Bravo Case	Lowndes, Mrs Belloc. *What Really Happened* (1926) Rickard, Mrs Victor. *Not Sufficient Evidence* (1926) Shearing, Joseph. *For Her to See* (1947) Jenkins, Elizabeth. *Dr Gully* (1972)
Burke and Hare	Byrd, Elizabeth. *Rest Without Peace* (1974)
Dr Thomas Neill Cream	Cashman, John. *The Gentleman from Chicago* (1974)
Dr Hawley Harvey Crippen	Bloom, Ursula. *The Girl Who Loved Crippen* (No date)
Samuel Herbert Dougal	White, R. J. *The Smartest Grave* (1961)
Christiana Edmunds	Carr, John Dickson. *The Black Spectacles* (1939)
The Starr Faithful Case	Scoppettone, Sandra. *Some Unknown Person* (1977)
William Gardiner	White, R. J. *The Women of Peasenhall* (1969)
Catherine Hayes	Thackeray, William. *Catherine* (1839)

Jack the Ripper	Lowndes, Mrs Belloc. *The Lodger* (1913) Barry, John Brooks. *The Michaelmas Girls* (1975) Gordon, Richard. *The Private Life of Jack the Ripper* (1980) Bloch, Robert. *The Night of the Ripper* (1984)
Constance Kent	Ford, Elbur. *Such Bitter Business* (1953)
Marie Lafarge	Shearing, Joseph. *The Lady and the Arsenic* (1937)
Henri Landru	Wiser, William. *Disappearances* (1980)
Jessie M'Lachlan	Goodchild, George & Roberts, C. E. B. *The Dear Old Gentleman* (1935) Muir, D. E. *In Muffled Night* (1933)
Maria Manning	Dickens, Charles. *Bleak House* (1853)
Florence Maybrick	Berkeley, Anthony. *The Wychford Poisoning Case* (1926) Shearing, Joseph. *Airing in a Closed Carriage* (1943)
Katherine Nairn	Duke, Winifred. *The Laird* (1925) Duke, Winifred. *Crookedshaws* (1936) Stubbs, Jean. *The Case of Kitty Ogilvy* (1970)
The Penge Case	Jenkins, Elizabeth. *Harriet* (1934)
Dr Edward William Pritchard	Ford, Elbur. *Flesh and the Devil* (1950)
Madeleine Smith	Lyell, William Darling. *The House in Queen Anne's Square* (1920) Lowndes, Mrs Belloc. *Letty Lynton* (1931) Lofts, Norah. *Lovers All Untrue* (1970) Ashe, Mary Ann. *Alas for Her That Met Me!* (1976) West, Pamela Elizabeth. *Madeleine* (1983)
Ruth Snyder	Matthews, T. S. *To the Gallows I Must Go* (1931) Cain, James M. *Double Indemnity* (1936)
The Mamie Stewart Case	Picton, Bernard. *The Thread of Evidence* (1965)
Edith Thompson	Jesse, F. Tennyson. *A Pin to See the Peepshow* (1934) Iles, Francis. *Ask for the Woman* (1939)
The Wallace Case	Goodchild, George & Roberts, Bechhofer. *The Jury Disagree* (1934) Duke, Winifred. *Skin for Skin* (1935) Rhode, John. *The Telephone Call* (1948) Hall, Angus. *Qualtrough* (1968) Goodman, Jonathan. *The Last Sentence* (1978) Hutton, John. *29, Herriott Street* (1979)
Robert Wood	Stone, Austin. *In the Shadow* (1953)